MOUNTBATTEN
of
BURMA

Published in 1996 as *The Princely Sailor – Mountbatten of Burma*

MOUNTBATTEN *of* BURMA

Captain of War, Guardian of Peace

IAN McGEOCH

Foreword by
Countess Mountbatten of Burma CBE MSC CD DL

Haynes Publishing

First published in 1996 by Brassey's (UK) Ltd as *The Princely Sailor – Mountbatten of Burma*

This edition, retitled *Mountbatten of Burma: Captain of War – Guardian of Peace*, published in 2009 by Haynes Publishing.

A catalogue record for this book is available from the British Library

ISBN 978 1 84425 686 0

Library of Congress control no. 2008943648

Published by Haynes Publishing, Sparkford, Yeovil, Somerset BA22 7JJ, UK
Tel: 01963 442030 Fax: 01963 440001
Int. tel: +44 1963 442030 Int. fax: +44 1963 440001
E-mail: sales@haynes.co.uk
Website: www.haynes.co.uk

Haynes North America Inc.
861 Lawrence Drive, Newbury Park,
California 91320, USA

Printed and bound in Great Britain

To

CLIO

In memory of

Doreen Brabourne, Nicholas Knatchbull and Louis Mountbatten, who were killed in cold blood because they were British, and with them a local boy, Paul Maxwell, who was in their boat off Mullaghmore, in the Irish Republic, on 27 August 1979.

CONTENTS

LIST OF MAPS AND DIAGRAMS

LIST OF PLATES

FOREWORD

Countess Mountbatten of Burma CBE MSC CD DL

My father, Admiral of the Fleet the Earl Mountbatten of Burma, had an astonishing and varied career from the age of 41 for the rest of his working life. But although he always put his great ability and whole effort into whatever was asked of him, such as Supreme Allied Commander South-East Asia or the last Viceroy of India, his first and abiding love and interest was always in the Royal Navy. There was never any doubt in his mind that his heart lay in his naval career. Had he been asked, at the end of his life, what career he would want to return to, there was never the slightest doubt!

So I am very pleased that Admiral McGeoch's excellent book concentrating on my father's naval and combined services career is being republished. Being a naval officer himself, who had served with my father in many different capacities, Admiral McGeoch was aware that the extraordinary other appointments he had filled had overshadowed a brilliant naval career which was in danger of being overlooked, even though he rose to the top as Chief of the Defence Staff.

The qualities needed and developed in a service life of loyalty, honesty, courage, dedication and hard work, also ensured success in any later employment, as well as being a firm foundation for character building. These characteristics, developed early on in his naval career, served him well in whatever other task he was asked to undertake, and enabled him to give of his best to his country.

PREFACE

Philip Ziegler, in the foreword to his indispensable biography of Lord Mountbatten, said he had compressed the superabundant material into a single volume because his subject's career 'flowed in such a way that it was exceedingly difficult to know where to make the break'. For me, writing as a naval officer, the problem did not arise. In professional terms Mountbatten, having proved himself in peace and war to merit promotion to the highest ranks of the service, then served with great distinction in no less than five senior appointments, each so different in character as to demand separate treatment. And just as Lytton Strachey, in *Eminent Victorians*, studied four individuals as representative of an age of which too much was known to be chronicled, so have I concentrated upon the five peaks of Mountbatten's career, hoping to illuminate the unique blend of royal nature and naval nurture underlying his achievement as a whole. I follow Strachey, also, in aiming to lay bare the facts in each case 'as I understand them, dispassionately, impartially, and without ulterior intentions'.

I joined the battleship HMS *Royal Oak* as a Midshipman on 2 February 1933, just in time to witness the celebrated wireless signalling demonstration given to the Mediterranean Fleet by the fleet wireless officer, Lord Louis Mountbatten, newly promoted to Commander RN; I was serving in a destroyer when he took command of HMS *Daring* in the same fleet; I met him when he took his flotilla to Malta in 1941; I was commander of a cruiser in the Mediterranean when he was Commander-in-Chief; I commanded a submarine squadron and served on the naval staff when he was First Sea Lord; and, while he was Chief of Defence Staff, I was captain of a cruiser and then became Admiral President of the Royal Naval College, Greenwich. The knowledge and experience thus acquired has enabled me to evaluate, as one who 'knows whereof he speaks', the opinions of Mountbatten expressed by those who were senior to him in the Navy, his contemporaries, and his juniors and subordinates.

In the wardrooms of warships talking 'shop' was discouraged and, when some matter of general interest was raised, conversation tended to take the form of 'confident assertion, followed by flat contradiction, met by personal abuse'. On the more controversial aspects of Mountbatten's career I cannot expect to command total agreement with my conclusions, but should disagreement amount in any instance to flat contradiction, I hope it would be supported by unassailable evidence, so that resort to personal abuse could be ruled out.

ACKNOWLEDGEMENTS

My warmest thanks must be accorded, in the first place, to Professor John Simpson, Mountbatten Centre for International Studies, Department of Politics, University of Southampton, for his help in obtaining for me a grant which facilitated my access to the Mountbatten Papers; and equally to Dr C.M. Woolgar and his colleagues at Special Collections in the Hartley Library of the university, for their unfailing courtesy and help in my use of the archive.

Next, I wish to acknowledge my debt to, and thank wholeheartedly, those who have provided me with recollections of Mountbatten and permission to use them: Rear Admiral I.G. Aylen; William Batters; His Honour Christopher Beaumont; Gus Britton; David K. Brown; David Chalmers; the late Captain J.O. Coote; Lieutenant General Sir Napier Crookenden; Admiral J.R. Crowe, Jr, United States Navy; Captain Raymond Dreyer; Captain E.T. Dunsterville; Captain R.D. Franks; Captain R.W. Garson; Vice-Admiral Sir Donald Gibson; Lieutenant Commander Langton Gowlland; Commander Geoffrey Greenish; Rosemary Grindle; Captain J.A. Hans Hamilton; Vice-Admiral Sir Ian Hogg; Professor R.V. Jones; Captain Barry Kent; Rear Admiral Peter La Neice; Captain W.R.H. Lapper; Vice-Admiral Sir Louis Le Bailly; Captain R.G. Lewis-Jones; Vice-Admiral Sir Hugh Mackenzie; Vice-Admiral Sir Hector Maclean; Captain J.E. Moore; Rear Admiral Sir Morgan Morgan-Giles; Captain J.W. Mott; the late Professor Peter Nailor; Sir Patrick Nairne; Lieutenant Commander Lewis Payne; Captain D.G. Robertson; Professor Clayton Robinson; John Roskill; the late Rear Admiral M.W. St Leger Searle; Adrian Seligman; the late Commander E.G. Tyrell; the late Lieutenant Commander Hugh St Aubyn Wake; Captain Christopher Wake-Walker; Commander John Watson, Royal Canadian Navy; Captain Gordon Wilson; Captain Mervyn Wingfield; the late Lord Zuckerman.

I am most grateful, also, to the following publishers (and to the authors or their executors) for permission to quote from the books and journals shown in the chapter notes, namely: Abacus; Arms & Armour; Barry Rose; Book Club Associates; Brassey's; Cassell; Charlton Press; Chatto & Windus; Clarendon Press; Collins; Constable; Doubleday; Guild; Hamish Hamilton; Harper Collins; Heinemann; HMSO; Hodder & Stoughton; Hutchinson; Leo Cooper; Macmillan;

ACKNOWLEDGEMENTS

National Maritime Museum; Nautical Publishers; Oxford University Press; Peter Owen; Putnam; Sidgwick & Jackson; Weidenfeld; Worcester; *The American Political Science Review*; *The Naval Review*; the *RUSI Journal*; The Navy Records Society; and the US Naval Institute *Proceedings*.

Finally, I owe much, and the reader owes even more, to my editors, and to my niece Christine McGeoch, for their skilled help in shaping a book out of my rough-hewn chapters. My thanks to them, and to my long-suffering wife and family to whom it has seemed that, in submitting to the discipline of writing, I have abandoned the slippered ease of retirement and resumed the rigours of active service.

Ian McGeoch
Kirk Deighton
20 June 1996

1

A NAVAL OFFICER IN THE MAKING (1913–34)

. . . an art beyond most of others, not to be snatched at, at idle times and on the bye, but rather requiring so full a taking up of a man in learning of it; as for the time nothing else is to be looked after.

Nathaniel Boteler (1685)[1]

Chapter 1

As a naval officer, Dickie knew that to be promoted he had to do everything
twice as well as anyone else.
Lieutenant Commander The Reverend Hugh St Aubyn Wake[2]

On the evening of Tuesday 4 August 1914, a father and son were dining
together, alone save for the servants, in Mall House, the official residence of
the First Sea Lord. Located at Admiralty Arch, within hailing distance of Trafalgar
Square, its use enabled the professional head of the Royal Navy to exercise
immediate personal control over the disposition and, thanks to wireless
telegraphy, the operations of the fleet. On the roof of the Admiralty building there
stood, adjacent to the wind-vane with its historic repeater in the boardroom,
several tall, slender masts between which were stretched a cat's cradle of wires –
aerials by which the Sea Lords could send and receive signals to and from the
greatest navy the world had ever seen, deployed all round the globe.

For the half-German First Sea Lord, Admiral His Serene Highness Prince
Louis of Battenberg, the drama of war now unfolding had the elements of Greek
tragedy. In the midst of the *Pax Britannica*, guaranteed by the Royal Navy, he had
married a granddaughter of Queen Victoria, the Princess Victoria, one of whose
sisters married the Grand Duke Serge of Russia, another the Tsar Nicholas II,
and a third Prince Henry of Prussia. It is not surprising that King Edward VII
and King George V, and through them the British government, were well
informed of the propensities, intentions and capabilities of both the Tsar and
the Kaiser, as revealed to Prince Louis in family conclave. Equally, Prince Louis
had warned the Kaiser that Britain could not remain neutral if Germany
attacked France and the Low Countries; and he had advised the Tsar of this. To
no avail. . . .

Through the dining-room windows in Mall House, on that August evening,
came the confused shouts of the crowd gathering in Trafalgar Square on their
way to the palace – patriotic, anti-German shouts – while the First Sea Lord and
his son, Naval Cadet His Serene Highness Prince Louis of Battenberg (Dickie to
the family) talked gravely of the predicament and prospects for a safe return
home of his mother and younger sister, Louise, who had been staying with the

Tsarina and were believed to have arrived in St Petersburg. They no doubt talked, also, of Dickie's much-envied brother Georgie, serving as a lieutenant in the battle cruiser *New Zealand* – already, thanks to the prescience of the First Sea Lord, at her war station under the flag of Vice-Admiral Sir David Beatty.

Shortly before Dickie's birth, on 25 June 1900, his father, while still a captain, was appointed Assistant Director of Naval Intelligence, following highly successful periods in command of the cruiser *Cambrian* and as flag captain in the battleship *Majestic* of the Channel Fleet. There being at that juncture neither a General Staff nor a Naval War Staff, properly constituted and established with trained officers, the appointment was of special significance and recognised Prince Louis's capacity to grasp the major issues of naval policy at the turn of the century.

No longer could Britain stand aside in 'splendid isolation' from continental combinations of power, the outcome of which could be a European hegemony, threatening her future as an independent state. By 1894 the Triple Alliance of Germany, Austro-Hungary and Italy had been confronted by the Dual Alliance of France and Russia, in response to the lapse of Bismarck's Reinsurance Treaty, whereby Russia promised not to back France in an attack on Germany in exchange for German support for Russian interests in the Balkans.

For Britain the strategic problem of whether to counter an invasion threat by coastal defences, or by keeping command of the Narrow Seas, was subsumed in the dilemma of how to ensure that the Low Countries, from which Britain's command of the Narrow Seas could be directly threatened, were not annexed by a hostile power. Would a commitment to intervene on the side of the weaker power, or alliance, on the continent prevent war; or would it merely deprive Britain of the strategic choices conferred by her sea power?

In January 1901 Queen Victoria died, having reigned for 63 years. She had held Dickie Battenberg, her great-grandson, in her arms at his baptism. It may be said that he belonged by nature to the 19th century, but was nurtured in the 20th – and to be a prince, even for only 17 years, in the century of the common man would both demand and help to fashion personal qualities of exceptional rarity.

It is mothers, for the most part, who take care of the early upbringing of children. Princess Victoria was not only loving and diligent, but a woman of strong principles and enquiring mind; a strong constitution and sanguine temperament enabled her also to take in her stride, as the wife of a naval officer, the frequent moves of home. The Battenbergs were not well off; even when both Louis and Victoria had inherited money enough to remove worry she continued to impress upon her family the need to manage expenditure with care. Engagingly, while conscious of her royal descent and happy in the company of her numerous royal relatives, Victoria retained throughout her life a more than patrician concern for the underdog, and was inclined to express her belief that monarchy was anachronistic. As Dickie Battenberg grew from infancy to boyhood his father, at the centre not only of naval but of foreign affairs, still found time to be with his wife and children, in London or holidaying at the Hesse family seat of Wolfsgarten, or the Battenberg estate at Heiligenberg.

Consideration of the naval appointments held successively by Prince Louis in the decade prior to August 1914 leaves little doubt that by the time war came he was worn out, mentally, emotionally and physically. Having commanded the Second Cruiser Squadron for two arduous years with conspicuous success, he was made second in command of the Mediterranean Fleet as acting vice-admiral, confirmed in rank on 30 June 1908, and five months later given command of the Atlantic Fleet.

David Beatty, then captain of the battleship *Queen* in that fleet, wrote to his wife:

> We have a very fine Fleet and the best materials. . . . But we have eight Admirals, and there is not one among them unless it be Prince Louis, who impresses me that he is capable of great effort.[3]

No wonder the formidable 'Jackie' Fisher intended to bring Battenberg into the Admiralty to be his own favoured successor as First Sea Lord. Here was a man sympathetic to his reforming zeal, a proven seaman beloved of his men, and also a technical innovator whose ingenious 'course indicator' was still in use during the Second World War (and still called a 'Battenberg').[4]

Having completed two years as commander-in-chief of the Atlantic Fleet, followed by a waiting period in command of the 3rd and 4th Divisions of the Home Fleet, Prince Louis was appointed Second Sea Lord by Winston Churchill, the youthful, ambitious and demanding First Lord, to whom Lord Selborne, a Tory and former First Lord wrote, congratulating him on his appointment of 'the ablest officer the navy possesses and, if his name had been Smith, he would ere now have filled various high offices to the great advantage of the country'.[5]

In December 1912 Prince Louis became First Sea Lord in succession to Admiral Sir Francis Bridgeman, who had lasted for only a year. Bridgeman had followed Sir Arthur Wilson who, when asked by Churchill to create a naval war staff, had presented him with 'a powerfully argued and unqualified refusal' to initiate the growth of an elite body of 'intellectuals' – 'land-lubbers remote from the problems facing commanders at sea'.[6]

By this time the urgent need for such a staff, to coordinate plans with the army if nothing else, should have been manifest to all. Although the Asquith government would give no formal commitment to either France or Russia to provide military aid if they were attacked by Germany, informal 'conversations' had been taking place between the British and French general staffs, on the understanding that at the outbreak of war Britain would deploy an army of six divisions to extend the left flank of the French army. No wonder 'Jacky' Fisher had resolutely kept naval planning under his hat. Having concentrated Britain's naval might in home waters, and ensured its numerical superiority to the German High Seas Fleet, he saw the army as 'a projectile to be hurled at the enemy' at a time and place of Britain's choosing, in accordance with traditional maritime strategy, once command of the sea had been established.

It fell to Prince Louis, without a trained staff in the Admiralty, to make the necessary radical adjustment of naval policy. But the burden on him was heavy, after a year of intense reformist activity as Second Sea Lord. Fortunately, he and Winston Churchill worked well together. By the beginning of 1914 they had succeeded, against Treasury objections, in improving the pay and conditions of service; opened an avenue of promotion to officer rank from the lower deck; set in train the conversion of the fleet from coal to oil burning; brought forward the flag officers who would fight the coming war at sea; established the Royal Naval Air Service; gained Government support for building towards a 60 per cent superiority in dreadnoughts over the German navy; organised and analysed major fleet exercises designed to provide a sound basis for war planning; and initiated the design and building of a squadron of fast battleships of the *Queen Elizabeth* class.

In response to their urging, a Standing Committee on Insurance of British Shipping in Time of War was set up – just in time. Above all the Admiralty, without abandoning various projects for independent offensive operations (for example in the Baltic, Scandinavia and the Low Countries), had concerted plans with the War Office for the movement of the British Expeditionary Force to France immediately on the outbreak of war.

Dickie Battenberg had joined the Royal Naval College at Osborne on the Isle of Wight as a naval cadet in May 1913, passing in 15th out of 83. Being still His Serene Highness Prince Louis of Battenberg, a cousin of the King, of Germanic descent, and son of the First Sea Lord, Dickie was fair game for the bullies in his term, the Exmouths, and those in the terms above. But he stood up to the rough and tumble, held his own and certainly never regretted his decision to join the Navy. He wore his uniform with pride and was photographed in it with his father and brother in theirs – the three Battenberg princes, all loyal servants of King George V and the British Empire.

Professor Sir Michael Howard, writing of 'Europe on the eve of the First World War', points out that in 1907 Oxford University had bestowed an honorary doctorate of civil law upon the Emperor William II of Germany – 'the Kaiser' – and that even in June 1914, of a total of seven Oxford honorands five were German, including Prince Lichnowsky, the German ambassador.[7] It was also in 1907 that Eyre Crowe, a resident clerk in the Foreign Office, whose mother was German, had submitted a lapidary memorandum, now a classic text, warning that if Germany tried to establish her hegemony in Europe, Britain would have to oppose her. For the British people, the traditional enemy was still France; and in any case at this time domestic rather than foreign policy mainly preoccupied government and people, with industrial strife and the Ulster rebellion the dominating concerns.

Against this background, and with commendable foresight, the First Lord and First Sea Lord between them planned a Royal Review of the Fleet, to take place in July 1914 and include a full mobilisation of the fleet reserves. It was to be, in Churchill's words, 'incomparably the greatest assemblage of naval power ever witnessed in the History of the world'.[8] Thanks to his father's influence Cadet Battenberg found himself on board his brother's ship, the *New Zealand*. It is hard to exaggerate the impact on Dickie of this experience, which included lunch with his father, the First Sea Lord, as guests of the captain; a visit to the Admiralty yacht *Enchantress*, where the company included Winston Churchill, Admiral Jellicoe and other Sea Lords; then proceeding to sea in company with that magnificent armada – 59 battleships and battle cruisers, with 133 cruisers and destroyers and numerous smaller warships.

The ships returned to their home ports on 23 July and in the ordinary course of events would have begun to send their ships' companies on summer leave next day, the reservists being due to pay off on the following Monday, 27 July. Given the worsening international situation, the test mobilisation was an indicator of Britain's alertness as far as the Navy was concerned, but even now the country was not committed by any formal alliance to go to war. As if to emphasise this the Prime Minister, Foreign Secretary, Chancellor of the Exchequer and other senior Cabinet ministers, as well as most of the senior people in Whitehall, left London for the weekend, despite the news that Austria had by this time issued a bullying ultimatum to Serbia.

On 25 July, before leaving for the seaside to join his wife and children, Churchill had discussed with Prince Louis whether or not to 'stand fast' the reservists. To do so might be read abroad as a signal that Britain was preparing for war, and thus add to the international tension. To release the reservists and immobilise the Third Fleet would leave the Navy that much less able to counter a possible 'bolt from the blue' – a surprise attempt at invasion by the Germans, as allies of Austria. Prince Louis, almost alone in the Admiralty on Sunday 26 July, awaited news of Serbia's response, having obtained by telephone Churchill's approval to act on his own initiative and cancel the demobilisation if the situation worsened. By 6pm it became clear that Serbia's moderate reply to the Austrians had nevertheless caused them to break off diplomatic relations with her. The First Sea Lord acted:

> At 6 o'clock Louis began writing out the orders himself in his own hand, assisted by the resident clerk, and within five minutes the top priority message was singing along the wires to Portland – cancel leave and demobilisation of Reservists, First and Second Fleets to remain concentrated.

7

Then Louis sent an urgent despatch to George V and another to the Foreign Office telling of what he had done.[9]

By 31 July the fleet in home waters – not until September was it to be known officially as the Grand Fleet – had been deployed to its war stations, and Churchill had also gone ahead with his plan, predetermined at the instigation of the long-since retired Fisher, to appoint Jellicoe on the eve of war to be Commander-in-Chief of the Grand Fleet in place of Sir George Callaghan. On this day the luncheon guests at Admiralty House included Asquith, the Prime Minister, who had assumed the additional office of Secretary of State for War. The other principal guest was Field Marshal Lord Kitchener, whose reputation stood high as a commander in colonial wars and proconsul in the Sudan – his ambition was to be Viceroy of India. He warned the company that a German attack on France was to be expected and that failure to support France when she was in mortal danger would inevitably deprive Britain of any real power in the future; but, he held, contradicting received opinion, it would be a prolonged war of attrition, in which armies numbering millions would be engaged and vast expenditure incurred.

Kitchener's unpalatable view gave a military slant to Eyre Crowe's 1907 memorandum, but still the Asquith Cabinet collectively refused to face the facts. It was left to the leaders of the Army and Navy to complete the preparations for war as best they could, supported by the comprehensive administrative measures for which provision had been made in the government War Book, prepared with foresight and assiduity by the Committee of Imperial Defence under the guidance of its celebrated secretary, Col Maurice (later Lord) Hankey.

During the first days of August, as news of Austria's unacceptable ultimatum to Serbia was published in Britain and its significance became understood by the people, patriotic feeling began to manifest itself, with Germany as the main threat – against France on land and Britain at sea. The anguish of Britain's Liberal Cabinet, of all governments the least disposed to lead the country into war, is apparent from the political memoirs of the period. On 1 August the following exchange of notes took place in Cabinet:

> David Lloyd George to WSC. What is your policy?
> WSC to David Lloyd George. At the present moment I would act in such a way as to impress Germany with our intention to preserve the neutrality of Belgium. So much is still unknown as to the definite purpose of Germany that I would not go beyond this. Moreover public opinion might veer round at any moment if Belgium is invaded and we must be ready to meet this opinion.[10]

Not until 3 August, when the German army was already pouring across his frontiers and the King of the Belgians had appealed directly to Britain for help, was a British ultimatum demanding the maintenance of Belgian neutrality sent to Germany by the government – eight days after Prince Louis, on his own responsibility, had indicated Britain's readiness to fight if need be by keeping the naval reservists under command. Imagine the advantage, as a preparation for service to the nation, of being present in the home of the First Sea Lord at this time of crisis. As Mountbatten recalled:

> In the evenings and at meals, the talk was often of the political and defence manoeuvrings of the nations that were to align against one another as the Allies and the Central powers. And it was highly informed talk. No one was better connected to top politicians and defence chiefs than Prince Louis.[11]

Churchill, having refused to appoint the professional head of the Navy, namely the First Sea Lord, also to be Chief of Naval Staff, had taken upon himself the latter role, for which he was totally unqualified by experience, knowledge or temperament. Moderating, and directing into fruitful channels, the impetuous pugnacity of the First Lord imposed a strain on Prince Louis which became unendurable. It was despite, rather than thanks to, the political direction of the war that, following the expiry of the ultimatum to Germany on 4 August 1914, British sea power ensured the transport of the British Expeditionary Force to France without loss by 12 August; imposed an effective distant blockade on Germany and her allies; drove the German merchant fleet from the seas which the British merchant fleet, amounting to some 43 per cent of the world's shipping, continued to ply; safely escorted large numbers of troops from Australia, Canada, India and New Zealand to the Near East and Europe to fight alongside the British Army; and sank a German minelayer, three light cruisers, four minelaying torpedo-boats and a U-boat by surface action, while a British submarine sank a cruiser and a destroyer.

Against such cumulative evidence of Britain's retention of her mastery at sea the German navy's successes during the same period were insignificant in material terms, although the loss of life was tragic and the adverse effect upon public opinion wholly out of proportion. Instead of an immediate and resounding victory at sea, in which the German High Seas Fleet had been annihilated – another Trafalgar – the headline news was of the escape of the battle cruiser *Goeben* and her light cruiser consort, the *Breslau*, into Turkish waters. Prince Louis had been unable to dissuade Churchill from intervening in the conduct of operations, and in consequence a message of critical importance sent by wireless telegraphy from the Admiralty to the Commander-in-Chief, Mediterranean was ambiguous. The draft, which was preserved, was in Churchill's hand.

The newspapers were soon full, also, of reports of the torpedoing by U-boat of four elderly cruisers and a light cruiser, and the mining of another. Spy mania began to sweep the country. Anyone with German connections was automatically suspect. German waiters were victimised and kicks were aimed at dachshunds. Even before the war Lord Charles Beresford and his friends in the anti-Fisher camp had been spreading calumny against Prince Louis. Now they vilified him openly in their clubs. Fisher himself scented recall to the Admiralty when the government, terrified by events, had on 3 August caught Kitchener as he was about to embark in a destroyer on his way back to Egypt and made him Secretary of State for War. Suddenly, the man who had brought the Navy into action in good shape and with high morale became the scapegoat for Britain's governing elites, political and military, hounded by press and public.

Churchill, sensing that his political life was at stake, thought to strengthen his own position in Cabinet and in the country by sacking his supposedly incompetent, and by inference Germanophile, First Sea Lord. On 30 October 1914 Prince Louis's dignified letter of resignation and the First Lord's reply appeared in the newspapers. Next day Churchill invited the 74-year-old Admiral of the Fleet, Lord Fisher, to resume the post of First Sea Lord which he had vacated four years before. In letters to his wife written at the time Admiral Beatty said that Prince Louis 'did not keep a proper check on Winston and run the show himself, instead of allowing him (W) to do it. . . . Prince Louis departed not for the reason given but to save the politicians.'[12]

Writing in 1928, Lord Hankey said of Kitchener:

> He understood sea power but little and . . . there was no one in the Admiralty to stand up to him. Prince Louis was past his prime, and a sick man hampered by his German connections.[13]

For Cadet Battenberg at Osborne, his outstandingly efficient naval brother George and their mother, Princess Victoria, the treatment accorded to father and husband by an ungrateful country called for every vestige of self-control, filial loyalty and wifely support. Dickie Battenberg's enthusiasm for the Navy became case-hardened by a determination to vindicate, in his career, his father's name and reputation. Moving on with his term from Osborne to Dartmouth, being not yet 16 he was then sent to Keyham, the Navy's long-established engineering college, where the curriculum had been broadened to include naval history and the elements of tactics. Having passed out of Dartmouth only 18th in his term, Dickie came out top from Keyham. Writing to congratulate him, his mother said:

> Georgie and you have never given us a moment's worry by your general life and conduct as cadets – for after all, to do well at one's work may be due a great deal to the natural gifts one has been born with, but to have come through the many temptations that assail a boy in his school life so well as you have done, is a sign of a

good character, and that is your own doing, therefore a better thing in our eyes than the highest place in exams.[14]

Had Dickie shown signs of exulting a bit too much in his success?

On 19 July 1916, at long last as it seemed to Dickie, he joined his first ship. It was less than three weeks after his 16th birthday. The ship, to his intense satisfaction and that of his father, was the famous battle cruiser HMS *Lion*, which since March 1913 had been the flagship of Sir David Beatty. On 9 August Beatty was confirmed in the rank of vice-admiral, aged 44 and years younger than many of the captains and flag officers who were delighted to be serving under him. To Dickie he was a heroic figure with élan and style, always firmly in command, inspiring all to give of their best, itching to get at the enemy.

As Beatty saw it, the German High Seas Fleet should not have escaped destruction at Jutland, and he was appalled when, on 19 August, the Grand Fleet, still under Jellicoe, failed once again to bring the High Seas Fleet to action. Being stationed on the bridge most of the time, as 'doggie' to Flag Captain Chatfield, Dickie saw and heard much of what went on as the opposing fleets closed for battle, including the forceful and colourful language in which Beatty expressed his disgust at the pusillanimous behaviour of the commander-in-chief in turning away from the enemy to avoid a possible, but highly improbable, minefield.

To serve as a midshipman in those days was an experience which combined immense pride at being responsible, even in a small way, for the fighting efficiency of a great ship, with continual reminders that as a 'snotty' one was the lowest form of life on board. Whether as assistant to the officer of the watch at sea or in harbour, in charge of a steam picket-boat with a crew of four, a launch crowded with rumbustious libertymen or a 12-oared cutter conveying the crucially important picking-up rope to a mooring buoy, or at action stations in a gun-turret, the tasks were exacting and failure was liable to result in corporal punishment. It was a rigorous apprenticeship.

When Beatty was appointed to relieve Jellicoe as Commander-in-Chief, Grand Fleet on 28 November 1916, and transferred his flag to the *Queen Elizabeth*, Dickie went also – George came over to the *Lion* with Rear Admiral Pakenham, and the Admiralty did not allow brothers to serve in the same ship.

Not long after Dickie joined the *Queen Elizabeth* he ceased to be known as Battenberg and lost his princely style and title. King George V and the government had sensed that press attacks on the royal family for being 'half-German' must be taken seriously. The German origins of the Battenbergs brought them within the scope of anglicisation measures. From June 1917 onwards, Admiral HSH Prince Louis of Battenberg became Admiral the Marquis of Milford Haven; Lieutenant HSH Prince George of Battenberg became Lieutenant the Earl of Medina (his father's second title); and Midshipman HSH

Prince Louis of Battenberg became Lord Louis Mountbatten, now the family name, and was known thereafter in the service as Mountbatten or, in due course, Lord Louis.

Life in the *Queen Elizabeth* was happier than it had been in the *Lion*, Mountbatten reported to his mother, although the midshipmen worked much harder. Time was found, however, to start a gunroom newspaper, *Chronicles of the QE*. The editor ('general work and stories, accounts etc., puzzles') was Mountbatten. It went on sale to officers and men in the ship and was a resounding success. Such efforts were invaluable in keeping up the morale of a fleet which, operating from its remote base in Scapa Flow winter and summer, exercising and carrying out sweeps, kept ready to fight a German fleet which prudently remained in harbour.

Apart from a couple of months in the large, steam-driven fleet submarine *K-6*, which he enjoyed, Mountbatten continued to serve in the *Queen Elizabeth* until 13 October 1918 when, having received his commission as a sub-lieutenant, he joined HMS *P31* as first lieutenant and second in command. It was no mean thing (though normal at that time) at the age of 18 to be directly responsible to the captain of an anti-submarine patrol vessel for the good order, welfare and discipline of a crew of 60 or so; and for the cleanliness, smartness and fighting efficiency of a steam-driven, twin-screwed ship 244ft in length, with a beam of 28ft and a useful armament.

Mountbatten learned a lot about the practical side of his profession in the year that followed, and was then sent with many of his contemporaries to Cambridge University, there to make good the deficiencies in education arising from being sent to sea at the age of 16. Mountbatten went up to Christ's College in October 1919 and chose as his special subjects the History of Geographical Discovery, and Ethnology (described as 'Savages, past and present'). As usual he threw himself into both work and play, and seemed particularly to enjoy the freedom to express an opinion, however heterodox, not normally vouchsafed to junior naval officers. Not that he was an intellectual, even *manqué*; but he had a furious thirst for knowledge and an extraordinary capacity for concentration.

Despite a hectic social life, centring upon pretty actresses but veering now and then towards more serious attachments, he managed to turn in the required essays, getting away sometimes with short stories – one was about the concern of a press baron to increase circulation rather than publicise the plight of a poor wronged woman – and he spoke effectively in that cradle of political leaders, the Cambridge Union. On 14 November 1919 the Milton Society debated the motion 'That in the opinion of this house, the Ulster Unionist Party is principally to blame for the present chaotic conditions in Ireland'; proposed by Sub-Lieutenant McCoy and opposed by Sub-Lieutenant Lord Louis Mountbatten.

One might think that to enjoy Cambridge to the full in those days a man would need to have a most generous allowance, if not personal wealth.

Mountbatten kept an account of his funds around this time which shows that his income was modest: his pay as a sub-lieutenant RN was £310 per annum; he had an allowance from his father of £300 a year; and his net income after tax was £510 per annum. To keep the purchasing power of the pound in perspective, a reputable gunsmith rendered an account at that time to the Marquis of Milford Haven, 'To: one 12-bore hammerless gun made to measure for Lord Louis Mountbatten . . . £23.10.0.' Not that Lord Louis, as he was now generally known in the service, ever became a keen shot. His favourite recreations hinged on high speed and manoeuvring, whether at the wheel of a motor car or speedboat, or riding a polo pony. But even these activities had to be crammed into the interstices of a life dedicated mainly to naval duties.

On 1 February 1920, perhaps while sitting in the bath, Lord Louis had the germ of an idea for 'Signal Training by Cinematograph', which he set out on the sheet of his host's embossed writing paper as reproduced on page 14. He developed the scheme, but it was too innovative to attract Admiralty support when he submitted it formally about a year later. By then he had completed an Empire tour in HMS *Renown* with the Prince of Wales – westward via the Panama Canal to New Zealand, then to Australia, Fiji, Samoa and Honolulu, back through the Panama Canal to British Guyana, the West Indies and Bermuda, and finally arriving back in Portsmouth on 11 October 1920.

Plans were already afoot for the Prince of Wales to make a second Empire tour in the *Renown*, and Lord Louis's naval career might have been put in jeopardy by an invitation from the Prince, which it would have been discourteous to refuse, to accompany him again as his personal ADC. Fortunately, owing to departure being delayed for a year, he was able to undergo the usual courses of instruction in gunnery, torpedoes, navigation and signals to prepare him for the rank of lieutenant; and once again, despite the distractions of a lively social life, he came out top.

The Prince of Wales's second tour, starting in October 1921, took them to Aden (unofficially), India, Burma, Ceylon, the Malay States and Japan. As before, Lord Louis kept a diary – a lively and illuminating account of an unrelenting programme of public occasions, which made gruelling and often inconsiderate demands upon the Prince and left little time for relaxation. It was a period of impending political and constitutional change, as the British Empire evolved into the British Commonwealth of independent nation states united under the Crown, with the monarch as head of state in each country.

During this tour Lord Louis became engaged to Edwina Ashley, whose father was a grandson of the seventh Earl of Shaftesbury (celebrated for legislating against the employment of women and children in coalmines), and whose mother was the daughter of the financier Sir Ernest Cassel. Louis and Edwina had met in England and been strongly attracted to each other. Although an

'Signal Training by Cinematograph'. Mountbatten's idea proved too innovative to attract Admiralty support when he submitted it in 1921.

heiress, Edwina was at that time almost penniless, but she contrived to travel to India where she was the guest of the Viceroy and Lady Reading during the stay in Delhi of the Prince of Wales and his ADC. The Prince, six years older than Lord Louis, envied his cousin the relative freedom with which he had been able to choose his future wife, and his good luck in meeting and falling in love with so marvellous a girl. The approval of the King would have to be sought, of course (and was not withheld), but he would certainly like to be Dickie's best man. Prince Edward himself was not lucky in love, and was a deeply unhappy young man. It was as much as anything because he felt able to open his heart to Dickie that he had asked for his company on this second Empire tour.

In Japan, perhaps because there was no polo, Lord Louis produced a remarkably comprehensive intelligence report on the Imperial Japanese Navy, including a description of the Japanese equivalent of Dartmouth for the education and training of aspiring naval officers. At a time when British naval opinion tended to discount the potential of the Japanese navy, and particularly of its air arm, he gave strong reasons for regarding it as a formidable force which would grow rapidly stronger.

The Prince's tour ended with a ceremonial arrival in London on 21 June 1922, and the engagement of Lord Louis Mountbatten and Edwina Ashley was made public to great acclaim. Their wedding at St Margaret's, Westminster, on 18 July was a scintillating occasion, attended by the royal family, nobility and aristocracy, with many naval officers resplendent in their full dress uniforms – known as 'cockers and frockers' (cocked hats, frock coats, swords and medals) – and a huge crowd of delighted spectators.

The ancient Teutons, we are told, had a practice of drinking honey-wine for 30 days after marriage. The young Mountbattens – both having Teutonic forebears – after a few days of bliss at Broadlands, the Hampshire seat of Edwina's father, went to the Ritz in Paris; to Spain as the guests of King Alfonso and Louis's cousin Queen Ena; followed by a nostalgic (for Louis) visit to Hesse where, sadly, they found the palace at Wolfsgarten shrunk in size, and Heiligenberg of happy childhood memory in grievous disrepair. For most couples, despite that note of disenchantment, this honeymoon alone would have been a fairy-tale beginning to married life. But Louis, with a serious naval career firmly in prospect and a wife who had vowed to support him in it, decided that never again would there be so good an opportunity to take extended leave without an adverse effect upon his promotion prospects.

Transatlantic air travel being still far in the future, the Mountbattens set off for the USA on board the *Majestic*, a huge White Star liner. In the first week of October 1922 they arrived in New York. The jazz age was already in full swing. Louis and Edwina were the talk of the town and revelled in it – the Ziegfeld Follies, baseball, dining and dancing all the way across the States to Hollywood and the fantasy world of film stars and studios. For Louis, now with his own 35mm cine-camera and his enthusiasm for using film for naval instruction, enjoyment of the fun and glamour of Hollywood was enhanced by the opportunity to learn from the world's leading cameramen and directors how to use the medium most effectively, while the friendships made with stars such as Charlie Chaplin, Douglas Fairbanks and Mary Pickford were fruitful and lasting.

Before these halcyon days in the USA ended, Louis had not only met President Harding, but been invited, as a mere lieutenant, to be a principal speaker at a Washington dinner of the American Navy League. Already, in the Cambridge Union and elsewhere, he had spoken well from a platform; and he had recognised in himself a talent to engage an audience, which he was happy to exploit. In 1922 the limitation of naval armaments, to be codified in the Washington Treaty, had led to acrimony between influential members of the British and American delegations. For so well known, if junior, a representative of the Royal Navy to be warmly received by senior officers of its first-ever rival for over a century was certainly helpful to the politicians in reaching agreement on thorny issues. When the Mountbattens left New York in mid-December 1922 for home, they had not only enjoyed themselves enormously, thanks to the generous hospitality of their American hosts, but had proved to be fine ambassadors for Britain.

In the period between the wars, when Lord Louis was determined to make his way as an ordinary naval officer, albeit with royal relations and married to an heiress, the Royal Navy still saw itself as the guarantor of an Empire 'on which the sun never set'. But, unlike the Navy of the early 19th century, it had not emerged triumphant from a series of hard-won victories in great sea battles, culminating in another Trafalgar; it was the beneficiary of the successful outcome of an Allied campaign on continental Europe, won at an enormous cost in blood and treasure. The sole great fleet action had been indecisive. Opinions as to the reason for this varied, but the captains of the battleships at Jutland, who became the flag officers of the 1920s, spent much time trying to ensure that next time – whenever and wherever that might be – the British fleet would gain a decisive victory.

The U-boats had been defeated by the introduction (almost fatally delayed) of the convoy system. As a result, the threat of unrestricted submarine warfare, which in any case had brought about the collapse of Germany by bringing the USA into the war against her, was virtually disregarded.

Above all, post-1918 Britain was impoverished. Drastic cuts in defence expenditure were ordained, and the resultant reductions in the size of Britain's all-volunteer armed forces had three dramatic effects. First, the competition between the Navy, the Army and the RAF for an adequate share of the total defence vote became acute; secondly, research and development almost ceased; and thirdly the rivalry for promotion, especially in the officer corps, became intense.

Owing to the strategic primacy of the Suez Canal, for access to India in particular and to the Persian Gulf for oil, the Mediterranean Fleet was at the zenith of its importance. Indeed, it had assumed many of the characteristics of a secular order, such as the Knights of St John. With its base at Malta; strict hierarchy from the commander-in-chief downwards; its task of being ready for war against the infidel, whoever he might prove to be; and the unmarried or unaccompanied status of most officers and men, this was a closed society. It was a society, moreover, secure in its belief that it served in the finest fleet, in the best navy, defending the greatest empire the world had ever known; and its members had little regard for riches. Everyone knew how much everyone else was paid. A few officers had 'private means'. Living on board HM ships was comfortable enough, sport was mostly free, and periodical exercises and cruises added interest and a change of scene.

What motivated people, and kept them happy, was competition – between groups in each ship, between ships in a squadron, and between individuals; at games, gunnery, or athletics; at evolutions, and above all, at the pulling regattas, in which crews of beefy, sweating, grimly determined sailors, stokers, Royal Marines and officers propelled heavily built whalers, cutters and galleys for long distances amid feverish speculation and much wagering upon the results.

Given that the ultimate competition, namely battle, was excluded, it was not surprising that success in competitive 'general drill', sports and games counted much towards the selection for promotion of the officers who could command it. But two other criteria counted even more, especially in the promotion of those in command of HM ships. The first was the behaviour of the ship's company when ashore, particularly when in a foreign port and 'showing the flag'; the second was good station-keeping. By always moving quickly to her correct station and maintaining it, by smartness of appearance and manoeuvre when leaving and entering harbour, and by meticulously correct ceremonial, the reputation of a ship in the fleet, and hence the promotion prospects of her captain, could be enhanced – because the commander-in-chief himself could observe these activities.

It was in this environment that Louis Mountbatten had to make good as a young officer. He had been tempted by, but rejected, the opportunities for early responsibility, excitement and extra pay offered by service in submarines or the Fleet Air Arm; instead, he had carefully considered the various specialisations open to him if he was not to remain what was termed a 'salt horse'.

The battle fleet was still the core of the Navy's power – 'a battleship is to an admiral', Liddell Hart once remarked, 'as a cathedral is to a bishop', and the *raison d'être* of a battleship was to mount huge guns, the manning of which – to load, control, fire and reload – occupied almost the entire ship's company other than the engine room. In 1930 Vice-Admiral W.W. Fisher, a gunnery specialist and then second in command of the Mediterranean Fleet, told an assembly of turret officers after firing practice that:

there were only 64 15-inch guns in the Royal Navy and that [each turret officer's] command consisted of one 32nd part of Britain's might. It is the 15-inch gun alone, he said, which is the sole bulwark of civilisation against the destructive force of

Communism and it is the sole weapon upon which England and consequently the World relies for security.[15]

Entirely in charge of this highly labour-intensive, powerful armament, responsible directly to the captain for training and in action for the effectiveness of the gunfire, was the gunnery officer. No wonder the gunnery specialisation was held to offer the best chance of early promotion to commander. The other specialisations differed little as far as promotion was concerned, in proportion to numbers, and each attracted individuals for whom the expertise to be acquired, and the type of service which would follow, appeared congenial, whether torpedo, navigation or signals.

Perceptively, Lord Louis chose signals. For centuries admirals, flying their distinctive flags in the most powerful and smartest-sailing warships, had used flags or lights to signal their orders, instructions, intentions and exhortations (remember Nelson before Trafalgar: 'I'll now amuse the Fleet . . . Mr Pasco, I wish to say to the Fleet "England confides that every man will do his duty."' And the signal lieutenant, unable to find a flag group meaning 'confides', asked if he might substitute 'expects', which Nelson approved). By 1923, when Lord Louis was making up his mind, wireless telegraphy had begun to supersede flag signalling. The technology was intriguing, the scope for innovation obvious, and the importance of good communications, in the broadest sense, hard to overestimate. But the role of signal lieutenant had evolved into that of a glorified personal assistant: the flag lieutenant, renowned in peacetime at any rate for sartorial elegance and *savoir faire*. It was time to restore the ethos of the true communicator. Lord Louis thus decided to apply for the Long Course in Signals, which would last for a year.

Not surprisingly, Their Lordships of the Admiralty required so junior a lieutenant to gain more experience as a ship's officer before specialising. Lord Louis was therefore sent to the battleship *Revenge*, joining her in February 1923 at Constantinople, where she formed part of an international naval force providing a stabilising presence in the region following the post-1918 outbreak of hostilities between Greece and Turkey. A confused situation was confounded by a nationalist revolution in the latter country, which led to the exile of the Sultan and his replacement by Kemal Atatürk. Thus ended five centuries of Ottoman rule from Constantinople, and in July 1923 peace was re-established by the Treaty of Lausanne. Because the naval force could not immediately be withdrawn, Lord Louis's main task in the *Revenge* was helping to sustain the morale of a ship's company yearning for 'England, home and beauty' now that the job which their ship had been sent to do appeared to have been completed. The officers, too, needed jollying along.

Since the 1770s, when Admiral Kempenfelt initiated the division of a warship's company into groups, each the responsibility of an officer who must ensure that they mustered each day 'taut and clean', the divisional system has been the key to happiness and efficiency in HM ships. Where the system has been but perfunctorily complied with, inefficiency and discontent – even refusal of duty – have occurred. As Lord Louis was to find throughout his service as a junior officer, it was not until he had proved in many ways his professional ability and 'officerlike qualities' that the wardroom would accept him as one of them and not just a playboy princeling favoured by palace influence.

It did not take him long to establish his credentials. Within a few weeks he had compiled a personal record of every one of the 160 men in the division for which he was responsible, together with the 15-inch gun turret that many of them manned; and he soon could put names to their faces. Whether inherited from his parents, or modelled on his father's style of leadership, this concern for his subordinates as individual human beings and keen interest in their welfare became one of the hallmarks of Lord Louis's naval career; so much so that in later years the occasional lapses of a Mountbatten memory system that had long since become institutionalised encouraged the belief that the whole thing was nothing but a public relations gimmick. This it certainly was not. Nor was there any element of patronising in this determination to know his people. But patrician it could hardly fail to be, given a lineage among the most ancient and illustrious in Europe.

The other aspect of Lord Louis's persona which came to the fore during his 18 months or so in the *Revenge* was his flair for organising entertainments. The ship's 'concert party', at which the natural comics were permitted to let off steam with caricatures of the officers, interlarded with ribald songs and indifferent instrumental performances, was traditional in ships stationed far from home. But Lord Louis wrote, produced and directed a black-and-white Pierrot show; and persuaded Douglas Fairbanks to let him have a print of his new film *Robin Hood*, which he then screened to the accompaniment of sound effects devised by himself, with music transcribed by C.B. Cochran and played by the Royal Marines band.

In the midst of all this activity Lord Louis found time to write frequently and at length to his wife of less than a year, to be parted from whom he felt as deeply as any other newly married young man. Early in 1924 the Mountbattens' first child was born, a girl, whom they named Patricia (now the Countess Mountbatten of Burma), and that autumn Lord Louis began his Long Course at the Signal School in Portsmouth.

Edwina was now the owner of Brooke House, a vast place in Park Lane, and had done it up in splendid style, including a bedroom for her husband fitted out as the replica of an admiral's cabin, with a *trompe l'oeil* outlook through a 'scuttle' to the Grand Harbour in Malta. She also acquired Adsdeane, a huge, ugly but well-appointed Victorian mansion 12 miles from Portsmouth on the way to London. This was convenient for Lord Louis, now engaged in the most strenuous life it is possible to imagine. Having seen to it that Adsdeane could provide for every outdoor pursuit from pheasant-shooting to golf, and a pit in which to practise hitting a polo ball, he and Edwina, now aged 24 and 23 respectively, proceeded to entertain and be entertained, relentlessly and on a lavish scale. Their activities were widely reported in the gossip columns of the popular press and society weeklies.

But few people, even in the Navy, realised that Lord Louis managed to apply himself to his Long Course work with such assiduity, aided by extremely fast driving between London and Portsmouth, that he came out top in the examinations and was nominated for the Higher Wireless Course at the Royal Naval College, Greenwich. This led to his appointment as Assistant to the Fleet Wireless and Signals Officer on the staff of the Commander-in-Chief of the Mediterranean Fleet which, as already described, formed a modern 'closed society'; the Reverend 'Tubby' Clayton (celebrated founder in the First World War of the Toc H soldiers' clubs), aptly christened it 'the City of Silver Grey'.

As always, Lord Louis brought not only energy and system to his work, but also inventiveness. A simple example was the use of glass tubing, into which different coloured inks were poured, as a visual aid in the course of a series of 12 two-hour lectures which he compiled and delivered to the junior officers of the fleet, describing how wireless telegraphy worked and its use in naval operations. The ability to communicate knowledge, as well as to acquire and apply it, is rare. It was not altogether surprising that Lord Louis's next appointment was that of Head of Wireless Instruction, once again at the Signal School, nor that his achievements in this post were exceptional. Among these were the introduction of sub-focal flashing lamps which made the transmission of Morse code feasible at a much higher speed; and the use of a typewriter keyboard for operating the mechanical semaphore arms, again with an increase in speed.

But his reputation as an instructor rested mainly upon his creation of a drawing-office at the Signal School for the production of simple, clear and comprehensive coloured display drawings of the circuitry of wireless sets; for his rationalisation of the haphazard handbooks and graphics associated with them; and for his never-failing attention to detail. He is remembered also for designing the Signal School tie, coloured blue (for blue blood, it was said) and grey (for grey matter); and still this phenomenal man found time to learn to fly a light aircraft.

In February 1929 Edwina bore a second daughter, Pamela (now Lady Pamela Hicks), so there was the nursery at Adsdeane to visit daily. Philip Ziegler has given a fair account of a marriage between two hyperactive people attracted to each other both physically and socially with a common liberal conscience in continual conflict with a strong hedonistic streak.[16] But whereas Louis's self-discipline, rooted in professional ambition, triumphed, Edwina had inherited from her grandfather Cassel not only a fortune but the entrepreneurial spirit and keen mind which enabled him to amass it. Unfortunately her upbringing and education as an English debutante were inadequate for so powerful a personality. Both her behaviour and her intellect remained undisciplined until the compulsion came, in wartime, to amend the one and exercise the other. She remained married to Louis because it suited them both for her to do so. But in his case what he brought to the partnership exemplified the Christian tradition of marriage to someone with whom one is in love 'till death do us part'; a family, and for the man a rewarding career, with a wife who would be his mistress when young, his companion in middle age, and his nurse when old. Given that his devotion to the Navy was accepted by Edwina, her independence was tolerable to Louis, but her infidelities were intensely hurtful, ameliorated though they were by 'laughter, learnt of friends'.

Lord Louis rejoined the staff of the Commander-in-Chief, Mediterranean, now Admiral Sir Ernle Chatfield, in August 1931, in the best job he could have been given at that stage in his career: Fleet Wireless Officer. He made the most of it. Within a few weeks he had visited every one of the 70 or so ships in the fleet; set up a most efficient system for monitoring every wireless telegraphy (W/T) transmission made in the fleet; set the highest standards for discipline on the air-waves, correct procedure and alertness; and made sure that they were matched by performance. His style of leadership was ideally suited to this task, based as it was upon one-to-one relationships, demonstration of his own ability to do the jobs of his subordinates, and the power to communicate his ideas and requirements effectively.

On 31 October 1932 Admiral Sir William Fisher, whose imposing presence led to him being dubbed 'the Great Agrippa' by flippant junior officers, took over from Chatfield as Commander-in-Chief, Mediterranean. That November the BBC announced that King George V would inaugurate an Empire Broadcasting Service with a speech on Christmas Day. Fisher decreed that everyone in his fleet should be enabled to hear the King's voice. In the few weeks available Lord Louis made the necessary technical arrangements, helped principally by a brilliant, if eccentric lieutenant named Robinson (later Captain J. Mansfield Robinson) in the battleship *Royal Oak*. Not only the Navy, but the Army, the RAF and many of the inhabitants of Malta heard the King's voice clearly, but it had been a close-run thing. Components from the UK arrived with less than 48 hours to spare, and the BBC's transmission faded badly a few minutes after the King had finished speaking. 'Dafty' Robinson, as he was known to his friends, at Lord Louis's instigation next designed a modification kit to enable 'talking pictures' to be shown to ships' companies by naval cinema projectors, at a charge of £60 to each ship instead of the £800 which the commercial equivalent would have cost.

Lord Louis was determined to bring to the notice of the fleet, and especially its more senior officers, the full range of skills, capabilities and technology which the W/T branch could provide in peace and war. Even as he was considering how best to put across this message, his promotion to commander was promulgated, with effect from 1 January 1933. Congratulations poured in: his 33rd birthday was almost another six months away, and he had been selected the first time that his 'batch' had entered the promotion zone.

In the highest spirits, therefore, he produced, scripted and directed a wireless signalling demonstration for the Mediterranean Fleet. The *mise en scène* was a warship's wireless office. Many years later he recalled:

> We demonstrated the speed of communication with the Admiralty. We showed the importance of wireless discipline, and how, if a ship breaks silence, she can be identified by the pitch of her morse, even if she only makes one dot! We simulated battle, by getting the ships themselves to transmit action signals; we had aircraft up and submarines submerged, and we fed in all their signals through loudspeakers as they came in. This is all old hat now; but it was very new then.[17]

Louis Mountbatten's early promotion to commander was almost inevitable in a system by which, imperfect though it was, officers were selected for advancement entirely on all-round merit as a naval officer. In Louis's case, he had managed to combine a hectic and glamorous social and sporting life with dedication to his profession. His particular contribution had been to bring about a marked improvement in radio communication in the fleet, both in training and the adoption of up-to-date technology. His fitness for further advancement was unquestioned. Now it was to be put to the test.

CAPTAIN OF DESTROYERS (1934–41)

Autumn 1939
From Admiralty to Destroyer:
PROCEED WITH ALL DESPATCH
From Destroyer to Admiralty:
REQUEST DESTINATION
From Admiralty to Destroyer:
ADEN REPEAT ADEN
From Destroyer to Admiralty:
AM AT ADEN

Captain Jack Broome
Make a Signal[1]

Time is everything; five minutes makes the difference between a victory and a defeat.

Nelson
Despatches[2]

Chapter 2

Keep on

Motto of HMS Kelly

A t the end of January 1933 Adolf Hitler became Chancellor of Germany. It was the moment, historically, when post-First World War became pre-Second World War. But whatever Lord Louis may have thought about the international situation at that time, his most earnest and immediate wish was to be given command of a destroyer. It was granted. He was told, on promotion, that he would command one of the most modern, HMS *Daring*, but not until the following spring. To fill in the time he qualified as an Interpreter in French, First Class. Then, in January 1934, he began a course at the Tactical School in Portsmouth, the highlight of which, despite the all but decisive impact of U-boat warfare in 1914–18 and the advent of aircraft carriers and naval aircraft with many functions, was still a re-enactment of the Battle of Jutland, using models on the floor.

Admiral of the Fleet Lord Jellicoe visited the school and, as Lord Louis recorded in his diary, demonstrated how, owing to bad visibility, he had never seen more than 4 out of the 22 battleships of the German High Seas Fleet. The information he received from his own ships was generally so poor that at no time had he ever had any clear idea of what the High Seas Fleet was doing. 'The inescapable lesson of course,' Lord Louis recorded, 'was that our failure to make essential signals had been well nigh disastrous. . . . I certainly wasn't likely to forget the vital role of communications when I went to my own command.'

Lord Louis learned that *Daring*'s main armament, torpedoes, would be of a new type. He therefore arranged with the captain of the Torpedo School, HMS *Vernon*, to be given a week's instruction on them. The officer charged to provide this recalled:

What a charming character! – What a really brilliant quick brain! He took everything in very easily – and on at least two occasions queried the efficiency of some item (depth keeping, I think, and steering gear), and suggested an improved method! (I had no answers!) On leaving Vernon at the end of the week he very kindly wrote me a letter of thanks – which was a great pleasure for me.'[3]

On 29 April 1934 Lord Louis assumed command of HMS *Daring*. So far, his career had offered scant opportunity to practise handling a destroyer. The Mediterranean Fleet was concentrated at Malta for a weapons training period, and according to the Weekly Practice Programme *Daring* was detailed to tow a high-speed target for the First Cruiser Squadron. This could be a tricky job, and the Captain (D) of the flotilla, Baillie-Grohman, suggested to the Rear Admiral (D), A.B. Cunningham, that another destroyer, with a more experienced captain, should be given the task, particularly because the Commander-in-Chief would be embarking in the destroyer to witness the firings. But the C-in-C, Admiral Fisher, disagreed with the proposal, saying that he was confident that Lord Louis, having served under him, could carry out the task. As if to make the point, Fisher remained on board the *Daring* while Lord Louis berthed her in Sliema Creek. This manoeuvre, which involved proceeding stern first through a narrow space between lines of destroyers and stopping the ship exactly between her two mooring buoys, could test the most experienced captain. To carry it out perfectly under the critical gaze of the destroyer command and the C-in-C was a satisfactory conclusion to a day that had been a considerable test of seamanship – and self-confidence.

Before 1934 ended Lord Louis was required to steam the *Daring*, by now a well worked-up and happy ship (in major fleet exercises the *Daring*'s 'enemy reporting' was always impeccable), to Singapore with the rest of 1st Flotilla, and exchange her for the *Wishart*, one of the destroyers of First World War design that were being replaced. Having brought the elderly vessel back to the Mediterranean, Lord Louis soon had her in a high state of efficiency and morale. She obtained twice as many hits as the other destroyers in gunnery firings and, except for the soccer competition, won all the recreational trophies, culminating in the fleet regatta. By thinking out carefully what had to be done to win, and then practising it thoroughly, Lord Louis achieved outstanding results. But it must be said that, far from being modest about his successes in the manner favoured by Englishmen (especially, perhaps, those who have much to be modest about), this princely sailor delighted in proclaiming them. Senior officers and rivals for promotion were irritated by this.

Having made his name as a destroyer captain, Lord Louis was appointed to serve in the Air Division of the naval staff. It was a key job. By 1936 the prolonged and debilitating campaign waged by the Royal Navy to regain from the RAF control of naval aviation in all its aspects was reaching the crunch.

The formation of the Royal Air Force on 1 April 1918 had followed the recommendations of a committee under General Smuts, who stated:

> the day may not be far off when aerial operations, with their devastation of enemy lands and destruction of industrial and populous centres on a vast scale, become the principal operations of war.[4]

This speculation, prompted no doubt by the stalemate punctuated by slaughter on the Western Front which characterised the 1914–18 war, was the genesis of the pernicious theory that 'the bomber will always get through'. It was pernicious because the appeasement of Germany in the 1930s had its origin in the fear that the civil population could not be protected from large-scale aerial bombing; and because it ran counter to the axiom that the primary aim of one's armed forces must always be the destruction or neutralisation of hostile armed forces to the extent necessary to attain the war aim.

With this axiom in mind, the First Lord of the Admiralty had stated the naval view in a letter dated 31 January 1934 to the Under-Secretary of the Air Ministry:

> You say that the Fleet Air Arm is an integral part of the Royal Air Force. I say that it is an essential part of the Royal Navy. Aircraft are a necessary component of a modern navy, and a fleet opposed to one with a superior air arm must be at a very great disadvantage. You do not establish a right to a voice in the carrier requirements of the Fleet by calling a carrier a floating aerodrome, any more than the War Office could establish a right to settle our cruiser requirements and armaments by calling a cruiser a floating gun platform.[5]

It must be said, however, that in the Navy itself there was a school of thought which, while rejecting the thesis that a future war could only be won by the RAF on its own, with so-called 'strategic' bombing, argued, nevertheless, that battleships were obsolescent and that aircraft carriers were the capital ships of the future. And some senior naval officers regarded 'the daring young men in their flying machines' as, at best, a useful auxiliary to the battleships and cruisers, and at worst not proper naval officers. There was a conceptual problem, also. 'Find, fix and strike', in that order, summed up the tactical role of the Navy's air arm; but, paradoxically, the more effective naval aircraft were shown to be in immobilising and then destroying hostile battleships, the stronger the claim of the RAF that its 'indivisible air power' could supplant the need for battleships at all.

Lord Louis did not share the more extreme views of some naval aviators, but as a member of the Naval Air Division he had access to the facts; with these at his fingertips he produced a powerful paper setting out the arguments for transferring the Fleet Air Arm in toto from the RAF to the Royal Navy, and sent it to Winston Churchill. In a covering letter dated 26 March 1937 he wrote:

> As promised over the telephone I am sending you some arguments in favour of placing all craft concerned in the defence of trade, be they warships, flying boats or specialised shore-based aircraft, under the control of a single service. The enclosed memorandum has been prepared by officers who have had more experience of air operations over the sea than any other officers on the active list.[6]

In the end Sir Thomas Inskip, a former Attorney-General whom the Prime Minister, Neville Chamberlain, had appointed Minister for the Co-ordination for Defence the previous year, was called upon to adjudicate between the respective claims of the Navy and the RAF to command and control the Fleet Air Arm.

On 30 July 1937 Chamberlain announced the Inskip Award. He gave the Navy full responsibility for, and control over, the Fleet Air Arm, but this would consist solely of aircraft operable from ships; shore-based aircraft, even if fully employed on naval tasks, would remain part of the RAF. This ignored the crucial importance of shore-based aircraft in countering U-boat attacks on merchant ships. Yet analysis had shown that during the final years of the First World War, only four ships were sunk in convoys escorted by aircraft as well as surface ships: the U-boats were forced to dive on sighting an aircraft, and their slow speed when submerged precluded successful approach and attack. It was for this reason that Lord Louis had stressed the need for specialised shore-based aircraft for the defence of trade. As a direct consequence of the Inskip Award the Royal Navy could not, and the RAF would not, design, produce, arm, equip, man and train the 'specialised shore-based aircraft' called for by Lord Louis, the absence of which was primarily responsible for the ascendancy of the U-boats in the first three years of the Battle of the Atlantic, despite the assumption by the Admiralty of operational control of RAF Coastal Command's aircraft.

Lord Louis's promotion to the rank of captain on 30 June 1937, just after his 37th birthday, was generally conceded in the Navy to be well merited. The cascade of congratulatory letters included one which, at the height of the clash between the Commander-in-Chief, East Indies, and the Supreme Allied Commander, South-East Asia, in 1943–44, may have been wryly remembered by both author and recipient:

From: Rear Admiral James Somerville CB, DSO

Dear Mountbatten,
I suppose some misinformed bandmaster will say – 'Oh he got promoted because he's a Lord' but those of us who know you all agree that no promotion was more fully deserved. . . .
   For some time past I've asserted that most of us on the Flag List are too old. I'm therefore very glad to see that in due course we shall have a Flag Officer who is still very much in his prime.[7]

Being junior in naval rank had never inhibited Lord Louis's efforts to place his views before the highest authorities, but he was well aware that first and foremost he must 'conduct himself to the entire satisfaction' of his immediate superior. Having achieved this in the Naval Air Division, he now espoused a cause almost as important as the transfer of the Fleet Air Arm to the Navy; namely, the adoption of the Oerlikon gun.

Until 1941, when the Gunnery Division was formed, the Training and Staff Duties Division (DTSD) was responsible for all gunnery aspects of the work of the naval staff. When Stephen Roskill (official historian of the war at sea, 1939–45) joined DTSD as a commander early in 1939 he was given the anti-aircraft 'desk'. As he wrote later in *The Naval Review*:

> The desperate shortage of close-range A-A weapons had become apparent well before my arrival in Whitehall, but there was intense opposition to 'buying foreign' in the Naval Ordnance and Armament Supply Departments, aided and abetted by Vickers-Armstrong, which of course had a virtual monopoly for the supply of British-made weapons. . . .
>
> As regards the Oerlikon, my first 'active' experience was gained in the gunnery firing ship . . . we fired at 'Queen Bee' wireless-controlled targets, and quickly shot down so many of them that the trials had to be stopped. The superiority of the Oerlikon over the Vickers weapons plainly lay in the fact that whereas the latter were laid and trained through clumsy and heavy gearing . . . the Oerlikon was swing-laid by one man from the shoulder.
>
> . . . Lord Mountbatten claimed to have been responsible for getting the Oerlikon accepted for the RN. Where and how he can have been introduced to the weapon is a mystery to me.[8]

In the course of further correspondence in *The Naval Review* the mystery was solved, in a letter from Rear Admiral George Ross in the issue of January 1981. While serving as British naval attaché in Tokyo in October 1935, he was approached by an Austrian named Antoine Gazda, who said, 'I represent the Oerlikon Machine Tool Factory in Switzerland. Have you heard of the Oerlikon gun?' Ross confessed that he had not. Having then witnessed most impressive Oerlikon firing trials in October 1936, Ross promised Gazda that he would do his best to interest the Royal Navy in it. Because there was no gunnery division in the naval staff at that time he could not find anyone in the Admiralty to take an interest until he called on his 'old term mate, Lord Louis Mountbatten, who was then in the Naval Air Division . . .'.

Ross described the most determined efforts made by Mountbatten to persuade the Admiralty to give the Oerlikon a fair trial:

> All to no avail until the breakthrough when Admiral of the Fleet [*sic*] Sir Roger Backhouse became First Sea Lord. . . . Until this decisive moment Toni Gazda had had 238 meetings with Admiralty officials and it was now almost too late. Delivery of guns from Switzerland ceased when France was overrun in 1940.
>
> . . . had it not been for the foresight of Dickie Mountbatten and Roger Backhouse, the gun would never have been heard of. But for their vision and decisiveness, many more ships and lives would have been lost during the war.[9]

With the introduction of the Oerlikon Lord Louis could see a satisfactory, if scandalously delayed, result. A combination of good luck, skill and daring enabled a British naval commander, Steuart Mitchell (later Rear Admiral Sir Steuart Mitchell), to bring out of Switzerland and through Turkey the Oerlikon drawings and parts needed for the manufacture of the guns, first in the UK and then in the USA.

A similar saga, which reflected equally badly upon the ethos and professional competence of the Royal Navy in that crucial pre-war period, was the refusal of the Naval Staff Signals Division to advise the Board to adopt the Typex signal ciphering machine. The consequence was grave. Prior to mid-August 1940, when the Admiralty at last realised what was happening and changed the codes and ciphers, the enemy could read the Navy's ciphered messages. Roskill quotes a postwar German comment:

> The insight into British operations, which had lasted so long, thus came to an end. Knowledge of British movements had spared German vessels many a surprise encounter with superior forces and this had become an element in operational planning.[10]

Correlli Barnett, writing in the late 1980s when all the sources were open to him, had this to say:

> Even in the 1930s, and despite urging by Captain Lord Louis Mountbatten, little technical research was conducted into crypto-analytical technology. Although the Admiralty conducted trials with enciphering machines (the prototypes of the wartime German 'Enigma' and the RAF 'Typex'), the work was dropped.[11]

One area of professional interest – again quite outside his current responsibilities – for which Lord Louis found time, astonishingly, to follow up was destroyer design and construction. He had formed a high opinion of a member of the Royal Corps of Naval Constructors named A.P. Cole, and on joining the Naval Air Division in the spring of 1936 he renewed his acquaintance with Cole and gave him the benefit of his experience in command of *Daring* and *Wishart*. He had made notes on 'what was wrong with destroyer design and what should be done in the future'. Cole himself had ideas, some of them radical, such as reducing the number of boilers from three to two, and hence the number of funnels from two to one, thus reducing the silhouette, an important tactical factor before the advent of radar. But senior naval constructors objected, so Lord Louis had to win the support of the Controller of the Navy for the two-boiler policy in order to get it introduced. Neither he nor Cole gained in popularity in consequence; but future destroyers were better warships.

One of these, HMS *Kelly*, launched on the Tyne on 25 October 1938, incorporated another of Cole's initiatives, longitudinal hull framing, which had not hitherto been used in destroyers. Also, at the instance of Lord Louis, who was to be her first commanding officer, a bridge designed by him to offer some protection from the weather had been included by Cole in the plans. Having heard a year or two before from his brother Georgie that in the US Navy 'damage control' was being studied, Lord Louis had followed this up, and with Cole's help produced a damage control handbook for the 'K' class destroyers which were to form the 5th Flotilla under his command. In the war that was shortly to erupt, many damaged ships, including the *Kelly*, were saved from sinking by this technique – but many, it has to be said, were lost in the early years through its neglect.

While busy selecting and briefing officers to be appointed to the *Kelly*, and supervising her fitting-out, Lord Louis found time to bring into being, with the generous help of some of his Hollywood friends, such as Jack Warner, the Royal Naval Film Corporation. This was to ensure a supply of up-to-date films at minimal cost for the Royal Navy's ships and shore establishments, with a correspondingly good effect on morale in peace and war. As Captain (D) 5, he was responsible for the administration of all the ships of the flotilla once they were in commission; but long before then he and his staff officers were busy preparing the flotilla orders, administrative, technical and operational, to cover the full range of activities which could be foreseen.

The imminence of war spurred everyone on to eliminate all possible delays. Even so, when Lord Louis visited the other ships of his flotilla – *Kashmir* and *Kimberley* at Thorneycroft's yard, *Kingston* at White's, *Kelvin* at Fairfield's, *Kipling* at Yarrow's, *Kandahar* at Denny's, and *Khartoum* at Swan Hunter's – some were behind schedule. All he could do was exhort, and set an example. But to ensure that all the flotilla's captains, engineer officers and first lieutenants would become a 'band of brothers', following Nelson's precept, and know what would be required of them, he invited the respective groups to stay with him at Broadlands. He also managed to get to know personally every member of the *Kelly*'s company as they joined her: first those standing by her during building and fitting-out; then the 'steaming party' which took her over for sea trials. These were satisfactorily completed and HMS *Kelly* arrived in Chatham, where the remainder of her ship's company joined her next day to be greeted individually by Lord Louis. The ship was now fully in commission.

Next morning he addressed the assembled company of the *Kelly* in the terms and manner made memorable by Noel Coward, who impersonated him in the film *In Which We Serve*. Three days later, having taken on stores and ammunition in about a fifth of the time normally allowed in peacetime, the *Kelly* was on her way to Portland, where she would 'work-up' to operational readiness and be joined by the rest of the 5th Flotilla as soon as they too had been commissioned.

On Sunday 3 September 1939 came the sadly disillusioned, broken voice of Neville Chamberlain announcing on BBC radio that as from 11am Great Britain was at war with Germany. On board the *Kelly*, as in the other HM ships present, preparations for covering her shining enamel with matt paint to help render her inconspicuous were put into effect. Before long her captain, suitably clad, was over the side with his sailors wielding a paintbrush. Later in the day came a message sent to the fleet by the Admiralty: WINSTON IS BACK. It probably meant more, personally, to Lord Louis, formerly His Serene Highness Prince Louis of Battenberg, than to anyone else in the Royal Navy; professionally, it was soon to mean more to him still.

For the Royal Navy the first few months of the Second World War resembled those of the First. The British Expeditionary Force was transported to France without loss and sustained there; the German merchant fleet was swept from the high seas; a distant but effective blockade of Germany was established; troop convoys were brought safely from Canada to Britain; British shipping, both coastal and ocean-going, was brought under control; the German main fleet stayed in harbour; minefields were sown; and a *guerre de course* was begun, with U-boats in the approaches to the British Isles and powerful raiders at large in the wider oceans. But as before, the inexorable pressures of sea power were brought to bear upon the enemy largely unnoticed by the British people. And although the torpedoing of the liner *Athenia* on the evening of 3 September heralded unrestricted submarine warfare against shipping, it was not until November that its full rigour was unleashed and neutral shipping was warned not to enter a designated war zone east of longitude 20° west.

There was, however, a new factor of decisive importance in the conduct and outcome of the war at sea: the capacity of shore-based aircraft to dominate sea areas within their radius of action. The Sea Lords, just as they had ignored the potential of shore-based anti-submarine aircraft in the defence of merchant shipping, failed to appreciate the potential of shore-based enemy aircraft to dominate naval operations within range of their airfields. Yet the evidence was there. On 22 February 1934, for example, fighter aircraft from HMS *Glorious* obtained about 30 per cent hits in dive-bombing attacks from around 5,000ft on the radio-controlled target battleship HMS *Centurion*; in high-level bombing from 8,000ft the torpedo-spotter-reconnaissance aircraft scored 10 per cent hits.

Lord Louis had done his best both to bring shore-based anti-submarine aircraft under naval command and improve the close-range air defence of ships, without success in the first instance, and too late in the second. Ironically, it was Winston Churchill who, having supported Lord Louis in his efforts, when war came once again imposed his amateur impulses upon a compliant First Sea Lord. He demanded, for example, that hunting groups were formed 'to work like a cavalry division on the approaches, without worrying about the traffic or the U-boat sinkings, but could search large areas over a wide front. . . .'.[12]

It was only by chance that on 14 September the *Ark Royal*, the Navy's only purpose-built fleet aircraft carrier, was not sunk by *U-39*, whose torpedoes exploded prematurely (owing to a fault which saved many of HM ships from destruction before it was eliminated). Three days later the fleet carrier *Courageous*, also hunting submarines, was hit and sunk by the torpedoes of *U-29*. Thus the Navy lost a quarter of its operational fleet carriers and 15 per cent of its front-line aircraft, as well as over 500 well-trained officers and men. Lord Louis, in the *Kelly*, was about 40 miles from the stricken *Courageous* when he got the signal giving her position, some 350 miles west of Land's End, and reached the spot in time to embark some of the survivors and bring them back to Devonport. Martin Gilbert states that 'The carrier *Courageous* had been on temporary escort duty.'[13] On the contrary, she had been sacrificed in 'searching large areas over a wide front'.

Having known in peacetime that he 'had to do everything twice as well to be promoted', when war came Lord Louis was bent – hell-bent, one may say – on 'seeking the bubble reputation even in the cannon's mouth'. And why not? As far as he was concerned it was a just war: 'Thank God I am not a German,' he had written in one of his many pre-war attempts to assure influential Germans with whom he was acquainted that Britain would fight. As a junior captain he could not normally expect to reach flag rank for another seven years. By that time the war might well be over. Although bursting with ideas about how the war should be conducted, and prone to press them on the most influential people, unashamedly using his royal connection, he was determined to do his job as a Captain (D) outstandingly well and thus be assured of the command, in due course, of one of the Navy's 'great ships' – preferably a fleet aircraft carrier. This was an entirely legitimate and laudable ambition – Nelson never concealed his thirst for glory. But, as in peacetime, Lord Louis was in competition for a rare appointment; and, as before, he had his detractors.

It was hard for them to fault his ship-handling. As an example, while operating in the Western Approaches he visited Dartmouth in the *Kelly*. The naval cadets (including, incidentally, his nephew, Prince Philip of Greece) were still in training there. One of them, Charles Poynder, recalled

the way Lord Louis . . . handled the large Fleet destroyer *Kelly* when he took her to two buoys in the small and difficult harbour. He even put the forward buoy jumper on the first buoy by sliding him down a boathook, instead of sending him there in a whaler.[14]

A less exemplary episode was Lord Louis's failure in the *Kelly* to intercept the American merchantman SS *City of Flint*, which had a German prize crew and a number of British seamen on board embarked from ships sunk by the German raider *Deutschland*. The Norwegian authorities were exercising strict neutrality, and so, as the *City of Flint* made her way south towards a German port, she could not be boarded provided she remained within Norwegian territorial waters where the depth of water permitted. Rejecting the standard search plan proposed by his navigator, Lord Louis went at full-speed straight to where he estimated that the *City of Flint* would be, and failed to find her. Although he acknowledged his error to his officers, Lord Louis unfortunately turned his ship homeward much too sharply for the speed she was doing, and despite the heavy sea which was running. In consequence the ship rolled excessively, and nearly to the danger limit: two ratings were washed overboard, one of whom was drowned; the other, miraculously, was swept back aboard. The ship also suffered considerable, if superficial, damage. The result was that the *Kelly* found herself back in the Tyne, where she had been built. The opportunity was taken to strengthen her hull plating against the ice that might be met during an operation in the Baltic which Churchill had in mind at that time.

In mid-December, two days before the *Kelly* was due to go back to sea, a signal was received by Lord Louis from the Commander-in-Chief, Rosyth Area, Vice-Admiral Charles Ramsey, that two British tankers had been torpedoed off the entrance to the Tyne and were sinking; he was to take any available destroyers and proceed to sea as soon as possible to hunt the submarine. But the destroyers being still under repair, it would be several hours before they could raise steam and get to sea. In any case, having looked at the depth of water on the chart where the ships had supposedly been torpedoed by a U-boat, Lord Louis became convinced that they had in fact struck mines. He put this to the Flag Officer Tyne, Rear Admiral Maxwell, who thought it reasonable and telephoned the Commander-in-Chief. To no avail. Ramsey instructed him to tell Mountbatten to stop bellyaching and get to sea.

Some hours later, the *Kelly*, with the *Mohawk* half a mile astern, cautiously approached the burning oil-tankers, the *Ethel Templar* and the *Inverlain*. A mine, laid by a German surface force several nights before, was heard bumping along under the *Kelly* before exploding under her stern, wrecking her propellers. This put Lord Louis's ship out of action for another 11 weeks. As it was shortly before Christmas 1939, most of *Kelly*'s company had already used their free rail travel warrants and spare cash. Philip Ziegler describes how 'Lady Louis stepped in and offered to pay the return fare for any member of the crew who wished to go home'.[15]

The cruiser *Naiad* was completing at the same yard and Lieutenant (E) Le Bailly (later Vice-Admiral Sir Louis Le Bailly) recalled lecturing to her engine-room department on the merits of the Mountbatten station-keeping gear, as the ship was the first cruiser to be fitted with this:

> Rear Admiral King (no friend of Mountbatten) on being proudly shown the gear by the chief of *Naiad* at once ordered its removal. Cruisers are for scouting ahead of the

Fleet and station-keeping will not be a wartime requirement. So the gear was landed and we did little else but station-keep until sunk.

On completion of repairs to *Kelly* MB gave a party for the whole of her ship's company (and *Naiad* officers) introducing each sailor by name to his wife. As a very junior Lt I found this impressive.[16]

Until the *Kelly* was ready for sea again Lord Louis transferred with his flotilla staff to the *Kelvin*, then at Portland. In the meantime two of his flotilla, *Kashmir* and *Kingston*, had helped the *Icarus* to sink *U-35* off the Orkneys, the entire crew being saved. But Lord Louis was most unhappy to learn later that the captain of the *Kingston*, Lieutenant Commander Peter Somerville, had been 'quietly ticked off for having treated the prisoners so well'. It was Lord Louis's custom, in common with most captains of HM ships when taking religious services on board, to include Nelson's prayer before Trafalgar, ending: 'And may humanity after victory be the predominating feature of the British Fleet.' Long after the war he found out that the captain of *U-35* had himself acted humanely by ensuring that the crew of the SS *Diamantis*, which he had sunk, were landed safely in Ireland, and corresponded with him.

At sea once again in the *Kelly*, early in March 1940 Lord Louis found himself in charge of the destroyers screening the fleet. A revealing sidelight on the efforts made to catch him out in some lack of alertness or faulty manoeuvre is the clear recollection of a former naval rating, at the time a signal boy in HMS *Nelson*, the fleet flagship. On two occasions, when *Kelly* was forming part of the screen, he was instructed to attach her signal pennants (the numbers, he recalls, were 01) to the inner halyards and keep them just out of sight on the flag deck, ready to be hoisted instantly 'at the dip' should the *Kelly* be the slightest bit slow in hoisting her answering pennant or repeating a signal from the flagship. But this performance was never instigated when any other Captain (D) was in charge. For a ship's pennants to be hoisted in that manner – known as 'a pair of kippers' – was 'considered quite an insult'.[17] The opportunity to hoist them was not provided by the *Kelly*.

Unfortunately on 9 March the *Kelly* was in collision, during a snowstorm, with the destroyer *Gurkha*. Lord Louis had given a standing order to his radio watchkeepers that immediately the ship seemed to have been struck they should signal 'Have been hit by mine or torpedo.' The *Gurkha* replied, 'That was not mine but me.' The fleet much enjoyed this good joke at Lord Louis's expense. To his credit, although *Kelly*'s officer of the watch was to blame, he treated him, as Ziegler puts it, 'with striking charity'. The *Gurkha*, it transpired, was far out of position.

Lest it be thought that the *Kelly*'s series of misfortunes betokened incompetence on the part of her captain, it is well to recall that by this date 'the dangers of the sea and the violence of the enemy' had claimed two destroyers of the 7th Flotilla badly damaged in collision; several Home Fleet ships damaged in a gale; the destroyer *Duchess* run down and sunk by the battleship *Barham*; and the destroyer *Jersey* torpedoed by the German destroyer *Erich Giese*. Much worse was soon to come.

Lord Louis had written on 15 February to the Foreign Secretary, his friend Anthony Eden, in the strictest confidence, warning him, on the basis of private information, of 'the strong likelihood of France not being able to hold out another winter'. He continued:

> How long could Germany hold out if we decided to violate International Law to a relatively mild extent by stopping the whole of her iron ore trade from Narvik, if necessary in Norwegian Territorial Waters?
>
> I know that it goes against the grain to violate in the smallest degree International Law, but to divert enemy ships into contraband control bases from neutral waters is surely a very small crime compared with the sinking of neutral ships on the high seas, in which our enemy are indulging.[18]

The War Cabinet needed no prompting from Captain Mountbatten to try to deprive Germany of the ore being shipped from Narvik. But Churchill's proposal was to lay mines in Norwegian waters and force the ore ships to seaward, where they could be captured. This being ruled out as unacceptable politically, an Anglo-French expeditionary force was to be sent to Narvik on the pretext of passing through to northern Sweden (where the ore lay), ostensibly to aid the Finns, who were being invaded by Russia. On the eve of the expedition Finland made peace with Russia. Hence Churchill got his way and an operation was set in train to lay the mines on 8 April.

In the meantime Hitler had ordered the invasion of Norway. By 9 April his troops had established themselves as far north as Narvik, transported by warships and supported by the Luftwaffe. From 14 to 17 April Allied troops were landed north and south of Trondheim, but the War Cabinet could not decide whether Narvik or Trondheim should be the primary objective, while Churchill, as First Lord, continually interfered with the Commander-in-Chief, Home Fleet's operations. The result was 'order, counter-order, disorder', compounded by the success of the Germans in deciphering a high proportion of the Royal Navy's operational signal traffic. Owing mainly to German air superiority the plan to take Trondheim had to be abandoned and the main effort directed towards Narvik.

On 29 April Lord Louis arrived at Scapa Flow in the *Kelly* to join an Allied cruiser and destroyer force commanded by Vice-Admiral J.D.H. Cunningham in the *Devonshire* which, with three French transports, was to evacuate the British and French troops from Namsos. It was expected that two nights would be needed to achieve this. Then on 1 May, when the force arrived in the area, fog imposed delay. However, Lord Louis, hoping that the fog would provide concealment from the German bombers which had been devastating Namsos, obtained permission to take the *Maori* and with two other destroyers attempt to negotiate the 70-mile passage up the fjord, utilising his sonar and echo-sounder as navigational aids.

All went well until, nearing Namsos, bombs began to land near the ships and it was realised that their mastheads were visible above the fog. Then suddenly the sky cleared and the air attack was redoubled. The destroyers had to reverse course and the *Maori* was hit before they could get back into the fog.

That night, 2/3 May, the fog cleared, and Captain Vian in the *Afridi* was able to lead in the transports, with the *Nubian*, the cruiser *York* and the French destroyer *Bison*. Being free to act independently, rather than held back by the slower transports, Lord Louis raced ahead in the *Kelly* and began to embark the Chasseurs Alpins. In just three hours nearly 6,000 troops were evacuated, but before the ships could escape beyond the range of the Ju87s they were heavily attacked. The hopeless inadequacy of the fleet's close-range anti-aircraft armament, to which Lord Louis had pointed so frequently but in vain when trying to get the Oerlikon gun adopted, was now tragically apparent. Down came wave after wave of Stukas. First the *Bison*, with her embarked soldiery, was sunk; then the *Afridi*, last to leave Namsos, was herself sunk going to the rescue of *Bison*'s survivors. Even so, nearly the whole of 'Maurice Force' was brought home. As its brave and colourful commander, General Carton de Wiart, wrote later:

> In the course of that last, endless day I got a message from the Navy to say that they would evacuate the whole of my force that night. I thought it was impossible, but learned a few hours later that the Navy do not know the word.'[19]

Of his part in this stirring and successful operation, Lord Louis's only published recollection is laconic but evocative:

> We took part in the evacuation of Namsos. It was a dark night, with dark blue sky overhead and black, towering cliffs on each side, as we entered the deep, magnificent fjord. At its head stood the town of Namsos. Built entirely of wood, and blazing like a Hollywood film set. We ran alongside the pier, collected our soldiers and brought them out.[20]

On completion of the Namsos operation Lord Louis in *Kelly* was sent to the Clyde to refuel. Almost immediately, on 8 May, he was told to take *Kimberley* and proceed 'with all despatch' to join the cruiser *Birmingham*, bearing the flag of Vice-Admiral Sir Geoffrey Layton who, with four destroyers, had orders to search for an enemy minelaying force in the vicinity of the German island of

Sylt. Having steamed at 31 knots, as ordered, to cover the 800 miles or so to the rendezvous, Lord Louis received a signal saying that the *Birmingham* would be two hours late reaching it, so that he could have steamed at less than full speed and conserved fuel; as it was he had to send the *Kimberley* to refuel.

Having met the *Birmingham*, the *Kelly*, with other destroyers, was stationed 3 miles ahead of her as an anti-submarine screen. At 0718 hours a patrolling aircraft reported a submarine ahead of the force, adding that she had caused it to dive, but failing to say how far ahead. Ten minutes or so later, when this had been established, Lord Louis was detached in the *Kelly*, with the *Kandahar*, to hunt the supposed U-boat. In his Report of Proceedings dated 20 May 1940 he stated:

> I had to decide how long to remain hunting this submarine without prejudicing my chance of rejoining the *Birmingham* before she made contact with the enemy.
> . . . At 8.18pm an enemy report of four minelayers, three destroyers and one torpedo boat was received from an aircraft. I proceeded to rejoin *Birmingham*, who was only just in sight on the horizon and signalled that she was doing 28 knots. . . .
> Visibility fairly good to Eastwards, very good to Westward but hazy to North. At about 10.30pm visibility to the North (port) became very bad. Speed 28 knots to allow *Bulldog* to catch up. At 10.44pm a blurred object was sighted by a number of people (including myself), about 3 or 4 cables on the port beam in the mist – almost simultaneously I saw the track of a torpedo. . . .[21]

The torpedo hit abreast the *Kelly*'s forward boiler room and exploded, causing a 50ft hole and immediate rapid flooding, with many men killed or severely wounded. With commendable coolness, presence of mind and skill, Lord Louis took the action necessary to prevent his ship from capsizing, with the inevitable loss of most of her company. With his, at that time exceptional, knowledge of damage control, for which his crew were organised and trained, no time was lost in eliminating topweight – torpedoes, ammunition (except close-range AA) and boats (except lifesaving floats) were ditched and all possible measures taken to maintain the watertight integrity of the ship, while the wounded were given first aid and preparations made to be taken in tow by the *Bulldog* (to which Lord Louis later paid a glowing tribute). Almost four days later, by then in tow of tugs, the *Kelly* arrived safely back in the Tyne.

At a time when the British people were hungry for better news, after the debacle in Norway, the epic story of how the *Kelly* lived to fight another day was a welcome boost to morale. Lord Louis was a public figure, whom the press were happy to lionise. But several senior officers, and some of his contemporaries, rather than immediately recognising the novel and potent threat posed by the German E-boats (fast inshore torpedo-boats), and the vital importance of good damage control, chose to criticise Lord Louis for being torpedoed. They were wrong to do so.

In the first place, this was the first-ever attack by E-boats on units of the fleet. Hence there was no reason to doubt that what the aircraft had reported was a U-boat; having dived ahead of the force, it was an immediate threat to the *Birmingham* and must therefore be hunted remorselessly. Given that the cruiser still had four destroyers screening her, Lord Louis was correct in prosecuting the U-boat hunt for as long as he could without losing touch with the flagship; and it was understandable, since a dived U-boat had been reported, that the hydrophone effect which had been detected was classified as emanating from a U-boat, whereas in fact it was from an E-boat at high speed, invisible in the haze. Indeed, Commander Robson (later Vice-Admiral Sir Geoffrey Robson) in the *Kandahar* was evidently in no doubt about the presence of a U-boat, as he did not risk submarine attack himself by remaining with the *Kelly* to pick up survivors but left her vicinity at full speed. He may have regretted this later, when it became clear that what he thought was a U-boat turned out to have been an E-boat.

Lord Louis was criticised unjustly, also, for having made an unnecessary signal by bright Morse lamp to the force commander, thus indicating the *Kelly*'s position to the E-boat, which then attacked her. Given that he had hunted what he, and everyone else, thought was a U-boat until it was no longer a threat, when the *Kelly* set off at full speed to rejoin the flagship, the problem was to remain in V/S (visual signalling) distance while resuming station. As it was already dusk, and the visibility to the eastward somewhat limited, the *Birmingham* could barely be discerned on the horizon; yet to the westward it was not dark enough to use a dimmed flashing lamp as in complete darkness. So *Kelly*'s bright Aldis signalling lamp was used to indicate her position as she pounded after the admiral, hoping to catch up with him before the enemy was encountered.

In the event, Admiral Layton did not make contact with the enemy, despite having increased speed, so that the destroyers he had detached to hunt the U-boat would have taken hours to rejoin him. As he sped past the near-sinking *Kelly* on his return to base the Admiral suggested to Lord Louis that he should scuttle her, as not being worth the trouble and danger of trying to salvage. But seven months later the *Kelly* was at sea again. To have built a new destroyer would have taken 18 months at least, and used about 2,000 tons of steel. Not worth salvaging?

Now without a ship of his own, Lord Louis established himself and his staff ashore at Immingham, going to sea in one or other of his flotilla, now comprising both 'J' and 'K' class destroyers. During the evacuation of the troops from Dunkirk at the end of May, Lord Louis's destroyers were deployed in the eastern approaches to the Channel against the expected incursion of German naval forces. Surprisingly this did not occur, perhaps owing to Hitler's expectation that Britain would sue for peace once France had fallen.

On 22 June 1940 the French government of Marshal Pétain at Vichy accepted the German's terms for an armistice, which came into effect on 25 June. Thenceforward the coast of Europe from the North Cape to the Spanish frontier was in enemy hands. The prospect of invasion was very real. Lord Louis and Edwina (now rapidly rising in the St John Ambulance hierarchy) had to decide whether or not to evacuate their children to the USA. There was no doubt that if the Germans invaded and the Nazi political police began to operate, prominent people such as Edwina, with her Jewish blood, and indeed the whole family, would be in peril. So on 4 July Patricia and Pamela Mountbatten sailed for New York in the liner *Washington*.

On 31 August Lord Louis was aboard the *Jupiter*, with the *Javelin* in company, in support of destroyers laying mines off the Friesian Islands, when three of them, the *Express*, *Esk* and *Ivanhoe*, themselves struck mines. Should he risk yet another casualty by going to the aid of the damaged ships? With the *Jupiter* he succeeded in towing the *Express* back to harbour, but both the others had to be sunk.

In October, after victory in the Battle of Britain had denied the Germans air superiority over the Channel, and the invasion threat had diminished accordingly, the 5th Flotilla was moved to Plymouth. Its first operation from there, on 15 October, was to take part with the battleship *Revenge* in a bombardment of Cherbourg. Two days later, in company with the cruiser *Newcastle*, the flotilla had an indecisive engagement with four German destroyers at the entrance to the Bristol Channel. Lord Louis was critical of the conduct of this operation, as the enemy was able to use his superior speed to get away.

On 24 November three of the same group of German destroyers, operating from Brest, made a sortie to the area off Plymouth and sank two merchant ships. On 28 November they returned again, wishing no doubt to take advantage of the moonless nights to avoid interception. Sweeping from east to west in the same area they first found and sank two tugs, and an hour later sank a small steamer, in both cases by gunfire. Lord Louis, embarked with his flotilla navigator and signals officer in the *Javelin* (Commander Anthony Pugsley), with the *Jupiter*, *Kashmir*, *Jackal* (next senior ship) and *Jersey* in company, had reached the western limit of his patrol area south of the Lizard at 3.50am when gun flashes were seen to the east, below the horizon. He at once set off at 30 knots on a course south of east so as to make sure of getting between the enemy and their base. At 5.04am more gun flashes were seen, now to the north of east.

Certain now that he could cut off the enemy force, Lord Louis disposed his ships on an east–west line of bearing – roughly at right angles to the direction in which the enemy was expected to be sighted. This was the classic means of ensuring an interception, while remaining ready to re-form into line ahead if the tactical situation should require it. He then turned the flotilla north, to close the enemy as quickly as possible. Speed was of the essence.

Comparing the forces that were about to make contact with each other, five British destroyers were pitted against three German, but the latter were 3 knots faster and carried torpedoes which could be fired in a fan-shaped salvo, with advanced fire control. The British method, which had hardly changed since Jutland, required the ship when firing torpedoes to be pointing at right angles to the direction in which they were required to run. But by far the most telling advantage enjoyed by the Germans was the serviceable radar with which they were equipped. In a night encounter, to sight the enemy before he sees you is all important. Although two of Lord Louis's destroyers were equipped with radar (still known as RDF), in neither case was it serviceable.

The two leading German destroyers, *Karl Galster* and *Richard Beitzen*, turned south at 0530 hours to return to their base at Brest; the *Hans Lody*, having become separated, was hastening to rejoin them when radar contact was made with the rapidly closing British force at 0538 hours, range 7,000 yards. Two minutes later Lord Louis and others on the bridge of the *Javelin*, having made no radar contact, suddenly saw the German vessels 'ahead, crossing from right to left'.

Having achieved the exceptionally difficult task of intercepting the Germans as they headed for base after a hit-and-run raid, Lord Louis had now to ensure that, given their superior speed, they did not escape destruction. The forces were closing at well over 60 knots, so with the range under 1 mile he turned his force 90° to port together, which brought them into fine quarter-line on a parallel course with the enemy. His ships could now open fire with all their guns at the Germans without endangering each other, and be able to hit them hard before they could flee out of range.

Alerted by radar, the leading enemy destroyers had already launched salvoes of torpedoes, begun to turn away and were making smoke. Two of a 'fan' of four torpedoes fired by the *Karl Galster* at the British force hit the *Javelin* moments after she had steadied on her new course and opened fire with all her guns. At that stage, unfortunately, the British destroyers still lacked flashless cordite and in the mêlée only the next in line, the *Jupiter*, realised that the *Javelin* had been torpedoed. In particular, the captain of the *Jackal* remained unaware that he was now in command of the flotilla, so the Germans, having escaped behind their smokescreen with little damage, continued to elude the four unscathed but leaderless British destroyers and regain their base at Brest. The *Javelin* was towed to safety and subsequently repaired.

Ziegler says of this episode that Lord Louis was 'moving at full speed, and the resultant noise, coupled with the enemy's superior radars, gave the Germans ample warning of his approach'.[22] But noise (made by forced draught fans at full power) had nothing to do with alerting the Germans; their radar had everything to do with it. The essential fact to grasp is that unless Lord Louis had

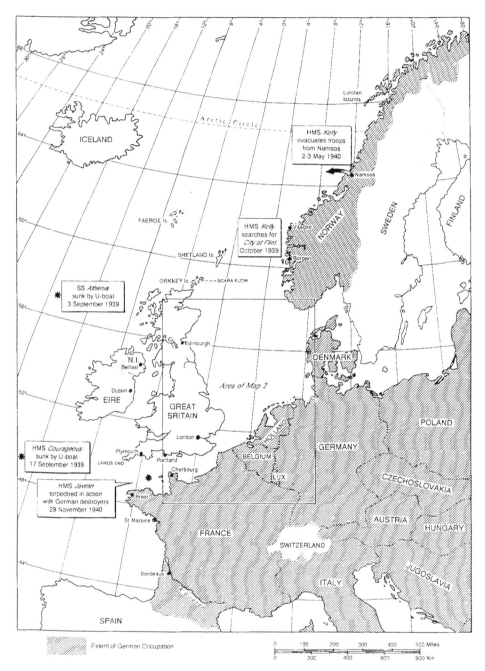

Map 1. Home Waters, 1939–43

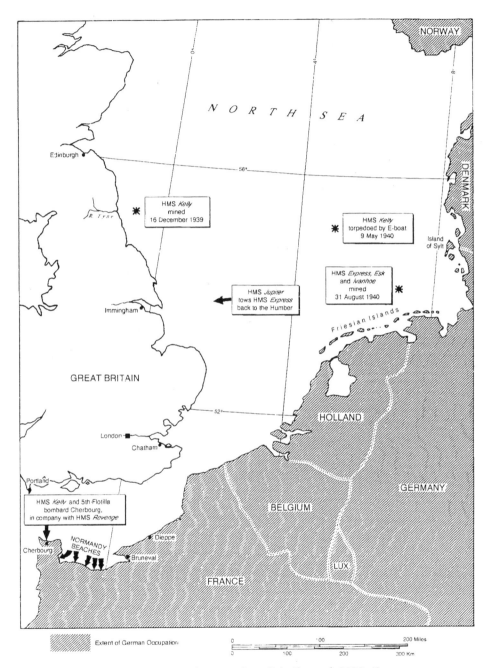

Map 2. The North Sea and English Channel, 1939–43

moved at full speed he would never, on a moonless night, have managed to intercept the Germans at all. No doubt 'the powers that be . . . concluded that Mountbatten had been at fault'. He had been right about too many matters too often; it was an opportunity to take him down a peg.

But a final, objective, Admiralty appraisal of the action was made when the logs of the German destroyers became available for study after the war:

> Although the German destroyers suffered no damage in this operation (except minor splinter damage from near misses) the conclusion of the German High Command was that 'the danger of operating in this area was very apparent, particularly as British air reconnaissance was very active while German air cover was but slight'. The unsuccessful outcome of this operation confirmed the Naval Staff's doubts about using destroyers in the Channel, and it was decided that operations would have to be avoided in view of the risks involved.[23]

If the outcome of the operation was, from the German standpoint, unsuccessful, the naval opinion upon which Mountbatten's official biographer based his judgement that 'Mountbatten blundered' merits re-examination. Not only did Lord Louis succeed in bringing the elusive German raiding force to action, despite his lack of serviceable radar, but his tactics were sound. To bring his superior force to bear decisively on the German destroyers before they could escape, he had to accept the risk of being torpedoed. The comment on this aspect of the action in the Admiralty study is cogent:

> The torpedo control of the German destroyers seems to have been either remarkably quick and intelligent or remarkably lucky.[24]

In 1940 the Royal Navy had not yet adopted operations analysis as a means of determining systematically what had taken place, and learning the appropriate lessons. Weight of brass equated with weight of opinion. On this occasion the heaviest weight appears to have been carried by the Vice Chief of the Naval Staff, Rear Admiral T.S.V. Phillips, who had not been to sea in wartime since 1918; who had obdurately refused to accept that it was suicidal to operate off an enemy-held coast without air cover; and in December was himself to lose the *Prince of Wales* and *Repulse* to Japanese air attack. As to the views of Commander Pugsley, the captain of the *Javelin*, chagrin at the torpedoing of his ship while carrying out Mountbatten's orders was understandable. But the instantly expressed desire of this self-styled 'Destroyer Man' to 'go straight at' an enemy force of faster ships suddenly sighted crossing his bow under a mile away revealed a surprising lack of tactical sense. Indeed, his brash exclamation, at a critical moment, was not helpful and may even have delayed for a few vital seconds Lord Louis's entirely correct decision to turn his ships to a course parallel with the enemy – a delay for which he blamed himself.

In December 1940 the *Kelly* was once again ready for sea, and on 31 December the award of the DSO to Lord Louis was gazetted. In early April 1941 he was ordered to take the 5th Flotilla to the Mediterranean, giving effect to Churchill's directive that the Axis supply lines to North Africa should be ruthlessly attacked. But by the time he arrived in Malta with his six destroyers, *Kelly*, *Kipling*, *Kelvin*, *Kashmir*, *Jackal* and *Jersey*, now designated Force K, the evacuation of the Army from Greece had already begun. The reversal of fortunes arising from the Greek adventure had been dramatic. Rommel's Afrika Korps had routed the hitherto victorious British Army in the desert and was driving it back to the Egyptian frontier.

Force K carried out sweeps, but without locating a convoy. Returning from a sortie on 4 May, *Jersey* struck a mine as she followed *Kelly*, *Jackal* and *Kelvin* into the Grand Harbour, and sank. There being no operational minesweepers to clear a channel, Force K was trapped in harbour. Adrian Seligman, at the time a lieutenant in the RN Reserve recalls:

> I only met the noble Lord once – when he sent for me in Malta to decide how to deal with a magnetic mine dropped by aircraft near the entrance to the Grand Harbour. . . . What impressed me most about him was his ability, without any effort or trace of insincerity, to make a very junior 'Rocky' feel at ease and wanted.[25]

However, on advice from the fleet torpedo officer, depth charges were used to blast a safe channel by counter-mining, and Lord Louis with his staff marked it by laying dan-buoys, precisely located. Luckily the magnetic-minesweeper *Gloxinia* soon came on the scene and exploded several more mines, so Force K was able to emerge from Malta just in time to meet a British convoy being run from Gibraltar to Alexandria, simultaneously with another from there to Malta.

Lord Louis's force was detached on the night of 10/11 May to shell the Axis shipping using Benghazi. The operation was successful, although most of the ships in that battered harbour had been sunk already. For the first time, however, the intrepid and skilful German dive-bombers attacked at night, as Force K was withdrawing. Admiral Sir Andrew Cunningham (the Rear Admiral at Malta who had questioned Mountbatten's ability to handle the *Daring*) was displeased, and wrote to the First Sea Lord:

> I was a little disappointed with the 5th Flotilla. They were dive-bombed by moonlight and legged it to the Northward. If they had gone South in accordance with their orders I think they would have picked up four ships which arrived at Benghazi next day.[26]

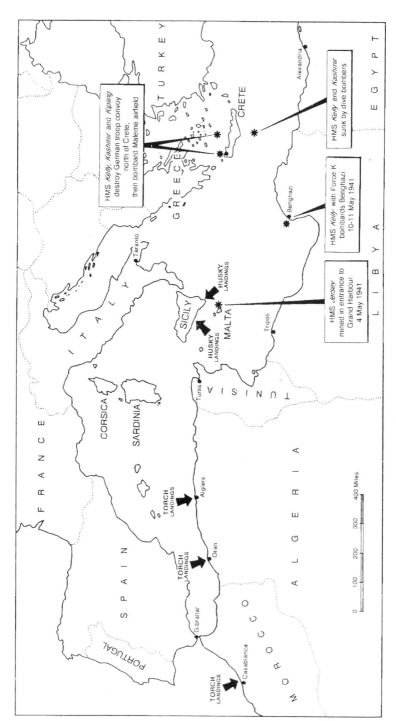

HMS *Kelly, Kashmir* and *Kipling*
destroy German troop convoy
north of Crete,
then bombard Maleme airfield

HMS *Kelly* and *Kashmir*
sunk by dive bombers

HMS *Kelly* with Force K
bombards Benghazi
10–11 May 1941

HMS *Jersey*
mined in entrance to
Grand Harbour
4 May 1941

TURKEY

EGYPT

CRETE

Alexandria

GREECE

LIBYA

Benghazi

ITALY

Taranto

HUSKY
LANDINGS

SICILY

MALTA

Tripoli

HUSKY
LANDINGS

CORSICA

SARDINIA

TUNISIA

Tunis

FRANCE

SPAIN

PORTUGAL

Gibraltar

ALGERIA

Algiers

TORCH
LANDINGS

Oran

TORCH
LANDINGS

MOROCCO

Casablanca

TORCH
LANDINGS

0   100   200   300   400 Miles

Map 3. The Mediterranean, 1941–43

Cunningham's faith in the offensive spirit as a substitute for air support gravely weakened his requests for more 'air' and led to the loss of many brave men and fine ships for no strategic gain. In any case it is hardly to be doubted that Force K would have gone for the enemy ships if their actual presence and position had been reliably reported. The imputation of a lack of courage and offensive spirit in Lord Louis was singularly unapt, as the next few days would show.

Ultra intelligence, combined with reports from agents in Greece, had by mid-May given warning that the Germans intended to seize Crete, using both airborne and seaborne forces. Sadly, no serious effort was made to provide adequate air defence for the island, whose garrison of numerous well-trained troops ought to have been able to hold it against the expected level of threat. About 3,000 German paratroops were dropped on Crete at 8am on 20 May. By 22 May the 5th Flotilla, no longer Force K, had joined the confused agglomeration of Cunningham's forces supporting the Army as best it could. Well aware by this time of the weight and effectiveness of German air attack on ships, Lord Louis had left behind in Malta a suitcase packed with uniform, as a precaution lest the *Kelly* should be sunk. This was certainly prescient.

Almost as soon as the 5th Flotilla had joined the main body of the fleet, west of Crete, its ships were ordered to rescue the survivors of the cruisers *Gloucester* and *Fiji*. The *Kingston* was already at the scene. The ferocity of the air attacks was devastating. Somehow *Kelly*, *Kashmir* and *Kipling* were not hit, and that evening Lord Louis was ordered to take them north of Crete and bombard Maleme airfield, a key position then in the possession of German airborne forces, albeit lightly armed and anxiously awaiting seaborne reinforcements. En route to the bombardment area Lord Louis's group intercepted and destroyed a couple of caiques carrying troops and petrol. The bombardment itself was also a success, and enabled the New Zealanders to recapture the airfield, although it could not be held for much longer.

It is necessary now to quote from the official history, *The War at Sea*, because the consequences of a failure of communications, for which Cunningham staunchly accepted responsibility, were disastrous:

> In the early hours of the 23rd, Admiral Cunningham gained the impression, from an error made in a signal, that the heavy ships had run out of ammunition and therefore ordered Admiral Rawlings back to Alexandria. This deprived Lord Louis Mountbatten's destroyers of support during their dawn withdrawal from the Aegean. At about 8am heavy air attacks started against his force, which was then only some 40 miles to the south of Crete. The *Kelly* and *Kashmir* were quickly sunk but the *Kipling* had seen the attacks, closed and managed to pick up 279 survivors from the two ships, including the flotilla's commander. She was heavily bombed while doing so but, happily, escaped unscathed.[27]

Sadly the *Kelly*'s first lieutenant, Lord Hugh Beresford, did not survive. He was lost when, with the first lieutenant of the *Kipling*, John Bush, he was trying to lower a boat to collect more men from the water.

Safely back in Alexandria, Lord Louis stayed for the next few days with Cunningham. All he could do was ensure the survivors from his flotilla were cared for, and gather those from the *Kelly*, bedraggled but unbowed as they were, for a farewell address. The fact that this was immortalised by Noel Coward in the film *In Which We Serve* should not be allowed to diminish its sincerity and force.

No doubt it was to ensure a 'warts and all' authorised biography of Mountbatten that it was entrusted to an author (Philip Ziegler) who, born in 1929, had no personal experience of the Second World War, let alone its higher direction, nor any first-hand knowledge of the Royal Navy between the wars. Considered from the point of view of the author, who joined the Navy in 1931 as a naval cadet, and left it in 1970 as a vice-admiral, it is clear that Ziegler's judgement of Lord Louis's professional competence as a captain of destroyers is hopelessly adrift. Posterity – and especially future generations of British naval officers – deserves to be better informed.

Winston Churchill, for all his faults as First Lord of the Admiralty in both world wars, did not err when he wrote, after the First World War:

> 'The Silent Service' was not mute because it was absorbed in thought and study, but because it was weighed down by its daily routine and by its ever-complicating and diversifying technique. We had competent administrators, brilliant experts of every description, unequalled navigators, good disciplinarians, fine sea-officers, brave and devoted hearts: but at the outset of the conflict we had more captains of ships than captains of war.[28]

It is evident, from his autobiography *A Sailor's Odyssey* (1951), that Andrew Cunningham, known to the Navy as 'ABC', was primarily a captain of ships. Having taken command of the destroyer *Scorpion* in January 1911, he remained in her until January 1918. Such action as he saw in that ship was mainly confined to bombardment at Gallipoli and convoy escort in the Mediterranean; that he 'never lost a single ship' he attributed to his insistence on 'exact station-keeping by the escorting destroyers'. His only engagement with enemy warships was an ineffectual brush with German destroyers off the Belgian coast when he was in charge of some British destroyers. 'To be 5,000 yards off the enemy and unable to hit them was exasperating and a poor reflection on our gunnery,' he wrote. But then, preoccupation with exact station-keeping was hardly conducive to effective use of gun and torpedo in action. It was not until after 'this distressing episode', as he called it, that Cunningham 'sought and obtained permission' for his sub-division to have even the most elementary gunnery practice.

Such were, and evidently remained, Cunningham's priorities, for in his memoirs he boasts that he 'conveniently forgot' that he should take the examinations prescribed for aspiring commanders of destroyers in gunnery, torpedo and signals – 'and so did the Admiralty'. Nor did he contribute 'between the wars' to improving the Navy's capacity to cope with the advent of aircraft and submarines as potentially decisive elements of naval power; he did not even pursue the development of radio-telephony, the dramatic possibilities of which, for the coordination of warships' movements, he had witnessed in a night destroyer exercise in 1923. Cunningham's attitude to technical innovation was summed up in his favourite comment upon any novel equipment: it was too 'velvet-arsed and Rolls Royce'. He was content, also, to be without radar in his flagship, *Warspite*, and it was *Valiant*'s radar that detected a large ship at 6 miles range, in the action off Cape Matapan on 18 March 1941, which led to the destruction of three Italian cruisers, although their supporting battleship, damaged by the Fleet Air Arm, escaped.

Rivalry between 'captains of ships', the 'salt-horse' non-specialist destroyer captains, and the potential 'captains of war' – newly promoted gunnery, torpedo or signals specialist commanders who were the subdivisional leaders – was at its height in the 1930s in the Mediterranean Destroyer Command under Cunningham. Typical was an exchange over pink gins in the wardroom one Saturday morning: a senior ('been in destroyers man and boy') divisional commander, seeking to scupper a 'specialist' subdivisional commander, thought he would have the last word: 'I'll tell you this, Max – I'm a seaman.' 'Yes, Roland,' came back the other, 'but surely you've got some brains as well.'

In this context 'brains' meant, in the words of the founders of *The Naval Review*, 'knowledge relevant to the higher aspects of the naval profession'. Moreover, it implied a readiness to express opinions, in the presence of an admiral, on such 'higher aspects'. There is no doubt that Lord Louis was prone to range widely in his conversation over aspects of the conduct of the war which he believed to be unsatisfactory, and give his opinion as to what should be done. And when he left Alexandria he took with him personal messages from Sir Andrew Cunningham to the Prime Minister, emphasising in particular the desperate shortage of air support for the fleet. But he appears also to have exasperated the Commander-in-Chief by failing to show even a semblance of the deference to which that dignitary was accustomed.

A lieutenant who had been Flotilla Signal Officer in the *Kelly* also stayed with the Commander-in-Chief, remaining after Lord Louis had left. It seems, even allowing for the stress which Cunningham was under at the time, singularly inappropriate that he should have said to him, one of Mountbatten's officers: 'The trouble with your flotilla, boy, is that it was thoroughly badly led.' This was the comment of an admiral whose own style of leadership was modelled on that of the pre-1914 era, and who, like his close friend Dudley Pound, would not have attained the highest commands had it not been for the untimely deaths of great naval leaders and potential captains of war such as Sir William Fisher, Sir Roger Backhouse and Sir Reginald Henderson, and the invaliding of Sir Geoffrey Blake. Furthermore, despite being served by many able staff officers, Cunningham failed to achieve the severance of the Axis supply line to North Africa, ending up with only a few cruisers and destroyers out of the formidable fleet with which he had been provided.

It was unwise of Ziegler to seize upon such remarks as that of Cunningham quoted above. He should not have paraded these as 'the unanimous feeling' of Lord Louis's 'peers', nor can he claim that, as a wartime commander of destroyers he was, 'by the highest standards . . . no better, than second rate'. In war, as in peace, he had proved himself to be a first-rate naval officer by any standards, and his potential to become a great captain of war was about to be realised.

3

CHIEF OF COMBINED OPERATIONS (1941–43)

In America I have heard much of a man who has been intensively studying amphibious operations for many months. I understand that his position is Chief of Combined Operations, and I think his name is Admiral Mountbatten. Anyone will be better than none; such an operation cannot be carried out under committee command. But I have heard that Admiral Mountbatten is vigorous, intelligent and courageous, and if the operation is to be staged initially with British forces predominating, I assume he could do the job.

General Dwight D. Eisenhower, May 1942[1]

Chapter 3

I want you to turn the south coast of England from a bastion of defence
into a springboard for attack.

Winston Churchill to Captain Mountbatten, October 1941[2]

Captain Mountbatten arrived back in London from the Mediterranean on
18 June 1941. Three days later he was lunching with the Prime Minister
at 10 Downing Street. He had been invited so that he could convey personally
the message with which he had been charged by Sir Andrew Cunningham.
The only other guest was Lord Beaverbrook, lately Minister for Aircraft
Production. It was the eve of Hitler's invasion of the Soviet Union. Churchill's
warning of it seemed to have been totally ignored by Stalin. He and
Beaverbrook both expressed the view, shared by the Chief of the Imperial
General Staff and many other well-informed people, that the Germans would
quickly destroy the Russian armies. What would happen then? The Tripartite
Pact had been designed by Hitler to ensure that Japan would threaten the
interests of Britain and the USA in South-East Asia and the western Pacific.
This in turn would prejudice, perhaps fatally, American support of Britain and
her Empire.

Mountbatten, whose maternal grandfather had served with distinction in the
Russian army, believed that the Communist dictatorship was even more ruthless
than that of Hitler, more absolute than that of the Tsars, and better able than
Nicholas I had been when Napoleon attacked, to mobilise and arm the masses
in defence of Mother Russia. Whatever the outcome of the Russo-German
conflict, he affirmed, Britain needed the wholehearted support of the USA; and
military aid must be given to the Soviet Union in every practicable way. On
these key elements of policy there was no disagreement. The Prime Minister's
mood was genial; towards Captain Mountbatten he was avuncular. This boded
well for the realisation of Mountbatten's most ardent desire – to be given
command of a fleet aircraft carrier.

In the course of Louis's well-earned leave, spent mainly at Broadlands, the
Mountbattens were reunited. They had much to tell each other. Among those
present to hear the story of the *Kelly* and her end, so dramatic and tragic, was

Noel Coward. Between them they conceived the idea of making a propaganda film about a destroyer in the war, her captain, officers and men. Its origins may be traced even further back to the summer of 1935, in Malta, when Noel Coward had written, in response to an invitation: 'Dear Dickie, I should love to be bounced about in a destroyer under your supervision. . . .' In due course the classic *In Which We Serve* was born, its title taken from a prayer ordained since Victorian times 'to be used in Her Majesty's Navy every day':

> O Eternal Lord God, who alone spreadest out the heavens and ruleth the raging of the sea; who hath compassed the waters with bounds until day and night come to an end; be pleased to receive unto thy Almighty and most generous protection the persons of us thy servants, and the Fleet in which we serve. . . .

Edwina was glad to be able to tell her husband about her war work in the Joint War Organisation, which coordinated the activities of the Red Cross and the St John Ambulance Brigade. The Mountbattens' marriage, which had nearly run on the rocks owing to the propensity of two exceptionally strong and energetic characters each to go their own way, was stabilised by the impact of war – the sharing of experiences, being parted from the children, and the sense of duty prevailing over self-regard and hedonism.

Having been offered, and accepted, command of the fleet aircraft carrier *Illustrious*, which was being repaired in the USA after being severely damaged by a German air attack in the Mediterranean, Mountbatten set off by air on 15 August for New York. It had been agreed that Edwina should accompany him to give talks on behalf of the Joint War Organisation, and generally seek American support for the much-blitzed British people. The visit would also give them both the chance to see their daughters, Patricia and Pamela, and meet the warm-hearted people who were looking after them.

After a visit to the *Illustrious*, where he made his usual strong impact on the officers and men standing by to man her, Mountbatten set off to meet the US Navy. One of his earliest engagements was to address 1,000 or so midshipmen at Annapolis, the US Navy's officer training academy. A British naval liaison officer wrote to him:

> I talked to several of [the midshipmen], and you have no idea how much they enjoyed your lecture there, they'd never heard anything like it in their lives before.[3]

The main strength of the US Navy in the autumn of 1941 was the Pacific Fleet, based at Pearl Harbor, Hawaii. By the end of an eight-day visit to it even Mountbatten, with his prodigious energy, admitted that he was exhausted. 'Carefully coordinated meetings, lunches, dinners and cocktail parties given by the Commander-in-Chief . . . etc.' enabled him 'to meet and talk shop with nearly all the 14 flag officers as well as many of the senior officers'.[4] But he spent most of the time at sea in the US aircraft carrier *Enterprise*, taking off in the dark with her air group, which 'attacked' Pearl Harbor at dawn on 27 September. He was invited to give a talk to 1,500 of her ship's company; Admiral W.F. Halsey also spoke, 'and when he mentioned the work of the British Navy during the present war there was a great demonstration'.[5]

Arriving in Los Angeles after his visit to the Pacific Fleet, Mountbatten was intercepted by the British consul with a message from the Admiralty ordering him to return to the UK immediately. Having a full programme of engagements he sought and obtained permission to remain in the USA for another week, but only because he had been bidden to dine at the White House, where Edwina would also be staying. It was agreed that she would finish her tour, in which Canada had been included, and return to England in December with Pamela, their younger daughter, while Patricia stayed on for her school's final examinations.

Mountbatten had been told only that he was required at once for 'something which you will find of the highest interest', as Churchill put it in a personal telegram. On 18 October, having said farewell to his beloved aircraft carrier, he left for the UK, carrying with him from Washington a letter from the American Chief of Naval Operations to the First Sea Lord:

> I wrote you a note this morning and, just after it was put in the mail, my Aide told me that Captain Lord Mountbatten was coming to say goodbye. . . .
>
> I want you to know that he has been a great help to all of us, and I mean literally 'ALL'. . . .
>
> If he carries back to you anything that will be nearly as helpful to you as what he leaves with us, we shall be very glad.[6]

And in a message to Winston Churchill, the President said of Lord Louis that he had been 'really useful to our Navy people'.

Having learned what his new appointment was to be, Mountbatten at once concentrated his mind on combined operations. Between the wars it had become a highly specialised and almost totally neglected area of study, development and training in the British armed forces. It was still a Cinderella. On 3 September 1939 the total number of motor landing craft (MLC) available was just nine. But, thanks to the foresight of the Deputy Chief of the General Staff, the Inter-Service Training and Development Centre (ISTDC), which had been disbanded on the outbreak of war, had been reactivated in December 1939.

In response to Churchill's urging to propose 'measures for a vigorous, enterprising and ceaseless offensive against the whole German-occupied coastline' after Dunkirk, the Chiefs of Staff had appointed Lieutenant General Alan Bourne as 'Commander of Raiding Operations on the coasts in enemy occupation and Adviser to the Chiefs of Staff on Combined Operations'. Churchill was almost alone in looking ahead to the day when, the threatened invasion of Britain by the Germans having been repelled or otherwise averted, a British Commonwealth and Empire army would re-enter the continent of Europe. But he was well aware, from his bitter experience of the Dardanelles disaster in the Kaiser's war, that the planning and execution of so vast and formidable an undertaking could not be left to the existing military leadership alone. A dynamic senior officer must be found, acceptable to the Chiefs of Staff of all three services, to work at their level in the development of Combined Operations at the pace and on the all-embracing scale required.

Despite the unhappy consequences attending the recall in 1914 of the almost-senile Admiral of the Fleet, Lord Fisher, to be First Sea Lord, Churchill once again sought a senior warrior figure to whom even the other Chiefs of Staff might defer, since it was inevitable that he would have to plunder all three services to build up the fourth arm envisaged. He appointed the 68-year-old Admiral of the Fleet Sir Roger Keyes as Director of Combined Operations in place of General Bourne. He was not a success. Before long he was adding to the burden of the tiny, toiling staff at Combined Operations Headquarters (COHQ), and creating friction in high places, by insisting that an operation should be mounted – preferably commanded by himself – to capture the Italian island of Pantellaria, at this stage a useless project.

The embryo organisation inherited by Keyes from Bourne, including the newly formed Commandos, plus training establishments on the south coast of England and in remote areas in the west of Scotland, was on the right lines, however, and in March 1941 a successful raid was carried out on the Lofoten Islands. The aim was to destroy a number of Norwegian fish-oil factories, which were being compelled by the Germans to supply glycerine, a vital component for munitions. It was briskly achieved.

Bourne had established representatives in the operations division of each of the service ministries, but Keyes, having asserted his independence by removing himself and his staff from the Admiralty to a nearby building in Richmond Terrace (which became, and remained, COHQ), set up a joint-service operations section. He left a captain in the Admiralty to form a Combined Operations Division of the naval staff, with an associated Director of Combined Operations (Materiel). And to cope with the provision of the large number of landing craft that would eventually be needed, the Admiralty set up a new department known as Director of Naval Equipment (Combined Operations). By the end of the war this had become a very big organisation, its director being Captain Sir John Reith.

In the nature of things, COHQ was called upon to plan and train the forces for a number of raiding operations which for various reasons were called off. In mid-August 1941 a major operation to capture the Canary Islands was prepared, in case Spain should enter the war as an ally of Germany. By this time Keyes had succeeded in antagonising the Chiefs of Staff and many officers in the service ministries. It had become evident that he was not the man to mastermind the eventual re-entry into Europe. To accommodate the insistence of the Chiefs of Staff that the turbulent Keyes be restrained, Churchill authorised a new directive according to which the old war-horse would no longer be Director, but Adviser. The role of COHQ would be limited to 'study of the intricate inter-Service problems involved, the working out of techniques, the development of ships, craft and gadgets; and to helping rather than directing Force Commanders in the training of their contingents'.[7]

Keyes refused to accept what he called 'such a sweeping reduction in status'. Churchill had no option but to inform his old friend, with deep regret, that he would be arranging for his relief. The departure of the gallant old firebrand was regretted by the stalwarts who had helped him to put combined operations on the map; and particularly by the Commandos, whose fierce, independent, fearless fighting spirit matched his own. But other young, thoughtful and equally courageous officers were far from content with the Keyes regime.

One such was Lieutenant Gerald Butler, who submitted to his commanding officer, Commodore Guy Warren, the Senior Naval Officer Landings, based at Largs, 'Some Reflections on Combined Operations', requesting that it be forwarded to the Adviser on Combined Operations. Unaware that Mountbatten had already been selected to take over from Keyes, Butler summed up thus:

(A) Let us have one permanent supreme commander designate and working under him joint Naval, Military and Air Commanders.

(B) Let us have AIR with a permanent RAF Commander designate of the highest rank and standing.

(C) Let us have one permanent Naval Chief of Staff designate of the calibre of Captain Mountbatten, Captain Ruck-Keene or Captain Charles Lambe.

(D) Let us have the Naval side of Combined Operations placed on a professional as opposed to an amateur status, i.e. let it be as much part of HM Navy as anything else.

(E) Let us plan for large numbers of small fast ships of reasonable endurance (i.e. *Queen Emma* class).

(F) Let us plan for permanent allocation of certain HM ships, possible old cruisers or battleships to be allocated as Operational HQ.[8]

This author would strongly have endorsed, from personal knowledge, Lieutenant Butler's high opinion of the captains whom he named; but there is no evidence that the views of junior officers influenced the choice of Mountbatten to take over from Keyes. As Churchill wrote later, he had reached the conclusion that:

the appointment of a new and young figure at the head of the overseas Organisation would be in the public interest. Lord Louis Mountbatten was only a captain in the Royal Navy, but his exploits and abilities seemed to me to fit him in a high degree for the vacant post.[9]

A revisionist view, expressed by Brian Loring Villa in *Unauthorised Action*, that 'Mountbatten had virtually no prior contact with Combined Operations' when Churchill appointed him, lacks force; the technique was in its infancy. And Villa is mistaken in saying that 'He had just lost his third ship, HMS *Kelly.*' She was the first and only ship under his command that was lost. Of real importance, given the necessity for the closest possible coordination with the American war effort, was Mountbatten's rapport with the President and his senior admirals. But Villa's lip curls, metaphorically, in reporting this:

> In October 1941 Mountbatten was invited twice to the White House, where one self-styled genius of the naval theatre regaled the other with tales of derring-do and royal shindigs.[10]

Some credence may, however, be attached to Villa's belief that Beaverbrook openly supported Mountbatten's appointment, as an earnest of Britain's determination to engage German forces in the west to relieve the weight of attack on the Soviet Union.

From the very day that the last British soldier was brought back from Dunkirk, Churchill had proclaimed that in due course the British Army would return to the continent – a combined operation on a massive scale. But in autumn 1941 the contrast between the ends proposed and the means available was stark. According to Bernard Fergusson, who was closely involved, the Prime Minister's verbal briefing to Mountbatten was on the following lines:

> I want you to start a programme of ever-increasing intensity, so as to keep the whole enemy coastline on the alert from the North Cape to the Bay of Biscay. *But your main object must be the re-invasion of France.* You must create the machine which will make it possible for us to beat Hitler on land. You must devise the appurtenances and appliances which will make the invasion possible. You must select and build up the bases from which the assault will be launched. Before that you must create the various Training Centres at which the soldiers can be trained in the amphibious assault. I want you to bring in the Air Force as well, and create a proper inter-Service organisation to produce the technique of the modern assault. I want you to consider the great problem of the follow-up, and finally, I want you to select the area in which you feel the assault should take place and start bending all your energies towards getting ready for this great day. . . . You are to give no thought to the defensive. Your whole attention is to be concentrated on the offensive.[11]

Lest the immensity and urgency of the task might encourage Mountbatten to exceed his authority and make peremptory demands, as Keyes had done, on exiguous resources of men and materiel, he was appointed formally as Adviser (not Director, as Keyes had insisted on being called) on Combined Operations, in the rank of Commodore First Class. And whereas Keyes had been responsible directly to the Prime Minister, as Minister of Defence, Mountbatten was required by a directive dated 16 October 1941 to work 'under the direction of the Chiefs of Staff' to:

a. Act as technical adviser on all aspects of, and at all stages in, the planning and training for combined operations.
b. Be responsible for co-ordinating the general training policy for combined operations for the three Services, and command the Combined Training Centres and Schools of Instruction.
c. Study tactical and technical developments in all forms of combined operations varying from small raids to a full scale invasion of the Continent.
d. Direct and press forward research and developments in all forms of technical equipment and special craft peculiar to combined operations.[12]

In the light of that comprehensive and exacting document, Mountbatten hardly exaggerated when, looking back 36 years, he told Stephen Roskill that when he took over Combined Operations from Keyes he inherited 'absolutely nothing' of value. According to Fergusson:

He looked first at his headquarters and was not impressed: including typists and messengers, it totalled 23, and was running on a hand-to-mouth basis. Most of the naval and air force officers were retired officers called back to service. There was a minute intelligence staff, no planning staff, no signals staff, no training staff; there wasn't even a Chief of Staff.[13]

Mountbatten, deprived of his aircraft carrier, did his duty. To him, intense, unrelenting and creative activity was the norm. Leadership by example, a flair for organisation, tact in dealing with older and in many cases more senior officers in all three services, and a gift for exposition were the main components of his style.

Putting people first, he obtained approval, given the backing of the Prime Minister, to recruit two of the best officers who could be made available from each service. 'Combined Ops' was not, professionally speaking, the most sought-after activity for naval officers, for whom service in destroyers or submarines, leading to command, had the most attraction; while the Fleet Air Arm and Coastal Forces could recruit the most daring spirits, including many of the best of the 'hostilities only' young men. The more senior officers, commanders and captains, both desired and were needed for important appointments on the naval and fleet staffs, with the prospect of a big ship command to follow.

But Keyes, as a notable naval figure, had been well served by the handful of senior officers, both active and retired, who had helped to get COHQ under way. In particular Rear Admiral H.E. Horan, who had been flag captain to Rear Admiral A.B. Cunningham in the *Coventry* and later commanded a cruiser, had a firm grasp of naval administration; and Commodore Guy Warren most ably looked after the rapidly expanding fleet of assault ships and craft of all types. The most pressing need was to appoint as Chief of Staff an officer of outstanding ability and at least some experience of combined operations. Brigadier G.E. Wildman-Lushington of the Royal Marines, who had been a pilot in the Royal Naval Air Service in the First World War and, like Guy Warren, had taken part in the abortive Dakar expedition, filled the bill admirably.

Five weeks after Mountbatten had relieved Keyes he submitted to the Chiefs of Staff his proposals, as Commodore (C), Adviser on Combined Operations. It was a seminal document, embodying in only nine paragraphs the nature and scope of the authority he required, and the practical steps to be taken to give effect to the directive he had been given.

'The Admiralty,' as he put it, 'wish me to take over the command and administration of all landing craft and crews', which would amount eventually to 500–700 tank landing craft (250 tons) and 2,000 smaller craft, manned by 2,000 officers and 20,000 men within the next 16 months, with suitable bases. For these responsibilities a Rear Admiral Landing Craft and Bases would be required, and under him a commodore as Senior Officer Assault Ships and Craft. He called for 'much closer relation with the Royal Marines (the traditional combined operations force)', to be facilitated by a colonel as Royal Marine Adviser; he requested the loan of staff officers 'to set up a small pool consisting of two teams of Operational Staff Officers' to be lent in turn to force commanders when appointed; he provided the draft of a brief explanation of the Combined Operations organisation to be published in the confidential orders of all three services; and he submitted a redraft of his directive.[14]

The Chiefs of Staff approved this document on 9 December 1941 with an amendment which delineated clearly the two separate, but complementary, aspects of Mountbatten's responsibilities: as Adviser on Combined Operations and in an executive capacity as Commodore, Combined Operations.

Mountbatten did not await the formal approval of his proposals before beginning to give them effect. Under Keyes, following the successful raid on the Lofotens, further operations against the German-occupied Norwegian coast were being planned when he took over as CCO. But it was under his auspices that, for the first time, 'all three Services had been completely interwoven in planning and execution'.[15] Two raids were carried out almost simultaneously between 26 and 28 December. The more important of the two was to destroy German installations on the islands of Vaagsö and Maalöy, and shipping in the harbours. Under the general charge of the Commander-in-Chief, Home Fleet, with a rear admiral as naval force commander and a brigadier commanding the soldiers, forming an effective joint command, with air support organised by a group captain at COHQ, the operation was a resounding success. Bombardment and bombing silenced the coastal batteries and shore-based long-range fighters countered air attacks on the force.

Significantly, the simultaneous operation to raid the Lofoten Islands for the second time was beyond the range of fighter protection, with the result that when heavy air attack threatened the admiral prudently abandoned it. This displeased the Prime Minister, but the critical necessity of air cover was the lesson taken to heart in planning future operations.

COHQ's next success followed, as it happened, a request from the Air Ministry to carry out a raid on Bruneval, on the Normandy coast, to seize key elements of a new German radar stationed there. Again, total success was achieved. On this occasion the modus operandi was to drop paratroops to landward of the objective, and deal with it while establishing a small beachhead through which the force was embarked in a landing craft and withdrawn. The radar components were then transferred to a fast motor-boat and conveyed to Portsmouth, whence they were rushed to London. Two prisoners were brought back, also, one of whom was a radar operator. Sadly, two British soldiers were killed and six taken prisoner; ten Germans were killed and two wounded. According to Professor R.V. Jones, we gained:

A first-hand knowledge of the state of German radar technology, in the form in which it was almost certainly being applied in our principal objective, the German nightfighter control system.[16]

News of the Bruneval raid on 27 February 1942 came at a moment when the war was going badly for Britain. On 7 December 1941 the Japanese had bombed the US Pacific Fleet in Pearl Harbor; on 10 December they had sunk one of Britain's newest battleships, the *Prince of Wales*, and her older consort, the battlecruiser *Repulse*, in the South China Sea. On 11 December Germany and Italy had declared war on the USA, and world war became a reality. From 11 to13 February 1942 the German battlecruisers *Scharnhorst* and *Gneisenau*, with the heavy cruiser *Prinz Eugen* in company, made the transit of the English Channel from Brest to the North Sea almost unhindered, although both battleships struck mines and had to be docked. The lack of commitment to, and training for, the naval task by the RAF exposed in this episode, and the absence of effective cooperation between the Navy and the Air Force, gave rise to the demand for unified command of the armed forces in each theatre of war.

At this time the Battle of the Atlantic was also going badly, owing to a change in the ciphering system, which denied Britain's operational intelligence much data about U-boat dispositions and movements. The battleships *Valiant* and *Queen Elizabeth* were disabled in Alexandria after attack by Italian frogmen, reducing Cunningham's Mediterranean Fleet to three light cruisers and a few destroyers. In Russia the Germans were preparing for another great offensive, and in North Africa the German Afrika Korps was once again advancing. Singapore had fallen. Churchill's conduct of the war was being questioned.

Since early 1942 the Admiralty had been aware that St Nazaire possessed the only dry dock capable of taking the *Tirpitz*, menacing sister-ship of the mighty *Bismarck*, if she should break out into the Atlantic and be damaged but not sunk. An operation to put the dock out of action was therefore planned at COHQ. By 23 March the necessary force had been assembled and the complicated operation thoroughly rehearsed, under the supervision of the Commander-in-Chief, Plymouth, who had approved the plan and provided the escorts. On 28 March the elderly ex-American destroyer HMS *Campbeltown*, was driven into the dock gates and detonated, demolishing them completely. The Commandos who had been landed also destroyed various targets, and the force was withdrawn after suffering heavy casualties. It had been a most successful operation, though costly, in which total surprise was achieved and all arms co-operated admirably. The news of this feat greatly heartened the British people.

As is usually the case, those responsible for the higher direction of the war reviewed events as they unfolded, mainly in the light of their probable effect upon other operations planned many months in advance. By the time of the St Nazaire raid Churchill had already proposed, in a letter to the First Sea Lord dated 6 March, that Mountbatten should become a full member of the Chiefs of Staff Committee, to

exercise influence upon the war as a whole; upon future planning in its broadest sense; upon the concert of the three Arms and their relations to the main strategy; upon Combined Operations in the largest sense, not only those specific Operations which his own organisation will execute.[17]

Next day, he told the Chiefs of Staff that henceforth Mountbatten's title would be Chief of Combined Operations, and that he would have full and equal membership of their committee with the acting rank of Vice-Admiral; he was also to be permitted to assume the honorary acting ranks of lieutenant general and air marshal.

On 18 March the CCO provided the Chiefs of Staff with an appreciation, with which the Commander-in-Chief, Home Forces concurred, of the preparations which should be put in hand at once for 're-entry to the continent'. The Director of Plans in the Admiralty at that time was Captain Charles Lambe, a close friend of Mountbatten's, which helped to ensure that COHQ's ideas were in accord with those of the naval staff. This was particularly important at a time when the rapid expansion of Combined Operations was beginning to excite the hostility of one-track-minded senior officers who feared and resented what they regarded as the advent of a 'private navy'.

Concurrent with these developments, Operation IRONCLAD was being mounted: the capture of Madagascar. The plan had been put in cold storage since January, but COHQ was called upon to activate it at short notice. It had been estimated that it would take 91 days from the issue of the preparatory orders before the assault could take place; actually the period taken was 52 days. The landings were made on time, the subsequent operations against the French were successful, and the island was quickly captured.

While this was going on, five raids were planned by COHQ to take place simultaneously against the Cap Gris Nez to Le Touquet area of the Channel coast:

Operation TURNSCREW to capture or kill German military personnel at Ambleteuse; ROUGHSHOD to destroy the German military headquarters at Wimereux; EARTHQUAKE to immobilise German gun batteries at Equihen; BUSYBODY to capture or kill German military personnel at Hardelot; and DEARBORN to capture and bring back to England the new German radar equipment installed at St Cécile, together with its personnel.[18]

This activity brought to the fore the conflict of priorities in the allocation of the few landing craft so far available between raiding, and the training of assault forces for the major landing now envisaged. On 27 May 1942 it was agreed by the Chiefs of Staff that a cross-Channel operation on the scale now being demanded by the vociferous proponents of a 'second front' to take pressure off the Russians could not be undertaken in 1942, short of a complete collapse of civilian morale in Germany, which was most improbable. Raiding must continue as part of the 'second front' campaign now being concerted with the Americans, following the vitally important visit to Britain in April of President Roosevelt's personal envoys, Harry Hopkins and General George Marshall.

Marshall had been impressed by the intense and purposeful activity at COHQ, where Mountbatten explained what was going on and enabled him to see staff officers of all three services working together in harmony – a sight barely credible to an American general, given the total absence of cooperation between the armed forces of the USA at that date. The outcome of this visit was a proposal by General Marshall to send American officers to work at COHQ to further Allied unity in planning and procedures. It was accepted with alacrity. He was also persuaded to accelerate the equipment of the American forces with landing craft, the availability of which, inevitably and inescapably, would govern the Allied grand strategy, together with follow-up shipping and – the key to reinforcing the assault forces fast enough to prevail – the means of unloading the ships.

Anglo-American views on the conduct of what was now a world war being waged, as Roosevelt proclaimed, by the UN on behalf of freedom, crystallised in the spring and early summer of 1942 – but not without dust and heat. While Hopkins and Marshall were secretly conferring with Churchill and the British Chiefs of Staff, Litvinov, the Soviet ambassador to the USA, was calling publicly for the opening of a 'second front' as soon as possible. On the most fundamental point of all, Churchill and Roosevelt were in accord: that priority in the allocation of resources must go to the defeat of Germany. Unfortunately Marshall still believed, despite the misgivings of British military leaders, that preparations for Operation SLEDGEHAMMER should continue, to land even a few divisions in France in the event of a German collapse.[19] But the prospect of deliberately sacrificing thousands of soldiers in what was bound to be a military disaster could not possibly be entertained by the British. It was the moment, Mountbatten felt, to take advantage of Marshall's invitation to visit the US Chiefs of Staff to discuss future plans and see something of the American army.

It testifies to the trust that Churchill reposed in Mountbatten, and his knowledge that Roosevelt also had confidence in him, that the Prime Minister made of him a personal envoy. Mountbatten stayed at Chequers on 12 June, immediately after his return, and wrote to the President with tact and concision:

> I was so very grateful to you for giving me the opportunity of such a long and interesting talk last Tuesday, and I did my best to convey all that you told me to the Prime Minister and the Chiefs of Staff. In order to make sure that I correctly conveyed your points I propose recapitulating here what I told the Prime Minister.
>
> I pointed out that you had stressed the great need for American soldiers to be given an opportunity of fighting as soon as possible. . . .
>
> . . . that you had asked for an assurance that we would be ready to follow up a crack in German morale by landing in France this autumn and that I had given you an assurance that such an operation was being planned and was at present held at two months' notice.
>
> . . . that you did not wish to send a million soldiers to England and find, possibly, that a complete collapse of Russia had made a frontal attack on France impossible.
>
> . . . that you were sure, in any case, that when the operation came off we should have to secure the Atlantic ports. . . .
>
> . . . that you did not like our sending out divisions from England while American troops were still being sent in. . . . In the latter connection, I told the PM how much you had been struck by his remark in a recent telegram: 'Do not lose sight of GYMNAST.'[20]
>
> . . . I said that you and General Marshall were anxious that two British carriers with their destroyer screens should join the American naval forces in Australia.[21]

The grand strategy now taking shape brought to mind the aphorism of Francis Bacon: 'He that commandeth the sea may have as much or as little of war as he will.' He could hardly have foreseen that in 1942 unless 'he that commandeth the sea' also 'commandeth the air' the option was closed. The failure of the Luftwaffe to overwhelm RAF Fighter Command in 1940 had deprived Hitler of the option of invading Britain; per contra, if the Allies were to re-enter the continent in force, they must first gain air superiority over the Channel. With this in mind the air staff had sought continually to wear down German air strength in western Europe. This, coupled with the bombing of German industrial areas, also helped to diminish the intensity of air attack on the Russian armies. It would be an important contribution to a 'second front', therefore, if a major air battle could be brought about as the by-product, as it were, of what Churchill had called a 'butcher and bolt' raid across the Channel. The preparations for such a raid were initiated in COHQ during April, with Captain John Hughes-Hallett in charge of the planning.

There was never any doubt in the minds of those responsible in Britain for the higher direction of the war that before a sound military plan could be made for re-entry into France it was essential to test the coastal defences – the Atlantic Wall so painstakingly and thoroughly put in place by the German army using enslaved labour from Organisation Todt. It is a familiar saying in the British Army that 'time spent in reconnaissance is seldom wasted'. The aim of the large-scale raid now proposed would therefore be 'to make a reconnaissance in force'. Given that in the early stages of a full-scale invasion it would be necessary to land about 12,000 tons of stores and 2,500 laden vehicles per day, increasing in the follow-up, the assumption was that a major port would have to be captured at the outset. The object of the raid thus became to land a force of about division strength, with tanks, in the vicinity of a selected minor port; then to destroy shipping and other selected targets, take prisoners, and re-embark 12 hours after landing. It would in effect be a rehearsal for re-entry into Europe.

For reasons established by careful research the port chosen as the target of Operation RUTTER, as it was named, was Dieppe. In August, when the operation was finally carried out, having been renamed JUBILEE, the aim was achieved; but heavy casualties caused the Dieppe Raid, as it came to be called, to be categorised as a disaster. It was of little solace to the widowed and bereaved that 'They never fail who die in a great cause'; but the facts are that of the 15,000 or so soldiers, sailors and airmen who took part in JUBILEE, 4,260 became casualties, of whom the vast majority were Canadian soldiers, 907 being killed and the remainder wounded or taken prisoner.

'Failure is an orphan, success has many fathers.' It was not surprising that the high proportion of casualties suffered at Dieppe called into question the necessity for the operation, and whether its planning, launching and conduct had been responsibly carried out in accordance with well-established procedures. And because most of the casualties were Canadians, it was in their country that feeling ran most strongly. The Canadian historian, Villa, already cited, wrote 'For many Canadians, Dieppe has assumed the same importance Gallipoli has for Australians.' And he quotes his countryman, Lord Beaverbrook, as having said to Mountbatten at a dinner party a few months after the raid:

> You have murdered thousands of my countrymen. You took those unfortunate Canadian soldiers. . . . They have been mown down in their thousands and their blood is on your hands.[22]

Villa, who is not a military historian (*Unauthorised Action* was, in any case, his first book), adopted as his standpoint the conviction that:

> Dieppe is a classic example of military failure – in decision-making, in planning, and in execution – that has its roots in an intricate network of motives that almost defies analysis by the historian or political scientist.[23]

He also states that 'some six years ago' he had concluded 'tentatively' that the British Chiefs of Staff had 'never formally approved the decision' to remount the operation against Dieppe. Taken together these propositions amount to a perfect example of 'situating the appreciation' – the most egregious error which a military planner can make, namely to set down the aim before systematically determining what it should be. The book's title, *Unauthorised Action*, says it all. The author, having formed the opinion that Mountbatten had launched the Dieppe raid without specific authorisation, set out to prove it. To him, the mystery to be solved was who made the decision to execute the raid:

> for it can easily be shown that the British government, and the Chiefs of Staff in particular, had been convinced for more than a year that this sort of operation made little sense: it was extremely hazardous and was unlikely, even if it were to succeed, to be worth the cost.[24]

And because the more sources he examined, the less evidence he could adduce in support of his opinion, Villa resorted to much argument ad hominem, saying of Mountbatten *inter alia*: 'indifferent naval career', 'ignorance of military administration', 'empty talker', 'poor judgement', 'inattention to detail', 'multiple meteoric promotions', 'brashness', 'egotism', 'spuriousness', 'slack supervision', 'very immature', 'unqualified', 'amateur', 'bravado', 'utterly untrained', 'spoilt child', 'stirring rhetoric', 'natural stubbornness', 'malleable', '41-year-old baby', 'driven by ambition', 'glamour boy', 'a shallow parody of real leadership', and so on. By contrast, Villa refers to the 'weight and authority' of Rear Admiral Baillie-Grohman, 'who had considerable experience of amphibious operations', 'had commanded the Combined Operations Training Headquarters in the Mediterranean', and 'would clearly have been a natural candidate to succeed Admiral Keyes as Chief of Combined Operations had not Mountbatten been so much better connected'.

In 1942 Baillie-Grohman's experience of amphibious assault operations was nil, although he had served gallantly as naval liaison officer with the Army during its evacuation from Greece the previous year. As to his Combined Operations Training Command, the first operation carried out following his departure reflected badly upon the legacy of his organisation, methods and policy. It was a combined operation against Tobruk, on 13 September 1942, which failed disastrously. No advice had been sought from COHQ. Two fleet destroyers, an anti-aircraft cruiser and six coastal craft were lost. Nothing was achieved. Roskill commented that the operation was rash in conception and that

an assault from the sea on a strongly fortified port must require far more specialised equipment and training than were available on this occasion.[25]

Villa, referring again to Baillie-Grohman's 'extensive experience with Combined Operations in the Mediterranean theatre', quotes his comment on the lessons learned from Dieppe that virtually all of them 'could have been acquired by anyone reading Admiralty background pamphlets on combined Operations'[26] (identified as naval staff manuals dated 1931 and 1938). But, *inter alia*, there was no radar coverage in 1938; and no thought of launching tanks directly over beaches.

The list of sources scanned by Villa in his attempt to find proof of his thesis that 'Mountbatten bears direct responsibility, as Chief of Combined Operations, for executing the raid on Dieppe' is comprehensive. But it contains no reference to *The Ultra Secret*, by Group Captain F.W. Winterbotham (London, Weidenfeld & Nicolson, 1974); nor is there any mention made of the vital importance of Ultra in the context of both the aborted raid in Dieppe, Operation RUTTER, and its remounting as Operation JUBILEE. Prior to 1974, when permission was given for the publication of *The Ultra Secret*, no one but those who had been engaged in the deciphering of enemy messages enciphered by the Enigma machine, and the handful of individuals authorised to see the deciphered messages, knew of Ultra, the name chosen to cover both the intelligence system and the intelligence itself.

In May 1940, when Ultra came into use, it was distributed only to the Prime Minister, the Chiefs of Staff, the Directors of Intelligence of the services, Fighter Command and the Commander-in-Chief, Home Forces. These individuals took the most stringent precautions to ensure that no one outside their immediate and authorised circle became aware of Ultra's existence, let alone of the intelligence that it provided, for which a covering nickname was used. In Churchill's case this was Boniface. As Ronald Lewin put it:

67

. Many of those who worked in offices or on staffs to which Ultra material was actually being supplied could only recall, as they looked back, information apparently emanating from 'a secret source', or 'from secret intelligence', 'an agent', 'prisoner interrogation' or some other cover. The trained eye, scanning wartime documents in the Public Record Office or the National Archives in Washington, will sometimes come across such shutters over the truth and realise that Ultra lurks behind them.[27]

It follows that, until 1974 at the earliest, access to any document referring to Ultra (or one of its nicknames) would have been withheld from the public domain. Hence none of the sources used by Villa, if written before that date, could have included Ultra material. This undermines his case.

It is evident that the Chiefs of Staff, force commanders and the Chief of Combined Operations, when mounting and preparing to launch Operation RUTTER, would have placed reliance upon Ultra traffic to alert them to any positive indications of German awareness that a raid was about to be launched, and of its target. We know now that no such indications were obtained, and that RUTTER was aborted on the advice of the naval force commander, Rear Admiral Baillie-Grohman, when bad weather was forecast for the last day upon which other conditions were suitable. Ultra gave no sign that the bombing of two of the loaded assault ships as they lay off the Isle of Wight indicated German foreknowledge of the operation.

Because the politico-strategic necessity to carry out a major raid on the Atlantic Wall was paramount, and the military requirement for a reconnaissance in force was undeniable as a preliminary to an Allied re-entry into Europe, the Prime Minister and the Chiefs of Staff approved Mountbatten's proposal – which was undoubtedly bold – to remount RUTTER as soon as practicable. His point was taken that to select a different target, plan, prepare for and mount an entirely new operation would not be feasible in 1942. It was therefore decided that, with the minimum of changes in plan, RUTTER would be remounted as JUBILEE in mid-August.

So much is documented. It is evident, however, that the maintenance of secrecy would be extremely difficult, given that thousands of soldiers, sailors and airmen (and women) had already been fully briefed for RUTTER. Not only were the most stringent measures taken to preserve secrecy about the intention to launch JUBILEE, restricting this knowledge rigorously to those who 'needed to know'; but the final decision to launch the operation would have to depend upon assurance through Ultra that the Germans remained unaware of it. Because of Ultra's uniquely limited distribution this could not be spelt out in any directive, even of the highest security classification, which would be distributed outside the Ultra circle.

The risk that the Germans would know that the force assembled in the first week of July was about to assault Dieppe was real. But Ultra intelligence had given no indication that, by 27 July, they had such knowledge. Information had been received of the transfer to France of two SS divisions, but this movement could not be associated with the aborted Operation RUTTER. It did, however, reduce the estimated time which would elapse before reinforcements could reach Dieppe once the assault had taken place. In consequence, the plan for JUBILEE was altered to allow for withdrawing the troops within 7 hours of landing, rather than 12 hours in the original plan. It was also decided that the task of silencing the coastal batteries east and west of the port would be carried out by Commandos instead of airborne forces.

Thus, when Churchill left England on 2 August on his way via Cairo to Moscow, Operation JUBILEE was, with his approval, being held in readiness at short notice. The telegrams sent by the Prime Minister to the War Cabinet, describing his talks with Stalin, are among the most fascinating of the war. During the first meeting, on 12 August, Stalin was at the outset both grim and sceptical of Britain's capacity to fight. He remained unmoved by Churchill's account of the problems associated with making an assault on the Channel coast in 1942. The Prime Minister then told Stalin that

> he proposed, 'this month', if the weather were favourable, 'to make a raid on France on a large scale in order to seek information and to test the German resistance. We might lose as many as 10,000 men on this operation, which would be no more than a reconnaissance. Another means of confusing the Germans would be a sham attack on Norway. No attack would be made, but we were going on pretending that we were aiming at it.'[28]

According to F.H. Hinsley, official historian of British Intelligence in the Second World War, 'The Chiefs of Staff gave their approval to JUBILEE on 12 August',[29] within a few hours of Churchill's statement to Stalin.

On 15 August Churchill once again informed Stalin that 'there would be a serious raid in August, although the weather might upset it'. He went on:

> It will be a reconnaissance in force. Some 8,000 men with 50 tanks will be landed. . . . As we intend to withdraw immediately after the operation, I am having leaflets prepared which will tell the French to stay in their houses, to prevent reprisals as at St Nazaire.
> The object is to get information and to create the impression of an invasion. Most important, I hope it will call forth a big air battle.[30]

It is not surprising that on 15 August, and again on 17 August, Churchill telegraphed General Ismay, his representative with the Chiefs of Staff Committee, asking for news of Operation JUBILEE. But it was not until he had returned to Cairo and was staying with General Montgomery at his desert headquarters that he received news that on 19 August:

a force of 5,000 men, mostly Canadians, but with some British and American troops in support, had crossed the Channel to land at Dieppe. The Dieppe raid took nine hours. Nearly a thousand of the attacking troops were killed, and 2,000 taken prisoner.[31]

It is on record that Mountbatten telegraphed Churchill next day: 'Morale of returning troops reported to be excellent', adding, 'All I have seen are in great form.'[32] Survivors often are.

As already noted, Churchill had given Stalin repeated assurances that there would shortly be a bold assault by an Allied force against German defences on the French coast, as an earnest of both the will to fight and the capacity to do so. It is hardly surprising that his first response reflected relief and satisfaction that the promised raid had actually taken place: 'My general impression of JUBILEE,' he telegraphed to the War Cabinet, 'is that the results fully justified the heavy cost. The large-scale air battle alone justified the raid.'[33]

It was not until December, following the success of the TORCH landings in North Africa, in which the Canadian army played a leading part, that Churchill felt obliged to justify the appalling losses which the Canadians in particular had suffered at Dieppe; he was at least equally concerned to ensure that the military lessons learned were not obscured by any concealment of the facts. After all, the main object of JUBILEE, as an operation, had been to test every aspect of the German defence organisation, equipment and methods. When Churchill had asked the naval force commander, Hughes-Hallett, on the eve of Operation RUTTER, whether success could be guaranteed, General Brooke told Hughes-Hallett not to reply, saying that if he or anyone else could guarantee success, there would indeed be no object to the operation. It was because no one had the slightest idea what the outcome would be that the operation was necessary.

Mountbatten was therefore dumbfounded when, dining at Chequers at the end of August, Brooke made a 'very outspoken criticism of the manner in which the Dieppe raid was planned'. On 31 August he wrote to Brooke:

> I had meant to come and see you about it after leaving the dining room but, before I could do so, the Prime Minister sent for me on the terrace and said: 'I heard CIGS complaining that the planning was all wrong for the Dieppe show; what did he mean?'[34] I replied: 'It was planned in accordance with the Chiefs of Staffs' own instructions; I am afraid I have no idea on what his complaint is based unless it is a fundamental objection to having a CCO and a Combined Operations Staff.'
> 2. The PM then said: 'Explain how the Military side of the raid was planned.' I gave him an explanation on the following lines . . .

There followed nine sub-paragraphs describing the successive steps in the planning process, the last one being:

To sum up, the only way in which the Army could be given any more control would be to disband the Combined Operations Headquarters.

The letter continued:

3. I have, as you know, always reported to the Chiefs of Staff any conversations of consequence with the Prime Minister and have therefore given you the above account.
4. So far as I am concerned your complaint raises a major issue. If you accept the explanation which I gave to the Prime Minister I know you will be generous enough to withdraw your complaint. If you don't I shall know that you no longer have confidence in me and were it permissible to resign my post I would do so and ask to be allowed to resume my Command at sea from which I was taken so greatly against my will.
5. Since serving officers are not permitted this luxury the only alternative open to me would be to ask the Minister of Defence (under whom I have been told I come) for a full and impartial enquiry into the Planning and Execution of the Dieppe raid and the conduct of all concerned.[35]

The letter ended with the customary courtesies. Since no such enquiry took place, it is fair to assume that Brooke withdrew his allegations.

It is unlikely that any more records with a direct bearing upon Operation JUBILEE will be unearthed. Given that the intention was to carry out a reconnaissance in force of the German defences of a Channel port, it cannot be denied that this was achieved. Nor has the selection of Dieppe as the port to be assaulted been seriously questioned. The authority of Mountbatten to remount Operation RUTTER as JUBILEE has been established beyond reasonable doubt as having been conferred personally by Churchill, with the concurrence of the Chiefs of Staff, though not recorded and known only to those whose 'need to know' was paramount, with due regard to the strict limitations of the Ultra list. The courage and determination of all who took part in the fighting, whether on the sea, on land, or in the air, was manifest. Why, then, were the casualties so heavy? To what extent was the success of the operation dependent upon surprise? Was surprise achieved? To what extent did inadequate or faulty intelligence contribute to the high rate of casualties? Of all the lessons derived from the operation was there one, above all, that must be learned if re-entry into continental Europe was to be achieved and sustained?

The answer to the first of these questions is provided by F.H. Hinsley:

As may be judged from the response from the German Air Force (GAF) the raid achieved tactical as well as strategic surprise and did so despite a chance encounter between the naval force of the eastern outer flank attack and the escort of a small enemy convoy.[36]

As to the adequacy and reliability of the intelligence provided to the planners, and to units in the assault force, a single but critically important lacuna was the failure of photographic reconnaissance to reveal gun emplacements in the cliffs enfilading the beach where the tanks were to be landed, preceded by infantry. It transpired that the guns in these emplacements were withdrawn during daylight hours, to be run out at dusk and manned until dawn. Apart from this, and the shock of encountering a most expert and vigorous defence force, which had to be experienced to be gauged, the intelligence could hardly be faulted, although proof of this did not emerge until after Dieppe had been captured by the Allies in 1944. On 7 December of that year a senior staff officer wrote to Wing Commander Casa Maury, senior intelligence officer at COHQ before and during JUBILEE:

> We have recently had some German reports about the Dieppe operation. Knowing how much trouble you took on the Intelligence side and how well this was done, I thought it might interest you to see the attached extract from a German report. . . .
> 'The enemy was provided with the very best maps, which were of great help to him in carrying out the operation. By means of perfect photographic reliefs, the German positions had been reproduced to the smallest detail. There were even shown the anti-tank walls barring passage to the sea-promenade.'[37]

The question remains, was there one lesson above all which had to be learned if re-entry to the continent was to be achieved? And if so, what was it? Could the lesson have been learned with far fewer casualties? Above all, could the lesson have been learned in time to create, by mid-1944, 'the machine', as Churchill had demanded of Mountbatten, 'which will make it possible for us to beat Hitler on land'?

Historians have a duty, in passing judgement on war leaders and their conduct of great affairs at decisive moments, to exclude rigorously from their minds knowledge which those leaders did not have, and could not reasonably have been expected to have, at the time. Wellington remarked that he never knew what was going on 'at the other side of the hill'; and as Nelson put it: 'In war something must be left to chance, in a sea affair above all others.' It is also owed to those subjected to 'the judgment of history' to re-create as nearly as possible an understanding of the simultaneity of events and the speed with which news of them could be communicated.

During Churchill's absence from the UK between 2 and 24 August, the disastrous dispersal, and subsequent decimation, of convoy PQ17 on its way to north Russia had occurred, calling forth Stalin's taunt to Churchill:

This is the first time in history the British Navy has ever turned tail and fled from the battle. You British are afraid of fighting. You should not think the Germans are supermen. You will have to fight sooner or later. You cannot win a war without fighting.[38]

Even as Churchill was being thus insulted by Stalin, the British Navy was hard at it protecting the Pedestal convoy, manned with matchless bravery by the Merchant Navy, through to Malta against the onslaughts of the Italian Navy and German Air Force, suffering the loss of 9 out of 14 merchant ships, 1 aircraft carrier, 2 cruisers and a destroyer.

On Churchill's express instructions, Mountbatten was being shown the war leader's own most secret signals – the 'Reflex' series – distributed to the individual Chiefs of Staff and members of the War Cabinet only. Mountbatten told the Chiefs on 20 August that the lessons learned at Dieppe would be 'invaluable' in planning for the future cross-Channel invasion. Admittedly at a fearful cost, it had been shown that an amphibious operation to re-enter and liberate enemy-occupied territory would be different not only in scale but in character from raiding the enemy-held coast. It had also been made clear that a major assault force, of air, land and sea elements, must be commanded by a 'supremo' with a fully integrated inter-service, inter-Allied staff. Above all, the crucial importance had been confirmed of the War Cabinet accepting nothing less than the total commitment, from the top down, of all three services to acting in concert in support of a clearly defined aim, in a truly combined operation.

These were lessons of the utmost importance for all concerned with the higher direction of the war, confirming the long-established views held in COHQ and the advice it gave. As to the technique of amphibious assault, thorough study of what had gone wrong (and also what had gone right) at Dieppe yielded fruitful guidelines for research, development and training. Furthermore, the confidence reposed in Mountbatten by Churchill, and shared by Roosevelt, far from being undermined by the outcome of the Dieppe operation, was seen to have been completely justified. Not only was the competence and potential of COHQ as an organisation proved, and its indispensability confirmed, but the weight to be accorded henceforth to Mountbatten's views on the conduct of the war would be no less than that of the other Chiefs of Staff.

The key decision had been to remount RUTTER on the assumption that even if the Germans had found out that Dieppe was the target, they would not expect the British, having aborted the operation, to mount it again with the same target. There is no doubt that Mountbatten pressed for this. He was fully justified, also, in proposing Captain John Hughes-Hallett as the naval force commander. Not only had he been associated with the planning of the operation since its inception, but he was one of the few officers in the Royal Navy, other than technical specialists, who thoroughly understood radar – still generally known as RDF (for radio direction-finding, a cover name) – having been chairman of the Chiefs of Staff sub-committee dealing with RDF, for which purpose he had served under Sir Henry Tizard. He was therefore fully aware of both the capabilities and the limitations of radar, whether shore based or shipborne, which played so important – and secret – a part in operations in coastal waters; Hughes-Hallett's expertise in this field, coupled with that of Mountbatten in radio technology, was invaluable in the electronic warfare which featured, always secretly, in combined operations.

The eventual success of the deception plan, which caused the Germans to believe that the Normandy landings in 1944 were a diversion from the real cross-Channel assault in the Pas de Calais, owed much to radio and radar. The radio communications organisation, equipment and training developed by COHQ was first-rate. Brigadier Derek Mills-Roberts, of No. 4 Commando under Lord Lovat, wrote:

> Messages were relayed to Headquarters Command ship from our own headquarters; on the beach was a special 'Phantom' link which signalled direct to Mountbatten, the Chief of Combined Operations, at Uxbridge.[39]

It is hard to believe that this main lesson, namely that the Chief of Combined Operations and his team were better qualified than anyone else to advise on amphibious warfare, could have been learned unless they had proved themselves in battle. As an example, after the Dieppe operation the Commander-in-Chief, Portsmouth, Admiral Sir William James, who had supervised JUBILEE, wrote to Mountbatten that 'Hughes-Hallett had handled the whole show quite brilliantly'. And it was Hughes-Hallett who said, at the debriefing: 'The next time we bring our harbour with us.' The idea of building an artificial harbour was not new; but, encouraged by Churchill and Mountbatten, with vast resources placed at his disposal, Hughes-Hallett developed the huge artificial harbour, code named 'Mulberry', which was crucial to the build-up following the OVERLORD landings in Normandy over open beaches. It was he, also, who obtained and adapted for naval use the RAF precise radio navigation system known as 'Gee' (outfit QH). Without this it would have been impossible to ensure that the 237 vessels taking part in JUBILEE arrived at the right time and place after a night-time passage across the strong tidal streams of the Channel, negotiating accurately swept approaches through minefields en route.

It is true that, owing to a navigational error, the force detailed to assault the inner eastern flank of the main beach was 16 minutes late. Surprise, on which success depended, was therefore lost at this critical point, with terrible results. But the success of the novel electronic navigational system had been proved in action, and more advanced equipment, known as 'Decca', similar in principle, was used to ensure the precise minesweeping and navigation needed in OVERLORD to achieve the safe and timely arrival in the assault area of an armada of 4,266 vessels.

Still dealing with the specifically naval aspect of combined operations, the increased authority with which requirements could now be stated by the CCO led without delay to two more ships being converted to headquarters ships on the lines of HMS *Bulolo*, with a comprehensive communications outfit devised by Captain Michael Hodges and his signals specialists at COHQ; the formation of a standing naval assault force to be used in raids, rather than relying, as hitherto, on an ad hoc group of whatever vessels happened to be available at the time; the development, production and bringing into service of landing craft equipped with guns or rockets to provide the overwhelming naval support fire without which, as Dieppe had proved, an opposed landing must not be contemplated; the organisation of specially trained and equipped beach parties, called Beach Commandos; and the establishment of a Beach Pilotage School.

It will be recalled that, in terms of grand strategy, the 'reconnaissance in force' at Dieppe was intended to help the Russians by keeping German troops in the west, manning coastal defences and supporting them with mobile forces. It was also confidently expected to cause a large-scale air battle and impose substantial attrition on the Luftwaffe. The extent to which this was achieved, based upon the most reliable British and German data, is assessed by Norman Franks in *The Greatest Air Battle* (London, Kimber, 1979).

In the course of Operation JUBILEE the RAF flew 3,000 sorties from 71 squadrons and were supported by 4 US Army Command B-17 units. One hundred aircraft were lost; the Luftwaffe lost 48, and were prevented from interfering with the assault force. Unfortunately the contribution made by air power to the suppression of the enemy's defences at Dieppe was minimal, despite the punctual execution of the planned close-support sorties. The effect of smoke, so helpful to the attackers at certain moments, was to add to the difficulty experienced by aircraft in identifying their targets. It was also amply demonstrated that the effective use of aircraft in close support called for the integration of their control with the naval and landing force joint command. Air Vice-Marshal Trafford Leigh-Mallory, Air Officer Commanding No. 11 Group and the Air Force commander, had not employed the fighter-direction facilities provided by COHQ in the destroyer *Calpe*, the JUBILEE headquarters ship, although she had embarked qualified RAF officers for the purpose; the experience of the operation confirmed the COHQ view, and for this reason, fighter-direction ships, equipped accordingly, were made ready in time for future operations.

Since the CCO's primary task in mid-1942 was still to build up the expertise essential for planning a successful re-entry into Europe, it was in his interest to examine with objectivity and care every aspect of the results obtained from the reconnaissance in force of Dieppe. To compile the Dieppe Report the services were obtained of Hilary St George Saunders, a former Clerk to the House of Lords, who had already written *The Battle of Britain* (London, Wingate-Baker, 1969). According to Mountbatten:

> He was given free access to every person and every document concerned with the Dieppe operation and checked through all the details with the most meticulous care, and no attempt was made to influence his Report.[40]

In forwarding a copy of this report to General Ismay, for the Prime Minister, on 24 December 1942, Mountbatten wrote:

> The fact that the COHQ plan originally aimed at avoiding a frontal assault and taking Dieppe by a pincers movement was stated by me to the CIGS at Chequers, I also told him that although General Montgomery favoured a frontal assault preceded by an air bombardment and that this had influenced my decision to adopt it, I had no desire to evade any responsibility in the matter. . . .
>
> I feel I must be guided by the desires and opinions of the Army Commander so long as the Navy and Air agree that the Military plan is feasible from their point of view. . . .
>
> After the appointment of the Force Commanders the work of detailed planning devolved on them and they brought the result of their labours to the notice of periodic meetings. . . . At the 5 June meeting, for example, they advocated what I regarded as a very important alteration indeed – the elimination of an air bombardment on Dieppe. I took this point up with them several times and again on 17 August but was unable to alter their opinion.[41]

From the naval point of view, by far the most important failure was the refusal of the First Sea Lord to accede to Mountbatten's request, on behalf of the naval force commander (first Baillie-Grohman, and then Hughes-Hallett), to provide adequate gunfire support, either in weight or quantity. Pound's non-cooperation was matched by that of Sir Charles Portal, the Chief of the Air Staff, who accorded overriding priority to the demands of Air Chief Marshal Harris in refusing to provide adequate bomber support for Operation JUBILEE.

As we have seen, under Churchill's indomitable direction the outline of a plan for re-entry into the continent had been conceived by the British Chiefs of Staff as early as December 1941, when the USA was brought into the war. In April 1942, Vice-Admiral Sir Bertram Ramsay, who had distinguished himself commanding the evacuation of Dunkirk, had been appointed Flag Officer Expeditionary Force and instructed to confer, in complete secrecy, with General Sir Bernard Paget and Air Chief Marshal Sir Sholto Douglas, nominated respectively as army and air commanders-in-chief of the proposed expeditionary force.

In June of that year Ramsay was promoted to 'Naval Commander-in-Chief, Expeditionary Force, with the acting rank of Admiral', and in a letter from the Admiralty dated 9 July 1942, Ramsay's duties and responsibilities were defined in the following terms:

(a) In conjunction with Commander-in-Chief, Home Forces, Air Officer Commanding-in-Chief, Fighter Command, and Chief of Combined Operations, he is the planning authority for the invasion of France and the Low Countries.

(b) He will be responsible for the general direction of all naval forces engaged in large-scale landing operations on the coast of France and the Low Countries, and for the transport of the Expeditionary Force across the sea and its landing and establishment on the enemy coast.

(c) In co-operation with the Army and Air Force and with the Chief of Combined Operations, he will be responsible for the training of the Expeditionary Force in Combined Operations.[42]

Thus was created a minefield of conflicting responsibilities and authority between Ramsay and Mountbatten, the negotiation of which could only be achieved by common sense and a good personal relationship. For not only was the latter, as CCO, still in administrative command of all landing craft and their crews, now numbering hundreds of vessels and thousands of men, but he and his staff were the repository of virtually all the knowledge and experience of combined operations in the British services. Given that Ramsay had joined the Navy 14 years before Mountbatten and had retired as a rear admiral four years before the latter was promoted to captain, the potential for friction was considerable; to compound this was the fact that Mountbatten was a member of the Chiefs of Staff Committee and hence a member of the inner circle directing the war, from which Ramsay was excluded. But thanks to the outstanding professional ability of both these naval officers, their strength of character, integrity and shared dedication to winning the war, a modus vivendi was quickly established and maintained.

Mountbatten lost no time in writing to congratulate Ramsay on his promotion to full admiral, and hence his senior in rank; both of them held acting rank only, but whereas Mountbatten was on the active list, even if only as captain, Ramsay was still technically a retired officer. His biographer, W.S. Chalmers, noting that Mountbatten had been made responsible for 'the planning of raids, the training of seamen and soldiers in amphibious attack and the development of equipment in collaboration with the Service Ministries', said that in fulfilling these tasks Lord Louis had 'made one of his greatest contributions to the winning of the war'.[43]

To begin with, it must be said, Ramsay was somewhat critical of the

state of training and discipline among personnel of special surface ships and landing-craft and beach parties . . . [which] naturally affects me very closely, as the whole success of ROUNDUP depends upon it. . . . I must, therefore, in some way have a say in it, with access to establishments to inspect and report, etc.[44]

And he made it clear that he did not think that Mountbatten could at the same time be CCO and be 'tied by the heels to the Chief of Staff's meetings'.[45]

However, these reservations were forgotten when, at the beginning of August, Ramsay was detached from planning ROUNDUP and assigned to the more immediate task of planning Operation TORCH (the Allied landings in French North Africa), as Deputy to Admiral Sir Andrew Cunningham, who had been appointed Allied Naval Commander, Expeditionary Force. Mountbatten, credited by at least one historian as having 'originally suggested' the North Africa landings,[46] had already formed five planning syndicates, which had begun work on the outline plan; and when General Eisenhower was appointed Allied Commander-in-Chief for TORCH, the entire planning resources of COHQ were placed at his disposal. He asked immediately for the use of the Intelligence Branch and the Directorate of Experimental and Staff Requirements (DXSR).

It is said that appetite grows with eating. This was certainly so with TORCH: the table shows requirements first notified in August and the actual numbers which sailed in October:

Notified	Ships	Sailed
1	Headquarters Ship (LSH)	2
15	Landing Ship, Infantry (Large) (LSI(L))	25
3	Landing Ship, Gantry (LSG)	3
3	Landing Ship, Tank (LST)	3
15	Mechanical Transport Ship	34
37	Total	67

Notified	Craft	Sailed
91	Landing Craft, Assault (LCA)	140
13	Landing Craft, Support (Medium) (LCS(M))	12
93	Landing Craft, Personnel (LCP)	120
43	Landing Craft, Mechanised (Mk I) (LCM(I))	49
42	Landing Craft, Mechanised (Mk III) (LCM(III))	87
282	Total	408

An Admiralty report stated:

It can be said that during this period of mounting TORCH, the Admiralty lost control of the situation. It should be remembered, however, that speed of mounting and secrecy were essential factors and the contribution of COHQ to this mounting operation was immense. . . . That this force started mounting in September and carried out the operation early in November was in itself an extraordinary piece of work, and was only achieved by the relatively independent initiative of every individual responsible. There was no time for tidy co-ordination.[47]

The coordination may not have been tidy enough for the typical Whitehall warrior, but it was of the spontaneous kind achieved by highly motivated people given a clear aim, brisk encouragement, rapid decisions when required, and allowed to get on with the job; in other words, first-rate management and inspiring leadership. The individual responsible for providing this was the Chief of Combined Operations, namely Mountbatten.

The planning of TORCH did not at first go smoothly. An American group led by the Chief of Naval Operations, Admiral Ernest J. King, sought to keep the US naval forces under American command, and were chary of committing them inside the Mediterranean. For political reasons it was decided that the Americans would be less likely to get a hostile reception in French North Africa than the British. The American Chiefs of Staff were chary, also, of attempting to take Algiers, and wished to concentrate their forces to take Casablanca first; only if that went well would they land at Algiers. The British view was that, given such warning, the Germans would get to Algiers first. Churchill decided to send Eisenhower, Ramsay and Mountbatten to Washington to sort matters out. Mountbatten was to take a letter from Churchill to Harry Hopkins, couched in terms somewhat stronger than he could use directly to the President:

An amphibious operation like this has to be fitted together like a jewelled bracelet; for each particular landing place the right ships must be chosen, and these ships must be chosen in accordance with the needs of the particular work each landing party has to do.

At any rate, all was going forward, and until a week ago there was no reason why we should not have made the date 15 October. Then suddenly out of the blue arrived the shattering memorandum of the United States Chiefs of Staff, which altered the whole character and emphasis of the operation. . . .

What is the use of putting up an Allied Commander-in-Chief or Supreme Commander if he cannot have the slightest freedom in making his plan or deciding how, when and where to apply his forces? We are prepared to accept his decisions and to obey.[48]

In the event, Roosevelt once again exercised with wisdom his prerogative as Commander-in-Chief of the US armed forces, and on 4 September telegraphed to Churchill that he had accepted the British plan, adding, 'I am directing all preparations to proceed.'

During the next four weeks planners on both sides of the Atlantic worked feverishly to meet an assault date, for the first major Allied overseas operation, of 30 October 1942. A total of about 70,000 troops were to be used initially: Algiers was to be taken by a mixed British and American force under American command, followed up by the British 1st Army; and Oran by American troops, also under American command, followed up by Americans. All these forces would be trained in Britain and transported in British ships. Simultaneous landings at Casablanca would be by American troops transported direct from the USA in American ships.

According to Chalmers, 'Ramsay lost no time in putting the lessons of Dieppe to good account in planning TORCH and later large-scale operations.'[49] Despite his disappointment at being deprived of command of the naval forces he served Cunningham loyally, gladly accepting the help of some of the brilliant staff officers upon whom 'ABC had always had to rely'. It was one of these in particular, Commander M.L. Power, who, receiving the finally approved plan from the Chiefs of Staff on 2 October, 'dictated continuously for several days to Wren stenographers working in spells of four on duty and four standing by',[50] so that by 8 October the operation orders were ready for distribution. In all, some 200 warships, 350 merchant ships and 1,000 aircraft were taking part, as well as the troops.

TORCH was a resounding success, not least because of the deception plans which led the Germans to believe that the operation in prospect was another descent on Dakar; politically, the judgement was confirmed that Spain would not react, although the prediction of the Americans that they would be better received than the British by the French in North Africa was proved mistaken. Operationally, the failure, against the advice of COHQ, to reconnoitre the landing beaches resulted in setbacks that could have led to disaster had there been serious resistance. It was also unfortunate that the proud, pistol-packing Major General Patton did not accept Mountbatten's offer of one of the specialised headquarters ships. He chose instead to remain on board Admiral Hewitt's flagship, USS *Augusta*, which at the critical moment had to go and deal with a French force sallying forth from Casablanca. What happened then is described by Chalmers:

> At this critical moment, all communication between the Gibraltar Headquarters and Hewitt broke down. Eisenhower and Cunningham could get no news of how things were going on the wide stretch of surf-bound beaches north and south of Casablanca. Aircraft flown from Gibraltar over the scene were shot down either by French fighters or trigger-happy Americans. In desperation, Cunningham sent the fast (40 knots) minelayer *Welshman* with Rear Admiral Biere USN, to report on the situation, and it was learnt from him that for a time the fate of the expedition hung in the balance.[51]

But these were comparatively trivial errors in comparison with the wealth of experience gained, especially in bringing to prominence the differences in tradition, style and method between the armies, navies and air forces, with benefit to inter-service cooperation in future operations. Eisenhower set the proper tone for inter-Allied cooperation by declaring that a member of his integrated staff might call a colleague a 'son of a bitch' – but if he were to say a British or American 'son of a bitch' he would be out of a job.

Mounting TORCH denuded the CCO of landing craft. He was required to provide all the landing craft (LCA), called for by the US commanders of the assaults at Oran and Algiers, because at that juncture the US Navy possessed no armoured assault craft. COHQ also lost all its trained crews to TORCH. It was evident that the preparations for ROUNDUP had been set back. Furthermore, the swift and determined German reaction to the North Africa landings enabled them to make a stand in Tunisia, so the Allied invasion of Italy could not take place before the middle of 1943. It began to look as if the cross-Channel invasion of France, now fully occupied by the Germans, could not take place before the spring of 1944.

In the meantime, small-scale raiding continued under the auspices of COHQ. An example is Operation FRANKTON, in which the attackers, in six folding canoes launched from a submarine, sneaked up the River Gironde to Bordeaux and attached limpet mines to Axis blockade-runners unloading there. Only the leader, Major Hasler of the Royal Marines, and his canoe-mate Marine Sparks, survived and evaded capture, but it was disclosed after the war that ten limpets had been attached to four ships, all of which had been damaged. Many raids were planned and mounted, only to be cancelled before launch owing to a change of circumstances, bad weather, or fresh intelligence.

In this context, correspondence in the archives shows the pressure put on Mountbatten to sack the exceptionally able senior intelligence officer at COHQ, Wing Commander the Marquis de Casa Maury. Despite a strongly supportive letter from the Director of Naval Intelligence, and a direct appeal to the Chief of the Air Staff, Mountbatten was unable to obtain Casa Maury's promotion to group captain, which would have signified the confidence of the Air Ministry that he was worthy of it. In any event, it was intimated, 'they could supply a dozen' group captains or air commodores who were far superior to him.[52] As it turned out, Casa Maury was relieved in March 1943 by a lieutenant colonel.

Mountbatten's workload as CCO was extremely heavy, involving him continually in carrying out inspections of the numerous establishments and activities in his rapidly expanding command. The attack on his senior intelligence officer was one of a series of personnel matters to engage his attention. In the winter of 1942/43 the service ministries were becoming increasingly concerned as Combined Operations grew into a vast organisation, continually in competition for good officers, more skilled men, more vessels and more resources of many kinds. Rear Admiral Baillie-Grohman was particularly anxious that Mountbatten should recruit into Combined Operations more active service captains – about the scarcest commodity at the Admiralty's disposal – rather than retired admirals prepared to serve in a lower rank which would leave them nevertheless, in Baillie-Grohman's eyes, senior to him.

As planning for ROUNDUP continued, it became evident towards the end of 1942 that, owing to a restriction on recruitment by the Navy imposed by the War Cabinet, it was not possible to meet the normal fleet commitments and at the same time provide the rapidly increasing numbers of men required for Combined Operations ships and craft. The Admiralty having offered no solution to the problem, Mountbatten approached Ernest Bevin, Minister of Labour, directly. Bevin said that every man who could be recruited for the forces was needed in the Army for the invasion of France, whereupon Mountbatten pointed out that if it was not possible to man the invasion fleet the Army would be unable to get to the continent. Bevin saw the logic of this, and directed that the crews needed to take the Army to France should be regarded as part of the Army.

Preoccupation with such urgent matters did not prevent Mountbatten from writing to console the widows of friends killed in action, and some of their replies, preserved in his archives, should be read by a generation for whom marriage 'for better or for worse', selfless courage in adversity, and still less the ethos of *dulce et decorum est pro patria mori* seem to have little resonance:

> Thank you so very much for all your sympathy. I know *how* fond you were of XXX. The world will be a much less gay place without XXX won't it? I'm sad beyond words that the children will never know him and all the gaiety and goodness that made him. He so longed to come home and live a life of slippered ease and be with them, that I can't quite realise yet that it is never to be. However he has gone to where true joys are to be found and I'm certain that wherever he is will be richer for his lovable and laughable little person.
>
> In a way he seems closer to me than ever and so I pray I won't fail too hopelessly in trying to be all the best of two people rolled into one for our babes.[53]

The pressure on the planners to prepare for the invasion of France in 1943 was increased following TORCH. On 27 November Stalin telegraphed to Churchill a stern reminder of his promise 'to establish a Second Front in Western Europe in the spring of 1943'. In the light of Russian victories in the Caucasus and at Stalingrad it had certainly become essential to re-examine ROUNDUP.

Mountbatten attended the Casablanca Conference in January 1943, at which Churchill and Roosevelt, with their respective Chiefs of Staff, agreed upon Operation HUSKY to take Sicily in June; and in order to drive forward the planning for ROUNDUP, a Combined (Anglo-American) Chiefs of Staff group was established in London. Pending the appointment of a Supreme Allied

Commander, Lieutenant General F.E. Morgan was nominated as his Chief of Staff, soon to be abbreviated to COSSAC. At this stage the demands of the war in the Pacific for shipping were being met at the expense of needs in the Atlantic theatre. A closer look at the requirements for ROUNDUP also showed that it would have to be deferred until May 1944; in the meantime every effort would be made to knock Italy out of the war.

Training, and still more training, for these future combined operations took place at Inverary, at Djidjelli in Tunisia, and at Kabrit in the Middle East. Combined Operations Pilotage Parties were also being trained to land by folbot from submarines to survey and reconnoitre, in the utmost secrecy, the beaches of Sicily. The development of many projects was expedited, such as the Mulberry harbours; Pluto (Pipe Line Under the Ocean), which would in due course deliver a million gallons of petrol per day to the Normandy beaches; and means for demolishing underwater obstacles and waterproofing vehicles so that they could splash their way ashore.

Just as the Admiralty looked unfavourably upon the 'private navy' aspect of the rapidly growing Combined Operations fleet, so was the War Office less than enthusiastic about the growth of the Commandos. On 4 May 1943, after an exhaustive study of the relevant factors and consultation with the officers concerned, Mountbatten wrote to the CIGS:

> I am now forming up three Commandos for HUSKY and am most anxious to take full advantage of the lessons we learnt from the Commandos which took part in Tunisia.
>
> As you are aware, Commandos were originally raised to mount small raids. . . .
>
> They have now become a body of troops specialising in amphibious opposed assaults, in infiltration tactics and in operations against enemy flanks and L of C. They have also been trained to maintain themselves independently in enemy territory for considerable periods.
>
> In addition to this the Special Service Brigade has lately concentrated on co-operation with other arms to a far greater extent than was originally deemed necessary. . . .
>
> May I remind you in conclusion that every plan we see, whether made by the Planners at home or the Middle East Planners or the AFHQ Planners includes a certain number of Commandos, and I am most anxious not to fail in providing really first class Commandos. Morgan asked me only yesterday whether he could rely on Commandos being available for special tasks in the plans he is now producing.[54]

The remainder of the letter gave detailed proposals for a reorganisation, which would decentralise the command and administration of the Special Service Brigade and increase its firepower without 'an increase in British army personnel' in the brigade.

In the spring of 1943 the Sea Lords were still resentful at Mountbatten's sudden promotion to vice-admiral the previous March. But the force that he now commanded, as Chief of Combined Operations, certainly merited the rank. On 1 April 1943 it consisted of:

Officers: 5,489
Ratings: 44,275

	Home	Foreign	Total
Landing ships	28	61	89
Landing craft	1,678	923	2,601
Landing barges	1,019	—	1,019[55]

As Rear Admiral Horan remarked, with becoming modesty considering the important part he played:

Taken over a period of three years and starting from scratch this increase is something to look back on with satisfaction.[56]

It was evident that so great a part of the total strength of the Royal Navy ought to be reunited with its parent; but how could this be achieved without prejudice to the three-service integration, which was the *raison d'être* of 'Combined Ops'?

Meanwhile, Mountbatten was working in the closest collaboration with Lieutenant General Morgan (COSSAC) to lay the foundations for the OVERLORD plan. Between them they persuaded the senior officers of all three services and both nations who had been nominated for a key role in OVERLORD to attend a so-called 'study session'. It was to be held under the CCO's auspices in HMS *Warren*, occupying a hotel at Largs, the cover plan being to witness a large-scale exercise in the Clyde; its code name was RATTLE – suggested, it was said, by Morgan on the grounds that Mountbatten, always in the lead of progressive thought, was something of an *enfant terrible* to his more elderly colleagues.[57] During the four days from 28 June to 2 July every aspect of the forthcoming re-entry into the continent was presented to the assembled company in 23 papers, most of which emanated from COHQ. Discussion was chaired by Mountbatten, the youngest by eight years of the seven officers at the top table; the others were the force commanders designate – Admiral Little, General Paget and Air Chief Marshal Leigh-Mallory; Generals Devers and MacNaughton from the USA and Canada respectively; and COSSAC himself, General Morgan.

After a somewhat sticky start, in the course of which one of the force commanders designate argued strongly for a crossing at the Pas de Calais, a consensus was reached that 'the lodgement must be somewhere between the Cotentin Peninsula, inclusive, and Dieppe'. Within those limits, it was agreed, 'suitable assault landing beaches and an appropriate lodgement area could be, and would have to be, found'. The pros and cons of landing by day or by night, or at daybreak or dusk, were keenly argued; the use of airborne troops and Commandos; 'the administrative aspects of the build-up'; the artificial harbour – all the stratagems which became so familiar once D-Day had arrived and the world watched the greatest opposed landing ever carried out. It was revealed that the troops would have to start moving 'into and through their concentration, assembly and marshalling areas to their actual embarkation points' on D-Day minus 14. 'Once set in motion, the machinery could be stopped if need be up till the moment when the troops left their marshalling areas to embark. Thereafter they must be regarded as committed.'[58] This critical factor was put to the test when, on the eve of D-Day, unacceptably bad weather threatened.

Armed with the comprehensive data acquired at RATTLE, confident in the unity achieved, and fired by the enthusiasm generated for the operation in those who expected to participate in it, COSSAC produced the plan for OVERLORD for the British Chiefs of Staff within a fortnight. It was a bulky but most authoritative and detailed document. General Morgan concluded that, given the limitation of resources imposed by his directive,

> we may be assured of a reasonable chance of success on 1 May 1944 only if we concentrate our efforts on an assault across the Normandy beaches about Bayeux.[59]

Given the cardinal role played by COHQ in the preparations for OVERLORD, Mountbatten might have expected to be given command of one of the naval task forces in it. But this was not to be. Admirals who a year before would have spurned the offer of a job in Combined Operations were now eager to have control of a shoal of odd-looking craft, manned by 'Wavy Navy' (Reserve) officers and subject to the requirements of the 'Pongoes' (Army). The next best thing, as far as Mountbatten was concerned, was to be present when an assault was taking place, with the advantage of acquiring first-hand experience of an operation of this kind. So as soon as RATTLE was completed he set off for the Mediterranean to follow the learning curve leading from Dieppe, where lack of fire support was fatal; through TORCH, which succeeded because no follow-up over the beaches was needed; to HUSKY (the beach landings on Sicily), which would give proof of lessons learned or, in some cases, not learned.

With regard to fire support, of the two elements – bombardment by warships and bombing by aircraft – it was in the latter that the greater progress had been made. It had been necessary, as a preliminary to the assault on Sicily, to capture the small island of Pantellaria. Mountbatten had sent Professor Zuckerman to the Middle East in January 1943, at the request of the air staff, to make a scientific study of the efficacy of air support.[60] This proved to be most fruitful, if at first unwelcome to senior air officers. Based upon the new, systematic approach to the selection of targets and the effort required to destroy or neutralise them, Air Vice-Marshal Robb, who had been Mountbatten's air deputy at COHQ, produced a plan to reduce the defences of the island to an extent which would permit the landing of the ground forces without undue opposition. It worked. By the time the assault craft reached the beaches the white flag was flying. Unfortunately this success reinforced the belief, widely held in the Allied air forces, that bombing would enable them to win the war single-handed – the task of the navies being merely to transport the troops needed to occupy the territory of the defeated enemy.

As to bombardment by warships, not all senior naval officers yet believed that this was a suitable employment for their most powerful surface ships, which would thus be risked in mine-strewn waters and exposed to concentrated air and submarine attack. This was another aspect of the single-service thinking against which Mountbatten had continually to bring his influence to bear, indirect though it must be except in areas for which he had specific responsibility – Roskill gives examples:

In each of the British sectors a 'Senior Naval Officer Landing (SNOL)' was appointed to carry the responsibility for the naval side of the actual assaults. They were officers of Captain's rank who had, of recent years, specialised in the organisation and execution of combined operations. . . . During the period of preparation for the invasion of Sicily they had carried out all the training of their landing craft crews, and had established the intimate understanding with the senior officers of the Army units whom they were to put ashore, on which so much depended. The creation of this highly specialised body of experts had been a gradual evolution since the early days of the war, and the need had been reinforced by the experiences of the Dieppe raid. Latterly every effort had been made to keep together the staffs of all three services who were trained and experienced in combined operations, and to leave them in the same ships, thus making their experience in one assault fully profitable to the next. Another aspect of the organisation of combined operations to which considerable attention had been given since the North Africa landings of November 1942 was the provision of trained parties of specialists drawn from all three services, but principally from the Army and the Navy, to control the landing of vehicles, stores and ammunition.[61]

But Mountbatten could only regret, and do nothing about,

the failure of the respective Commanders-in-Chief to set up their Headquarters together. Cunningham insisted on being at Malta, Tedder on remaining at Tunis. . . .

Alexander finally decided to go with Cunningham to Malta. . . . After the 'critical period' Alexander joined Tedder at Tunis, while Cunningham went off to Bizerta.[62] Eisenhower was also in Malta initially; in fact, Mountbatten was with him when they heard a BBC announcer tell the world that he, Eisenhower, had just reported that the first wave of his Allied Forces had landed in Sicily. Eisenhower said: 'Well, thank God: he ought to know!' It was actually the first report that he himself had had.[63]

On the day before the HUSKY landings the weather suddenly deteriorated; instead of the calm, blue Mediterranean sea it blew up into half a gale. The defending commander thought the Allies would delay the expected assault, and stood his forces down. But Ramsay decided to press on. The weather abated and tactical surprise was achieved, although the sea was still rather rough to the west of Cape Passaro where the Canadians and the Americans landed.

Probably the most successful innovation, first tried out at Dieppe, was the tank landing craft which could fire a salvo of 2,500 rockets, each with an effect 25 per cent greater than that of a 6-inch shell; a number of these, once again well handled by Lieutenant Commander Hugh Mulleneux, gave overwhelming support to the Highland Division, enabling 'the Jocks', according to Fergusson, to get ashore 'with less than a dozen casualties'.[64] Also invaluable in the tideless waters were the naval lighter pontoons obtained by COHQ from the USA. Rafts of these were used to bridge the 'water gap', so vehicles could be driven to the shore from the landing ships with no delay. Mountbatten was also glad to see the Royal Marine Commandos, now part of the Special Service Brigade, deployed with good effect in the role that he had assured for them.

Although there remained a good deal to be learned about the conduct of large-scale combined operations, after HUSKY the time had come to transfer to newly formed divisions within the Admiralty the administrative duties of COHQ, retaining its advisory and planning functions. When, therefore, Mountbatten sailed with Churchill from the Clyde on 5 August on board the *Queen Mary*, prior to the Quebec Conference, he was aware that his term as CCO would probably soon be ended. In that event he would, presumably, cease to be a member of the Chiefs of Staff Committee. The Prime Minister had certainly toyed with the idea of offering Mountbatten the post of First Sea Lord; with Sir Dudley Pound's health visibly failing, that post would soon become vacant. But Mountbatten himself could see that the obvious successor to Pound was Sir Andrew Cunningham, and was well aware that his accelerated promotion to flag rank had created a strong animus against him in some naval quarters.

The Prime Minister's party in the *Queen Mary* included all three British Chiefs of Staff, with whom he wished to examine the main issues of policy and strategy for the year ahead 'before we meet the Americans'. The war plans to be considered included the twice-postponed and much awaited cross-Channel invasion, OVERLORD; the Mediterranean campaign to put Italy out of the war; and the war against the Japanese. The plan for an assault across the beaches of Normandy, for which Mountbatten and Morgan had obtained full backing at the RATTLE exercise, was explained to Churchill by Brigadier K.G. McLean and two more of General Morgan's staff officers; another day was spent in discussing options opened up by the successful invasion of Sicily, ranging as far as assisting the Russians to land in Romania, or to regain the Caucasus. 'Meanwhile,' added Churchill in a telegram to Eden, 'the war should be carried forward against Italy in every way that the Americans will allow. We do not have to ask their permission about bombing the towns in Northern Italy, and Harris should be limited by weather only.'[65]

Next came the need to agree 'on a general plan' for offensive operations in South-East Asia. At this stage Churchill revealed his hope that 'a specially constituted South-East Asia Command, under a British Supreme Commander' should be set up. There would then, he argued, be a chance of 'proving our zeal in this theatre of war, which by its failures and sluggishness is in a measure under reasonable reproach'.[66]

That the Prime Minister's strategic vision encompassed Burma the moment Sicily had been successfully invaded was marked by his order to Brigadier Orde Wingate to report to him in London. Wingate, who had become an expert in jungle warfare, arrived at No. 10 Downing Street the night Churchill was due to leave for Quebec. So impressed was he with Wingate's vigour and ideas that he decided Wingate must join the party on the *Queen Mary*. Wingate's protest that he had only got his tropical kit was brushed aside; and in reply to his further protest that he had not seen his wife for a long time he was told that he must bring her too. Miraculously, this was arranged, and Wingate was able to put before the Chiefs of Staff, with the Prime Minister taking the chair, his proposal for a long-range penetration force in Burma. It was Brooke's opinion that the operations of this specially devised force 'would have to be backed up by the main advance, so as to make good what he had gained'.[67] And he warned that if Wingate's plans were carried out, leading to the occupation of northern Burma, it would be essential to carry on in that theatre the following year and complete its conquest.

Churchill's restless mind, now fully engaged with the military prospects in South-East Asia, demanded the presentation of an operation to occupy the Andaman Islands. This was duly given by an expert on combined operations in the Indian Ocean, whose presence on board could not have been accidental. In any event he succeeded in convincing Churchill that the operation, code named BUCCANEER, was neither feasible nor necessary – but it was to become almost as much of an incubus at Combined Chiefs of Staff meetings as OVERLORD. Just as a 'second front' in Europe was called for to support Russia against the Germans, so an amphibious operation across the Bay of Bengal was held to be the key to supporting Chiang Kai-shek's China against the Japanese.

It is doubtful if any more congenial, and at the same time effective, environment could have been provided for conclave between Churchill and his chief military advisers than that provided during a five-day passage in the *Queen Mary*. The presence of Clementine Churchill and their daughter Mary promoted a differentiation between 'on' and 'off' duty. Plenary sessions, at which rigorous argument could lead to firm decisions soundly based, crystallised the lines of thought which had emerged during informal talk between members of the party in varying combination. Churchill was, of course, a warlord by temperament; no doubt this was why, under his leadership, there had not developed between him and the admirals, generals, and air chief marshals that mutual misunderstanding and mistrust between the 'frocks' and the 'brass' which had so tragically prejudiced the politico-military direction of the First World War.

For Mountbatten, aged 43, to be a member of this uniquely formidable group of military professionals testified to his own sheer professional ability. Whether in conversation or at a meeting, the facts he deployed and the conclusions he drew, together with the manner of his expression, ran the gauntlet of criticism by the head not just of one of the armed forces but the heads of all three. He passed the test. The *Queen Mary* arrived at Halifax, Nova Scotia, on the afternoon of 9 August. The Prime Minister's particular genius was then evidenced in the composition of his telegrams to Eden, giving guidance on the conduct of peace negotiations with Marshal Badoglio, as representing post-Mussolini Italy. As he put it, 'merely harping on "unconditional surrender" with no prospect of mercy held out even as an act of grace may well lead to no surrender at all'.[68] And he recommended use of the President's expression 'honourable capitulation'. Later the same day, as Gilbert goes on to record:

> Churchill also telegraphed to Attlee on August 9, about a suggestion made to him earlier by Leo Amery, that Lord Louis Mountbatten should be appointed to the South-East Asia Command. 'All would depend,' Churchill added, 'upon whether the Americans liked the idea. Personally I think he might well be acceptable to the President. He knows the whole story from the top; he is young, enthusiastic and triphibious.' Churchill telegraphed to Attlee and Eden two days later that Mountbatten's appointment 'would I think command public interest and approval and show that youth is no barrier to merit'.[69]

It would show, also, that being a great-grandson of Queen Victoria and having a First Sea Lord for a father were no barriers to such advancement.

Predictably, some people of influence were unimpressed. The post had, it seems, been offered around behind the scenes for the past couple of months. Among others Sir Andrew Cunningham had been considered, but had deemed it an 'unattractive job'. Later, and not untypically given his long-standing disdain of Mountbatten's innovative propensities, he wrote:

It rather defeats me how he can imagine he is the man for the job. It is the end of his service career. A political job, of course. . . . It is a poor business but I think most people in the service have just laughed.[70]

The opinion of the Secretary of State for War, P.J. Grigg, which he bruited around Washington, was even less flattering, and still further from the mark: 'an aristocratic playboy . . .'.[71]

But on balance, both in Britain and America, public opinion welcomed the establishment of a Supreme Allied Commander, South-East Asia, and the selection of Mountbatten for the job. He himself was elated at the prospect of so much power to put his ideas into practice, and overawed by the formidable difficulties of doing so. Nor can he have been comforted in that respect by a letter from Edwina:

You must be having a fascinating time . . . but for God's sake do something about the political set-up, otherwise all is useless.[72]

He told her that he would need her more than ever:

The more I think of this job the more it frightens me. . . .

I've got so used to leaning on you and hearing your brutally frank but well-deserved criticisms! But above all you have been such a help with all the people I have to deal with.[73]

On 23 September 1943 Mountbatten's appointment as Supreme Commander, South-East Asia Command, was gazetted. On 2 October he left Northolt airport to fly, via Baghdad, to Delhi.

4

SUPREME ALLIED COMMANDER SOUTH-EAST ASIA (1943–46)

In Singapore on 12 September 1945 I sat on the left of the Supreme Commander, Admiral Mountbatten, in the line of his Commanders-in-Chief and principal staff officers, while the formal unconditional surrender of all Japanese forces, land, sea and air in South-East Asia was made to him.

Field Marshal Viscount Slim[1]

As Aileen quietly entered the bedroom to warn the visitor that it was time to leave, she saw Mountbatten leaning over her husband and heard Slim saying, 'We did it together, old boy.' In the shadow of death plain words are spoken. 'We did it together.'

Ronald Lewin[2]

Chapter 4

There can be no doubt that, from the end of 1943, the whole of the Far Eastern campaign revolved around the Mountbatten–Slim axis, and the contribution of others, however great, was known and seen to be subsidiary.

Ronald Lewin[3]

Mountbatten arrived in Delhi on 7 October 1943 to take up his appointment as Supreme Allied Commander South-East Asia (SACSEA), buoyed up by the express good wishes and high hopes of both Churchill and Roosevelt. The Prime Minister had proposed him for the job and the President, warmly assenting, had told Mountbatten that he expected from him personal loyalty matching that evinced by Eisenhower, as Supreme Allied Commander in the Mediterranean, towards King George VI. But as time would show, this courtly relationship was to prove easier for 'Ike' than for 'Dickie' to sustain. For it lay at the heart of the struggle for resources with which to prosecute the war in their respective theatres, a discord compounded by divergent political aims.

On 9 March 1942, the day on which the last Dutch forces in Java had capitulated to the Japanese, Roosevelt had proposed to Churchill that, as Allies, the USA and Britain should divide operational responsibility: the USA would look after the Pacific; Britain would remain in overall charge of the 'middle area' stretching from Singapore across the Indian Ocean to the Persian Gulf, the Red Sea and the Mediterranean; and the European Atlantic area would be subject to combined Anglo-American control.

This geo-strategic consensus reflected the essentially maritime nature of the alliance: provided the war at sea was not lost, troops could be transported, landed and sustained wherever strategic gain dictated, and populations could be supplied with food and raw materials; but the political divergence remained. To his undying credit President Roosevelt accepted and never flinched from the policy of 'Germany first' urged upon him by Churchill, despite strong pressure from many quarters in the USA to devote more and more effort to the defeat of Japan.

By May 1943 Mountbatten had been a full member of the British Chiefs of Staff Committee for over a year; he had witnessed the success of the TORCH landings which led to the expulsion of Axis forces from North Africa; in Russia, after the defence of Stalingrad, the Red Army was ready to counter a new German offensive; and in the Pacific, since the resounding defeat of the Japanese fleet at the Battle of Midway, American predominance was assured. The grand strategy to bring about the unconditional surrender of Germany and the total defeat of Japan was beginning to take shape. But with confidence in military victory came political issues commensurate with the scale of events. In each case the aggressors had used war as an instrument of policy – to conquer, to dominate and to consolidate. For the victims, the achievement of military victory, with restoration of the status quo ante-bellum as a political aim, would not suffice. War is a catalyst. After it, things can never be the same.

When Britain declared war on Germany on 3 September 1939, to fulfil a pledge given to Poland, she was supported by the self-governing members of the Commonwealth and automatically took her colonies with her. Had peace prevailed these too would have attained self-government within the Commonwealth, as most of them eventually did. It was unfortunate but true that a view commonly held in the USA, and shared by President Roosevelt, was that the restoration of Britain's colonial empire would be contrary to both the political ideals and economic interests of the Americans; for them it was China – the so-called Nationalist China, where Chiang Kai-shek was bravely holding out against the ruthless Japanese armies on the one hand and the Communist revolutionaries on the other – that excited wholehearted sympathy and military support.

At the suggestion of General Marshall, the President had attached Lieutenant General Joseph W. Stilwell to Generalissimo Chiang Kai-shek as chief of a joint staff consisting of representatives of the American, British, Chinese and Dutch governments. His instructions were to increase the effectiveness of US assistance to the Chinese government; to assist in improving the combat efficiency of the Chinese army; to command all American forces in the China-Burma-India (C-B-I) theatre; to be the President's personal military representative to the Generalissimo; and to control and supervise the disposition of American Lend-Lease aid.

Stilwell, known from his acerbic manner as 'Vinegar Joe', had a good reputation as a commander in the field and had been provisionally chosen to command the first American overseas operations in Europe. But as he had extensive experience in China and spoke fluent Mandarin, his appointment to the C-B-I theatre made sense. In March 1942 he was put in charge of the Chinese forces in Burma, retreating, with the British Burma Corps, before the advancing Japanese. Two Chinese divisions managed to make their way into India; the third also disengaged and marched back into China. General Stilwell, at the age of 58, having been cut off by the Japanese advance, escaped through wild country into India. He did not conceal his view that British incompetence and defeatism had contributed largely to the debacle in Burma, which had not been regarded as essential to the defence of India; and believed that, as a matter of policy, Britain did not favour a strong China. Stilwell did not know that even before he had reached the sanctuary of Imphal, General Wavell, at that time the Commander-in-Chief, India, had told his chief of staff to put in hand straight away a study of an offensive to reoccupy Burma. As to the support of Nationalist China, British policy was based upon an appraisal of Chiang Kai-shek's character and prospects that proved to be far more realistic than Washington's perception of him.

The Japanese had halted their advance at the Burma–Assam frontier, which was to be the western limit of their Greater East Asia Co-Prosperity Sphere, but they did not wish to tie up large forces defending the perimeter of their conquests. To this end they sent a powerful naval force into the Indian Ocean to counter the threat, posed by the British Eastern Fleet, of attack upon their ships taking supplies to Rangoon, or of amphibious assaults on the Arakan coast of Burma; and above all, to demonstrate to the peoples of India and Ceylon the invincibility of Japan.

To preserve his much inferior fleet, Admiral Somerville, C-in-C East Indies, had withdrawn it to Kilindini in East Africa; and Madagascar had been taken from the Vichy French, to deny it as an advanced base to the Japanese lest they should be tempted to support the pro-fascist Free India Movement led by Subhas Chandra Bose, and the first Indian National Army under Mohan Singh. They may well have been heartened by the alacrity with which Gandhi, sensing that the British were 'on the toboggan', as he put it, initiated his 'Quit India' campaign. His intention that it should be non-violent was of little comfort to the authorities whose task it was to maintain civil order in a subcontinent with a population of 350 million, especially when famine threatened.

The military command to which Mountbatten had been appointed as SACSEA was set up by the British and US governments to control all Allied forces in Burma, Ceylon, Malaya, the Dutch East Indies, Siam and Indo-China, engaged now or in the future in fighting the Japanese. Inherent, therefore, was a divorce of administration from operations, in principle unsound. From his experience as Chief of Combined Operations Mountbatten was fully aware of this, and of the critical importance of command relationships, both personal and formal, in achieving a modus vivendi. The British Chiefs of Staff and the American Joint Chiefs, acting in concert as the Combined Chiefs of Staff, would be responsible for the strategic direction of the war against Japan and the allocation of resources between the relevant theatres; but orders and instructions to SACSEA would be issued by the British Chiefs of Staff. Unfortunately, either from negligence or pusillanimity, they did not place the respective commanders-in-chief of the sea, land and air forces in the theatre formally under the command of SACSEA.

This put Mountbatten in a difficult position. It had become obvious, following the numerous reverses suffered by British arms during the first two years of the war, that no single service could win battles without the closest cooperation of at least one and usually both the other services; and that this was true at the strategic as well as the tactical level. To achieve victory, all concerned, from the commanders-in-chief down to junior leaders, must think and act in terms of the combination of all arms to maintain a common aim – the destruction of the enemy's forces.

When offered this new Supreme Allied Command, at the age of 43, Mountbatten had already served as an acting vice-admiral for over a year, but he still ranked substantively as a captain of middling seniority. Even in the acting rank of admiral, therefore, he would be junior in service seniority, as well as by many years in age, to his sea, land and air commanders-in-chief. Not surprisingly, before accepting the post he sought assurance from the Chiefs of Staff, individually, that he would have their support if he should wish to sack a commander-in-chief. It was pointed out to him that only the Prime Minister could decide such an issue, and with that he had to be content. In consequence, Admiral Somerville, General Giffard and Air Chief Marshal Peirse were free to assume that Mountbatten's modus operandi would conform to that of Eisenhower in the Mediterranean, who acted as chairman of the commanders-in-chief in committee, rather than follow the example of MacArthur in the Pacific theatre, who had his own planning staff and made sure that his sea, land and air commanders were formally subordinated to him.

Ten days after being appointed as SACSEA, Mountbatten, sensing that for reasons of naval organisation, command and control, rather than any doubt about Somerville's competence – he was without exception the finest admiral of his generation – there could be misunderstanding between them, wrote to him:

> During any combined operation when the Army and the Air Force and our American Allies have a stake in your movements I hope that you will not mind that the Supreme Commander (who only happens to be Dickie Mountbatten by accident) will have a considerable say.[4]

To which Somerville replied briefly by signal, asking for the names of his 'military and air colleagues'. But friction came later, when the Supreme Commander proposed to make himself known to the men of the Eastern Fleet. Somerville did not welcome the youthful, princely Supreme Commander aboard his ships.

During the six weeks between receiving his appointment and arriving in Delhi, Mountbatten was fully engaged in selecting his personal staff and setting them to work, in determining the structure of the future SEAC staff and in getting suitable officers appointed. As Chief of Staff he was given Lieutenant General Sir Henry Pownall, who had been Wavell's Chief of Staff when the latter was Allied Commander-in-Chief of the American-British-Dutch Area (ABDA) established shortly after the Japanese attack on Pearl Harbor; thereafter he had been GOC Ceylon, then Commander-in-Chief, Persia and Iraq.

An American, Lieutenant General Albert Wedemeyer, who had served in Combined Operations planning, became Deputy Chief of Staff. And, given the vital importance of logistics, Mountbatten was thankful for the help of his principal logistics officer Lieutenant General Raymond 'Speck' Wheeler, who commanded the American services of supply in the Far East. Also, foreseeing that without the wholehearted and efficient support of India Command, SEAC's operations could not prosper, Mountbatten persuaded the Commander-in-Chief, India, Field Marshal Sir Claude Auchinleck, to create the post of Principal Administrative Officer GHQ (India) and appoint thereto a most able general, Lindsell.

In Delhi, the offices provided for SACSEA were initially quite inadequate; although Mountbatten intended to transfer his HQ to Ceylon, following a Chiefs of Staff proposal the previous June, he arranged acceptable accommodation for it in Delhi for the time being. In a series of meetings he quickly built up his own appreciation of the situation, while hearing a litany of difficulties: our troops could not stop the Japanese from infiltrating through the jungle and cutting off their supplies, so our advancing forces had to fall back to re-establish their supply lines; air supply was impossible owing to the lack of transport aircraft; it was impossible to prosecute the war in Burma for five months of the year (May to November) owing to the monsoon; tropical disease put 120 times more men in hospital than battle casualties; the lines of communication in Assam were hopelessly inadequate to support any form of offensive; morale was low.

Mountbatten's initial response to the challenge offered by SEAC was to identify three key elements in restoring the situation there – morale, malaria and monsoon – and of these three, the most important was morale. It was his intention from the outset to address personally as many as possible of the troops in his command as soon as he could – informally, and without interrupting work, as was his custom. The Eastern Army, soon to become the famous 14th, would no longer be the 'forgotten army'; and the Eastern Fleet, likewise, would be encouraged.

Making it clear, somewhat to the surprise of the commanders-in-chief, that he would deal with them as his subordinates in terms of military command, Mountbatten set out his response to their problems. He would ensure that enough transport aircraft were provided for air supply of forward positions; he would see that our forces fought on as hard in the monsoon as in the dry weather; he would organise a determined drive against disease by the medical

97

services, based upon vigorous research; he would get an American railway regiment to treble the capacity of the railway in Assam; he would visit the units in the front line, in particular, and talk to them to raise their morale; and he would create an inter-service daily newspaper, to be called SEAC, run by a former editor of the *Evening Standard* under the auspices of the editor of the *Sunday Dispatch*, who was to be attached to his staff.

A matter of special concern was the future of the long-range penetration groups, which had been raised by the fiery, fearless, eccentric Brigadier Orde Wingate, under the auspices of General Wavell, then Commander-in-Chief, India, to attack, destroy and disrupt enemy transport and communications, operating far behind Japanese lines and supplied as necessary by air. The name Chindit was adopted by Wingate from the word *chinthe* – the traditional lions at the entrance to Burmese temples. In February 1943 some 3,000 Chindits, organised into eight independent columns, had marched into Burma from Imphal in Assam, crossed the River Chindwin and later the Irrawaddy, penetrated 150 miles into enemy-held territory, destroyed many bridges and blown up the railway in 70 places. It had been a gallant and inspiring, but costly, effort, from which only 2,180 'shattered and emaciated' men had returned. But:

> After the campaign, the Japanese admitted that the Chindits were difficult to deal with effectively and had completely disrupted their plans for the first half of 1943.[5]

The Chindit operations had been designed to support a three-pronged advance of British and Chinese forces into northern Burma planned by Wavell, but this had been cancelled, so Wingate's forces had found themselves confronted by the whole weight of three Japanese divisions. It could reasonably be argued that future, and even enlarged, Chindit operations would be justified, provided they formed part of a general offensive.

Now well briefed, and having begun to establish his authority as theatre commander, Mountbatten flew on 16 October to Chungking in China. During a four-day visit, marked by the customary competition to gain 'face', the Generalissimo, for whom his charming and attractive wife acted as interpreter, seemed to agree with the strategic proposals put to him. These embraced a major amphibious operation across the Bay of Bengal, to be coordinated with Chinese advances into Burma.

Chiang Kai-shek's standpoint was that of a self-made political leader of a vast country in chaos, who sought continually to obtain the maximum possible support from both the Americans and British to bolster his regime and end Japanese occupation. To achieve his aim he was ready to promise the participation of Chinese armies in Allied offensives in Burma, subject always to conditions which would depend upon the favourable outcome of the war in other theatres. This was to be Mountbatten's main problem.

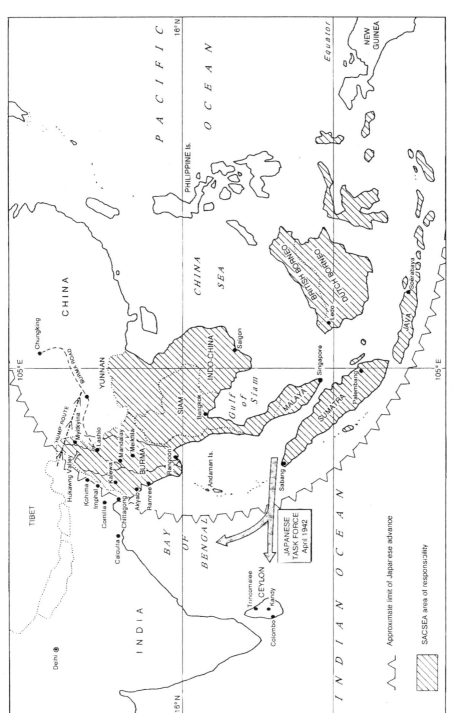

Map 4. South-East Asia, 1943–46

Between General Stilwell and Chiang Kai-shek relations were never cordial. But each had more to lose than to gain by a complete break. Stilwell was determined to maximise Nationalist China's contribution to defeating Japan; Chiang Kai-shek believed that, but for Stilwell, his credibility with Washington would be severely prejudiced. When Mountbatten met Stilwell in the course of his visit, his obvious fighting spirit impressed 'Vinegar Joe' favourably, and his contempt for the British was for the time being diminished. There is some evidence that Stilwell was at that time under threat of dismissal by the Generalissimo, and that Mountbatten intervened on his behalf, saying that he would not permit the Chinese, who were to be under SACSEA command, to fight under any other general. No doubt General Carton de Wiart was helpful. This most gallant officer had been commander of the Allied force evacuated in 1940 from Namsos, in Norway, by the Royal Navy, including Mountbatten's HMS *Kelly*, in the face of devastating attacks by the Luftwaffe. As Churchill's personal representative in Chungking he was well placed to know what was going on behind the scenes, and to keep his former rescuer fully briefed.

On his way back to Delhi Mountbatten took advantage of a fuelling stop at Dum Dum airport, near Calcutta, to visit the Joint Headquarters of the Eastern Army and the 3rd Tactical Air Force. He was received by the acting army commander, Lieutenant General W.J. Slim, and Air Marshal Baldwin. Pending the activation of the South-East Asia Command, Mountbatten was not in a position to issue orders to Slim, but accepted with alacrity the general's invitation to give a talk to some 80 of the most senior officers on the joint staff.

They were a sceptical audience. What, they wondered, could a semi-royal sailor, renowned mainly for dashing at the enemy and getting sunk, have to tell them? His message was clear and confident. He outlined to these hardbitten, disillusioned soldiers and airmen the principles upon which, in his view, a successful campaign for the recovery of Burma must be founded: he was aware of the terrible toll that tropical diseases took of their men, and had already set up a Medical Advisory Division of tropical disease experts to reduce their impact dramatically; there was to be no more retreat – if their lines of communication were cut he would arrange for the isolated troops to be supplied by air; above all, he was opposed to the custom whereby fighting stopped during the monsoon, and sought their support in keeping the battle going whatever the weather. He assured them, also, from recent conversations with the King and Prime Minister, of the high hopes placed in them, and of his intention to ensure that theirs was no longer the 'forgotten frontier'. He then had a private talk with Slim and Baldwin, leaving Brigadier Cobb, the Army Group Director of Plans, whom he had borrowed from Giffard to accompany him to Chungking, to assess the effect of his talk.

Since mid-1942 Slim, having shown skill and resolution of a high order in bringing Burma Corps out of Burma into Assam, had been in command of

XV Corps, responsible for internal security in the Indian states of Bengal, Bihar and Orissa – some 185,000 square miles – and for defending the Indo-Burmese frontier and the Bengal coast. In the 1942/43 mini-offensive launched by Wavell in the Arakan region of north-west Burma, in response to Churchill's querulous prodding, Slim had been called in at the eleventh hour to take charge of another retreat arising from the poor generalship of Irwin, whose relief in command of the Eastern Army by Giffard followed swiftly. Now, with the advent of SEAC, the 11th Army Group had been established, with Giffard in command and Slim acting as commander of the Eastern Army.

It did not take Mountbatten long to decide that Slim was the man he needed to command the new land force he intended to create for the Burma campaign, to be called the 14th Army. Before continuing his flight back to Calcutta therefore, he offered command of the new army to Slim – whose immediate reaction, while obviously delighted, was to accept subject to the approval of General Giffard. Mountbatten said that as he was the Supreme Commander Slim need have no concern, since Giffard was his subordinate, and in any case had reported favourably on Slim. In the event Giffard seems to have demurred, and asked for time to think it over. Sensing that he must exert authority commensurate with the responsibility laid upon him, Mountbatten suggested to Giffard that he should telegraph the CIGS asking whether he had to obey his orders or was permitted to protest. Giffard accepted Slim.

On 29 October the Prime Minister, as Minister of Defence, issued his directive to Mountbatten. Its main provisions were:

> As his 'prime duty' to engage the Japanese 'as closely and continuously as possible in order by attrition to consume and wear down the enemy's forces, especially his Air Forces, thus making our superiority tell and forcing the enemy to divert his forces from the Pacific theatre; and secondly, but of equal consequence, to maintain and broaden our contacts with China, both by the Air route and by establishing direct contact through Northern Burma *inter alia* by suitably organised, Air-supplied ground forces of the greatest possible strength. . . .'
>
> To use his air and sea power to seize some point or points which 'will induce a powerful reaction from the enemy' and at the same time give several options for a counter stroke to meet the enemy's reaction.[6]

The directive, with its unmistakable air of drafting in a postprandial euphoria redolent of cigars, large-scale brandies and small-scale maps, added that before the first amphibious attack was launched a battle fleet would be deployed for support, based on Ceylon. Field Marshal Slim recalled:

> From the Assam front I was called to Supreme Headquarters to attend conferences on the forthcoming general offensive. . . . New Delhi . . . was over-crowded . . .

I could sympathise with Admiral Mountbatten's desire to move his headquarters to some less congested spot and one within his own command. . . . This was the first conference I had sat through at SEAC Headquarters . . . I attended many in the next two years, and it was interesting to see how rapidly they became more businesslike and effective as Admiral Mountbatten learned the job of Supreme Commander. . . . His period as Chief of Combined Operations gave him an insight into the organisation and working of the other two Services that was of tremendous value to him. . . . It was as a member of the Chiefs of Staff Combined Operations Committee, where he came into contact with the wider direction of the war as a whole, that he served his apprenticeship for supreme command.[7]

Slim could have added that it was as Chief of Combined Operations, also, that Mountbatten became conditioned to his 'best-laid schemes' going 'aft agley' through the withdrawal of allocated forces more urgently needed elsewhere, or aborted by bad weather. Now, even as a Supreme Commander, his plans were to be set at nought by the dictates of grand strategy.

On 16 November 1943, South-East Asia Command was activated. Based upon a comparison of Allied and enemy forces in the theatre, plus the reinforcements he had been promised, and what could be gleaned of the Japanese intentions, SACSEA had already formulated a plan of campaign for 1943–44. It consisted of seven separate but related operations, some of which had already been set in train:

1. Capture of the Andaman Islands.
2. Advance in the Arakan with Akyab as the ultimate objective.
3. Advance on Central Front across Chindwin.
4. Advance by the Northern Combat Area Command (NCAC) to capture Myitkyina-Mogaung.
5. Advance by Chinese (Yunnan) 'Yoke' Force to Bhamo-Lashio.
6. Operations in support of items 4 and 5 by Chindits.
7. Airborne capture of Indaw followed by fly-in of a division to hold it pending arrival of NCAC forces.

A week later, at Cairo, in the presence of Churchill, Roosevelt, Chiang Kai-shek and the Combined Chiefs of Staff, Mountbatten presented these proposals. They were readily accepted by the heads of state, subject to the stipulation by Chiang Kai-shek that the advance of his forces from Yunnan would be contingent upon the launching of a major amphibious operation across the Bay of Bengal; but the Combined Chiefs of Staff had yet to confirm their allocation of resources to SEAC on the scale required if SACSEA was to have any prospect of carrying out the directive he had been given by Churchill.

From Cairo the Prime Minister and the President, with their military advisers, went on to Teheran to meet Stalin while Mountbatten returned to

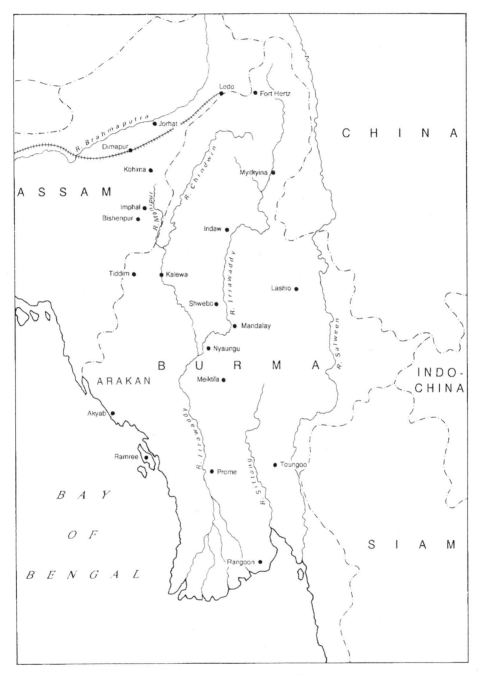

Map 5. Burma, 1943–45

India, confident that his campaign would form part of the war-winning Allied plans. But when the leaders came back to Cairo to confer further they had accepted the ineluctable necessity, imposed upon them by Stalin, to launch OVERLORD, the long-awaited re-entry into north-west Europe, in May 1944 or risk the withdrawal of the Soviet Union from the alliance.

The continuing requirement for amphibious assault operations in the Mediterranean – against the Germans in Italy and the Balkans, to recapture Rhodes without the aid of Turkey, and to mount a landing in the south of France in conjunction with OVERLORD – now convinced the Combined Chiefs of Staff that shortage of landing craft would govern the feasibility of the SEAC plans. As the chairman of the British Chiefs of Staff, General Brooke, put it, Mountbatten would have to do the best he could with what was left after the requirements of the European theatre had been met.

In the face of this setback, Mountbatten's resilience and leadership were severely tested. He recalled Churchill's paper of May 1943: 'Going into swampy jungles to fight the Japanese is like going into the water to fight a shark.' Confirmation that the SEAC campaign plan would have to be drastically revised was contained in the final report of the Cairo Conference, dated 6 December.

A succinct and reliable account of the effect of its provisions in relation to Mountbatten's seven related operations was given by Brigadier M.R. Roberts:

> Drastic modification of plans became necessary and, in spite of strenuous efforts to keep the whole programme in being, operations were finally whittled down to four:
> (i)   An offensive without landing craft in Arakan.
> (ii) An advance by NCAC [Northern Combat Area Command] from Ledo.
> (iii) A limited advance across the Chindwin.
> (iv) Operations by Chindits.[8]

The first of these operations would lead to the capture of Akyab, with its airfield of key strategic importance; the second would secure improved supply lines from India to China both by land and air; the third would remove the threat of a further Japanese advance into India; and the fourth would support the other three by interdicting the Japanese lines of communication.

It was therefore something of a triumph for Mountbatten, in contrast to the emasculation of his campaign plan arising from the second Cairo Conference, that the US Chief of the Air Staff, General 'Hap' Arnold, agreed to his request that the British and American air forces in SEAC, which had been operating quite separately, should be integrated to form Allied Air Command, South-East Asia, under Air Chief Marshal Sir Richard Peirse. A subordinate operational authority, Eastern Air Command, was to be established under his second in command, Major General G.E. Stratemeyer, commanding the 10th US Army Air Force, who became the Allied Air Commander for Burma. These arrangements were strongly contested. Mountbatten's Deputy Supreme Allied Commander, General Stilwell, had to be overruled by General Arnold in the face of lobbying by Stilwell's Washington friends. As Commanding General, China-Burma-India Theatre Stilwell continued to hold the Air Transport Command. The US Joint Chiefs of Staff reserved the right to reassign units to the 14th (Chennault's) US Army Air Force, also under Stilwell's theatre command; and he and Peirse agreed to coordinate its operations with those of Stratemeyer in Burma.

Mountbatten gave the order on 12 December for these new arrangements to be brought immediately into force. Not only did they prove to be workable, in a complex inter-Allied and inter-service environment, contributing decisively to the use of air power in the two theatres, SEAC and China Command, but they enshrined a seminal development of military staff doctrine in the application of subsidiarity to command relationships. Many years later, in NATO, the differing functions and status of full command, operational command and operational control were codified, introduced and utilised with good effect.

In restoring and sustaining the morale of his forces, and imbuing them with confidence that they could outfight the Japanese, Mountbatten's greatest ally was General Slim, who succeeded as Montgomery had done with the 8th Army, Rommel with his Afrika Korps and, to some extent, Patton with his American 3rd Army, in giving the 14th Army a sense of identity. Slim was less charismatic than they; he chose, and ensured that his commanders followed his lead, to talk 'to units, to collections of officers, to headquarters, to little groups of men, to individual soldiers casually met' as he moved around. Ronald Lewin wrote:

It was during these peregrinations, however, that his Army began to think of Lieutenant-General Slim as Uncle Bill. His technique – it was less a contrivance than a natural response – contrasted effectively with that of Mountbatten, who in his own idiosyncratic way contributed enormously to the restoration of confidence by his talks and speeches. The carefully planned casualness of Mountbatten's appearances was invigorating, but from the soldier's point of view this was the Supreme Commander descending to announce that 'God's in his Heaven. All's right with the world', before returning to the clouds. Uncle Bill, they came to see, was theirs and they were his, linked in the brotherhood of battle.[9]

And battle was soon to be joined. Slim and the rest of the SEAC high command had barely had time to appreciate the significance for 14th Army of the cancellation of BUCCANEER – the assault on the Andaman Islands – namely that Burma was to be retaken by land and air forces alone, when contacts with Japanese patrols provided information of great significance. It quickly became evident that the Japanese reinforcements of which warning had been received by secret intelligence were already deployed in menacing strength. By this time the 14th Army was itself almost ready to advance. To be caught on its start lines by an enemy offensive could be disastrous, with no time or space to adopt defensive positions; and mutual reinforcement by corps cut off from each other by mountain ranges would be impracticable – except by air. Could it be done?

During the early hours of 4 February 1944 a Japanese outflanking force cut into the rear area of Christison's XV Corps in the Arakan, and attacked the administrative box at Sinzewa, where large stocks of war stores had been established. The test had begun: this was the spearhead of *Ha-Go*, an offensive designed to threaten Chittagong and draw into that area a substantial part of the 14th Army. That achieved, a second and closely related offensive, *U-Go*, would be launched across the Chindwin towards the Imphal–Kohima–Dimapur area, where supply bases for the projected advance of Slim's army into Burma had been built up. General Mutaguchi, commanding the Japanese 15th Army – about 100,000 men – was relying on a speedy capture of Imphal, so that his men rather than Slim's should be reprovisioned. But this depended upon two assumptions, first that he could deploy his troops with minimal rations and supplies, relying on air support if need be; and secondly, that the forces now facing him were no more formidable than those which he had driven out of Burma in 1942 and defeated in the Arakan in 1943.

Both Mutaguchi's assumptions were mistaken. In the first place British superiority in the air over the battle zone severely limited his use of air transport; and secondly the 14th Army and its supporting air forces, the RAF and USAF, combined with General Stilwell's three comparatively well-trained Chinese divisions, forming the Northern Combat Area Command (NCAC), constituted a fighting force in no way inferior, and in some respects superior, to his own.

In the meantime Mountbatten and his planners, looking ahead to the defeat of a Japanese offensive in northern Burma, thus securing both the Ledo road and the strategic airfield at Myitkyina, were planning an amphibious assault in the northern Sumatra–Singapore area, with Singapore as the main objective. Accordingly a mission was dispatched on 5 February, called AXIOM, to seek the approval of the Combined Chiefs of Staff for such an operation, code named CULVERIN. It failed.

In the first place AXIOM incorporated a dissident view, insisted upon by General Stilwell who, despite being Deputy Supreme Commander, refused to accept any diversion of Allied forces from what he held to be their proper objective – the establishment and maintenance of full road and air links with China. Secondly, the British Chiefs of Staff did not share Churchill's enthusiasm for CULVERIN. Thirdly, it was learned that the Japanese were about to station a battlefleet at Singapore, which would have to be countered by a build-up of the Eastern Fleet. Fourthly, the assumption that victory would have been gained in Europe by the end of 1944 was questionable. Finally, as Martin Gilbert records:

For Roosevelt, the Anglo-American priority was on mainland Asia, 'a vigorous and immediate campaign' in Upper Burma. Churchill deferred to Roosevelt's insistence. 'I have given the President a personal assurance,' he telegraphed to Mountbatten that same day (25 February 1944), 'that you will not withdraw or withhold any forces from the campaign in Upper Burma for the sake of CULVERIN or any other amphibious operation.'[10]

General Stilwell, having sent his own envoys direct to Washington to plead his case without informing Mountbatten, had also presented it at a so-called 'off the record' press conference in Delhi. When General Marshall heard of this flagrant breach of trust he ordered Stilwell to apologise in person to the Allied Supreme Commander, which in due course he did, knowing that it had been left to Mountbatten to terminate his appointment as Deputy SAC if he wished to do so. Magnanimity prevailed. Stilwell was a good fighting general, even if rabidly anti-British; and in any case had the backing, as far as policy was concerned, of the American Chiefs of Staff. He kept his job.

While all this had been going on the Japanese *Ha-Go* offensive was proceeding, paradoxically, according to the plans of both sides. The two divisions of XV Corps which had been surprised and outflanked, rallied and held their positions, as directed by Slim, forming an administrative box supplied by air, thanks to the air superiority quickly gained by the newly arrived Spitfires. As the siege continued Slim brought two more divisions in from the Arakan, and an additional air transport squadron (borrowed from the 'Hump' route by Mountbatten with the concurrence of the US Chiefs of Staff), augmented the supply of the beleaguered 5th and 7th Divisions. By 12 February the battle had been decided, but this was not apparent until 24 February when General Hanaya, his men short of ammunition and food, ordered his 55th Division to retreat. He had achieved the aim of *Ha-Go* – to draw Slim's reserves into the Arakan – but in doing so his division had sustained 5,000 casualties, thus providing the 14th Army with its first victory and a corresponding boost to morale.

Having drawn in Slim's reserves, Mutaguchi made ready to launch *U-Go*, his main campaign, to capture Imphal and the surrounding plain. Again, a Japanese offensive-defensive was about to dovetail into an Allied defensive-offensive. For it was in Slim's mind to entice Mutaguchi's forces forward and expose their extended lines of communication to attack, while falling upon the Japanese with superior force where the terrain was most favourable. Stilwell, with his Chinese divisions, had already set off south from Ledo towards Myitkyina; and on 10 February the 16th Brigade, part of Wingate's Chindits, set out from Ledo under Bernard Fergusson with the aim of capturing Indaw.

Mountbatten had been called upon to moderate Wingate's intemperate, if brilliant, representations to higher authority, firmly rejecting his attempts to get the 14th Army to operate in support of the Chindits rather than the other way round. But he welcomed Wingate's proposed Operation THURSDAY, which involved flying in two brigades by glider to land behind Japanese lines in the Indaw area. Establishing 'strongholds', they would sally forth and disrupt the Japanese lines of communication both to the division opposing Stilwell's advance, and to those advancing into the Imphal–Kohima area.

On 5 March air reconnaissance of the selected landing areas showed that one had been blocked with tree trunks. Did the Japanese know they were coming? Should THURSDAY be cancelled? The final decision to go, but to fly the whole of 77th Brigade into the same landing area, was taken by Slim, with Wingate's concurrence. After a sticky start the operation went well. It was not the Japanese but local foresters who had pre-empted the landing area.

The key to success was the clearance and preparation by American engineers of an adequate runway for the Dakotas of No. 1 Air Commando, USAF, whose gallant pilots had to fly their slow, unarmed aircraft 400 miles across enemy territory. Over 100 Dakotas flew in every night, bringing in 12,000 men with their weapons, equipment, ammunition and food, together with over 2,000 mules. David Rooney quotes Air Marshal Baldwin:

> Nobody has seen a transport operation until he has stood on that jungle runway, under the light of a Burma full moon, and watched Dakotas coming in and taking off in different directions on a single strip all night long at the rate of one landing and one take-off every three minutes.[11]

Of singular importance for morale was the use of a dozen light aircraft to fly out men who had been wounded in the initial landing. Mountbatten's foresight at the Quebec Conference in asking General Arnold, Chief of the US Air Staff, to set up a special air unit to supply Wingate's men, was well justified:

> The admirable work of the Air Commando under Cochran not only safeguarded and supplied 'Broadway' and the other Chindit bases which followed, but by simultaneous attacks on Japanese airfields – in which 78 [enemy] aircraft were destroyed in the first two days – ensured that the fly-in and build up of 'Broadway' took place without any Japanese air attacks.[12]

Wingate expressed disappointment that Mountbatten was not present at the launch of Operation THURSDAY. But the supremo could not be everywhere at once. On that day, 5 March, he was in Delhi, politely but firmly informing the Commander-in-Chief, Eastern Fleet, that SAC had full responsibility for all clandestine operations in or into the SEAC theatre, adding:

I am just off to visit our mutual friend, Joe Stilwell, on the Ledo front . . . [then] I am going to see some more of Wingate's people and on another visit to the Arakan front, reaching Kandy about mid-April.

I realise what an anxious time you must be having with the Japanese fleet and only wish that they may send out a detachment of a size to ensure your winning a great sea battle in the near future, which after two years of waiting you have surely more than earned.[13]

Mountbatten, as an expert in radio communications, made use of a transport aircraft, which he named *Mercury*, equipped to his specification as a 'flying wireless and cipher station'. This accompanied him on his tours and enabled him to remain in immediate touch, through his headquarters, with the Prime Minister and Chiefs of Staff, while retaining firm control over events in SEAC.

The purpose of his visit to Stilwell was to re-establish a working relationship with him following his breach of trust in the wake of the AXIOM mission. It coincided with one of the most testing episodes in Mountbatten's career. On 7 March, as he was driving himself in a jeep along a jungle track, a bamboo sprang up from beneath a wheel and struck him in the eye. By good luck – and Napoleon believed that the best generals were lucky – an exceptionally skilled American eye-specialist attended him at Ledo. With both eyes bandaged, and in extreme pain, Mountbatten was immobilised for several days. But his determination to return to duty as quickly as possible was reinforced by reports he began to receive of a new Japanese offensive, this time on the Imphal front.

Although this had been expected, with indications from Ultra decrypts as confirmation, it was not at first appreciated that the attack in the Arakan was a deception, and that Mutaguchi's main attack would follow as soon as he had redeployed his tactical air force to support it. Furthermore, Mountbatten and Slim, in addressing the troops at the front, had emphasised that there would be no more retreat in the face of a Japanese advance. XV Corps in the Arakan had just demonstrated the new tactic of staying put, supplied by air, and letting the enemy exhaust his strength in costly attacks. And yet, with the two forward divisions of IV Corps in advanced positions on the central front, separated by 200 miles or more and ready, as the troops thought, to go over at last to the offensive, what was suddenly required was yet another fighting retreat. No wonder things at first went wrong.

An effort must be made to visualise the topography and conditions in which this campaign was being fought. No clearly demarcated front line existed. Contact had to be maintained with the enemy by continuous patrolling. The earliest possible confirmation had to be obtained that the Japanese offensive had been launched, so divisions could begin their orderly move back to the Imphal plain, there to concentrate and destroy the enemy by weight of numbers and superior fighting power. And the enemy was efficient, savage and fanatical.

How savage was exemplified when two muleteers were found to have been tied up by Japanese soldiers, beaten insensible and then, when they recovered consciousness, bayoneted to death as targets.

In the event, some four days elapsed after the Japanese had penetrated in force behind the 17th Division (IV Corps) before the corps commander, somewhat tardily, gave permission for it to retire. In consequence a reserve division had to be sent in to cover its retreat. The fighting was intense all the way back along the Tiddim road, recently completed under the supervision of the Bengal Sappers and Miners of the 17th Division. But for Allied air supremacy over the battle area, the Japanese might have gained the upper hand. This was not at all what Slim had had in mind. The situation had become both critical and complex. As he wrote of the battle for Imphal:

> [it] swayed back and forth through great stretches of wild country; one day its focal point was a hill named on no map, the next a miserable, unpronounceable village a hundred miles away. Columns, brigades, divisions marched and counter-marched, met in bloody clashes, and reeled apart, weaving a confused pattern hard to unravel.[14]

By throwing in the last reserves of IV Corps, Mutaguchi's attacks on Imphal were halted. But immediate reinforcements were vital if the threatened perimeter was to be held. The 5th Indian Division at Chittagong had been alerted, but its redeployment by road and rail would have taken far too long. Fully in touch with the situation Mountbatten, still in extreme pain and at the risk of losing an eye, discharged himself from hospital at Ledo on 14 March and flew to meet Slim at Comilla. Here, at 14th Army HQ, with Air Marshal Baldwin who commanded Third Tactical Air Force, the decision was made to move the 5th Division by air. To achieve this an additional 30 Dakotas would be essential.

Mountbatten had already borrowed and returned a number of aircraft from the 'Hump' transport force to supply XV Corps in the Arakan battle. But that was with the concurrence of the Combined Chiefs of Staff, which had taken ten days to obtain. This time any delay could result in Mutaguchi's forces taking Imphal. Having obtained the formal request from Slim by signal, Mountbatten at once initiated the loan of the necessary aircraft and the airlift of 5th Division to Imphal began on 17 March. With the route to China now directly threatened, covering approval was forthcoming from Washington within three days. But the time gained had been vital in the crisis.

Once again the airmen and their maintenance crews excelled themselves. A vivid description of the operation is quoted by David Rooney:

> These Daks were stacked up one behind the other, a quarter of a mile apart, touching down and those with troops were simply taxiing along and the soldiers rolling out

and then the Dak was straight off again. Then the others came in on the other side of the runway with mules, guns etc.[15]

And in Rooney's judgement:

At this juncture there is no doubt that without the determined actions of the crews and ground staffs of the RAF and USAF the battles of Imphal and Kohima would have been lost, and Dimapur would have fallen.[16]

The significance of Dimapur as a strategic objective, whether to be attained by the Japanese or defended by the Allies, could hardly be overestimated. Unlike the north-west frontier of India, with its admirable lines of communication dictated by considerations of defence, the north-east was served only by a fragile, narrow-gauge rail link with a peacetime capacity of 600 tons per day. By the time Mountbatten became SAC this had been quadrupled, but he insisted that it should be trebled again, and that vital sections of the line should be put under complete military control, using US railway troops, since there were no British railway troops to spare. The authorities in Delhi had not at first been helpful over this, but by March 1945 capacity had been vastly increased. The line ran from Calcutta to Dimapur, over 500 miles, then on another 200 miles to Ledo, where it ended.

Dimapur was the railhead for the road running about 40 miles south-eastwards to Kohima, then onwards another 45 miles or so to Imphal. The vast quantity of war stores of all kinds, amassed at Dimapur in preparation for the 14th Army's projected offensive, offered Mutaguchi a decisive prize. Its seizure would not only eliminate all possibility of an Allied advance to recover Burma, but would enable him to cut off the supply route to Ledo, and thus to Stilwell's forces operating from there southwards towards Myitkyina. But if Slim could hold on to Kohima and Imphal until the monsoon, when the extended Japanese supply lines would be unusable, defence could be turned into offence.

When Mountbatten returned to Delhi after his meeting with Slim and Baldwin on 14 March, he was thankful to find that General Giffard and Field Marshal Auchinleck were already considering the measures necessary to reinforce Slim with XXXIII Corps, now that the projected amphibious assault for which it was earmarked had been cancelled. Giffard had been slow to accept the necessity to transfer the 5th Indian Division north from the Arakan to Imphal, and much resented Mountbatten's intervention in support of Slim. But now even Giffard could sense that a desperate crisis was at hand.

In their appreciation of Japanese intentions Slim and the commander of IV Corps, Lieutenant General Geoffrey Scoones, had forecast a Japanese thrust at Kohima, and perhaps Dimapur, but for some reason had seriously underestimated its probable strength. In the event it was not just one regiment, the equivalent of a British brigade, which by the end of March was about to take Kohima, but an entire Japanese division, the 31st.

The planned, orderly retirement to the Imphal plain of the widely separated divisions of IV Corps had become a series of the most ferocious actions. Subordinate commanders also had to cope with the demoralisation arising from having to destroy vast stores of food, ammunition and petrol which had been built up in forward positions preparatory to the long-heralded offensive. David Rooney points to the key question:

> In a bitter message to Scoones, Gracey asked what was the point of building roads and building-up a colossal supply base at Moreh just to withdraw and hand it over to the Japanese without a fight. Gracey's comment raises a significant issue which has never been adequately explained. If Slim's strategy was to withdraw to the Imphal plain and fight the Japanese in the open country there, when did he make that decision, and why did 14th Army continue to pour supplies forward to the Moreh base?[17]

It was indeed fortunate – Slim's luck again – that the preparations for his offensive had caused the Japanese to carry out their feint against XV Corps in the Arakan sooner than had been intended; for this meant a longer interval before Mutaguchi's main offensive was launched against Imphal and Kohima. As it was, when he did so his 15th Division was incomplete. The odds were even.

Mountbatten, in Delhi, could see that both Imphal and Kohima would soon be under siege. If they were to fall, Dimapur would inevitably follow. The recovery of Burma might have diminished in priority as an element of Allied grand strategy; but the destruction of 14th Army, followed by a triumphant entry of the Japanese into India flanked by the new Indian National Army (formed in 1943 by Chandra Bose), would precipitate the collapse of order in the subcontinent – a calamity not to be contemplated, even by the Americans. General Wedemeyer had been instructed by Mountbatten to seek an opportunity in the course of his AXIOM mission to appeal to General Arnold to let SEAC have the greatest possible number of additional aircraft; at that time it had only 76, British and American. The argument was to be used that the American Chiefs of Staff directive, namely to clear the whole of northern Burma and push a pipeline through to China, would leave many of the troops in mid-Burma during the monsoon without any proper surface lines of communication; thus their policy could only be carried out if they provided adequate air transport.

As a result, General Arnold promised to set up four special combat cargo groups, each of 100 Dakotas or equivalent, on condition that it could be proved that these transport aircraft were essential for the operations envisaged. During the third week in March 1944, as Mountbatten recalled:

It now became clear that we were going to require air supply on an unprecedented scale. The whole of IV Corps was cut off in the Imphal Plain; the Manipur road was cut at Kohima in the North, and the Bishenpur trail in the South-West – the only other one – was also cut. 50,000 useless mouths [to the wry amusement of the fighting units, these did not include anyone in Corps HQ!] were flown out in the aircraft which brought in the supplies. We worked out that we wanted at least 70 more transport aircraft, and I asked if these could be taken off the 'Hump'. This request was refused, although I was told I could keep what I had already taken off the 'Hump' until June and that the remainder would be sent to me as soon as possible from the Middle East and the United Kingdom. In the meantime General Arnold informed me that the first combat cargo group of 100 Dakotas would arrive at the end of June. I put in an urgent demand for the second group to follow as quickly as possible, and this, too, was accepted.[18]

As Supreme Commander, Mountbatten had of course to keep under review all the operations in the area under his command. The activities of Wingate's Special Force, with its task of disrupting the Japanese supply lines, were of particular concern, given the need to reduce the pressure on Imphal and Kohima by every possible means. On 24 March the Chindits at 'Broadway' – their 'stronghold' about 50 miles north-east of Indaw – were greatly heartened when Wingate arrived to see them. After a busy day he flew on to Imphal for discussions with Air Marshal Baldwin, and then took off for Lalaghat, about 40 miles west of Imphal. Wingate did not arrive. His plane crashed and all on board were killed.

There is no room here to recount the ill-effects upon the morale and effectiveness of the Chindits of losing their charismatic and creative leader. Mountbatten knew that he had been deprived of a gallant and formidable fighter. Writing to Frank Owen, the brilliant editor of the *Evening Standard* whom he had recruited to produce *SEAC*, Mountbatten said:

> You will have heard the shattering news about Wingate. I am writing an Order of the Day which I should like published in *SEAC* at the correct moment.
>
> It has not been possible to identify for certain that Wingate has been killed and I only hope that rumours will get around implying that he is still alive and planning a bigger and better coup. That will give the Japanese something to worry about but it must be done with the greatest caution so do not mention it to anybody.[19]

In the same letter Mountbatten gave an example of his use of *SEAC* as a means of gaining support for his policies:

> It is most important that the correct note be struck about our move to Kandy. . . . I would be grateful if in your 'Good Morning' you could imply that this is a move 'in the right direction'.

If you could publish a little map showing the relative positions of Kandy, Delhi, Chittagong, and include from the North of Burma to the South of Sumatra it would immediately indicate how much nearer Kandy is to the whole of the South-East Asia front. . . .

Although you must be very cautious how you mention this I cannot help feeling that it is politically a good move to get out of the Government of India territory into a self-governing Crown colony . . . which, incidentally forms part of the South-East Asia Command.[20]

By 29 March the airlift of the 5th Indian Division to Imphal was completed – not a moment too soon. And on the previous day Lieutenant General Montagu Stopford, commanding XXXIII Corps, had reached Imphal to confer with Slim, who had put him in charge of operations in the Kohima and Dimapur sectors. An administrative error had already been made in placing the 161st Brigade, detached from the proud and highly trained 5th Indian Division, under the command of the area (garrison) commander. Similarly, the commanding officer of the Royal West Kents (RWK), arriving in Kohima on 30 March, found himself under the local garrison commander.

These uneasy relationships were compounded when Stopford, under pressure to make a quick decision, not unreasonably decided to accord first priority to the defence of the base at Dimapur and the railway to Ledo. In consequence the RWK had to leave Kohima the day after they got there and join the 4/7 Rajputs and 1/1st Punjabis, their fellow battalions in 161st Brigade, to defend Dimapur. There was strong disagreement about this and on 4 April, with the arrival of reinforcements at Dimapur, Stopford decided to send 161st Brigade back to Kohima. Frustrated and furious at being buggered about (the acronym SNAFU – Situation Normal All Fucked Up – was bandied about), the RWK advanced once again up the Kohima road, to meet hordes of panic-stricken soldiers and civilians. But, as David Rooney records:

Lieutenant-Colonel Laverty decided that, although the Japanese were at the outskirts of the town, his battalion would advance as rapidly as possible into Kohima. As they arrived, accurate Japanese shelling began, destroying much of their kit and most of their trucks. This was the unpromising start to one of the epic sieges of the Second World War.[21]

There followed a period of a few days before the hastily summoned XXXIII Corps had arrived and strengthened the position when the Japanese 31st Division under General Sato could have made a thrust for Dimapur which might well have succeeded. It was lucky for Slim, and Stilwell for that matter, that when Mutaguchi saw his opportunity and ordered Sato to commit his main force to the capture of Dimapur, General Kawabe in

Rangoon made him rescind the order on the grounds that Dimapur 'was not within the strategic objectives of the 15th Army'.[22] (An intriguing footnote in Lewin's biography of Slim indicates that Japanese intelligence had erroneously placed 'two or three' British divisions in the Shillong–Dimapur area – perhaps as a result of misinformation provided by Lieutenant Colonel Peter Fleming's D Division.)

Mountbatten seems to have sensed the urgent need to ensure coordination between Stilwell's operations in Northern Combat Area Command and those of Slim's 14th Army in countering what had become an extremely dangerous three-pronged thrust by Mutaguchi's 15th Army. He therefore flew on 3 April to Jorhat, about halfway between Dimapur and Ledo, to meet Slim, Stilwell (who had agreed to serve, at that stage, 'under' Slim), and Stopford. Faced with the immediate threat to the Dimapur–Ledo railway, his sole line of communication by land with India, Stilwell offered to provide Chinese-American forces to guard the railway and adjacent airfields. This would have slowed his advance down the Hukawng valley towards Mogaung and Myitkyina. The offer was refused. But, as support, a brigade of Chindits under XXXIII Corps was sent in to cut Japanese communications behind Kohima at Ukhrul.

By 20 April the Japanese advance had been halted everywhere. They had made the fundamental error of underestimating the enemy. But fighting continued with great intensity. In the third week of May the Japanese launched their most desperate attack, in the Bishenpur area about 10 miles south-west of Imphal. The orders for it, captured later, echoed Admiral Togo's signal to his fleet before Tsushima – 'The fate of the Empire depends on this one battle' – but this time they lost.

By now the Eastern Fleet had been considerably augmented and on 19 April a bombing raid on oil storage tanks, shipping and harbour installations at Sabang, on the north-east tip of Sumatra, was carried out by Admiral Somerville, flying his flag in the battleship *Queen Elizabeth*, with the battlecruiser *Renown*, the aircraft carrier *Illustrious*, four cruisers and seven destroyers of the Royal Navy, the US aircraft carrier *Saratoga* and three US destroyers, the French battleship *Richelieu*, the cruiser *Tromp* and one destroyer of the Royal Netherlands Navy, the New Zealand cruiser *Gambia*, and four destroyers of the Royal Australian Navy. Complete surprise was achieved and considerable damage was done, for the sole loss of one of the *Saratoga*'s fighter aircraft, the pilot of which was rescued by the British submarine *Tactician*. A similar operation against Surabaya, where an important oil refinery was the main target, was carried out by Somerville on 17 May with almost the same fleet. Again surprise was achieved and only one fighter was lost. But this time the results were meagre and Somerville regretted that he had not repeated the attack later in the day.

For many weeks Imphal had remained beleaguered, dependent entirely on air supply, and on 4 May Slim was told that the airlift of stores was so far below what was essential that if road access were not reopened by mid-June the situation would be critical. On the same day he heard that Mountbatten had been instructed by the Chiefs of Staff to return to the Middle East by 8 May the 79 transport aircraft that he had borrowed to save the situation early in March. In Ronald Lewin's words:

> If the demands of the Chiefs of Staff had been met it is difficult to see how victory could have been achieved at Imphal. Neither Giffard nor Slim had the status, vis-à-vis London, to ignore it, and in any case the matter did not lie within their scope. But once again Mountbatten exercised that imperious and self-confident authority which, like a core of high quality steel, strengthened the SEAC command. Once again he acted on his own responsibility, ordering that the aircraft must not be released without his permission. Stirred by the struggle at Imphal, Churchill warmed to this gesture, signalling to Mountbatten: 'Let nothing go from the battle that you need for victory. I will not accept denial of this from any quarter, and will back you to the full.'[23]

Even so, it was not until mid-May that covering approval was prised out of the reluctant Chiefs of Staff, preoccupied as they were with final preparations for the mightiest seaborne assault ever to be carried out, Operation OVERLORD. But Slim had been able to keep the airlift going, and on 22 June the advanced guards of IV and XXXIII Corps met north of Imphal. Twenty-four hours later road convoys were running. The corps commanders immediately met and concerted their operations to ensure the destruction of the Japanese 15th and 31st Divisions as they retreated. Some got away, but by the end of June there could be no doubt that the Japanese army had suffered a disastrous defeat. Of the force of three-and-a-half Japanese divisions and one Indian National Army division, about 84,000 men, more than 50,000 had perished in battle and from hunger, disease and exposure. British-Indian losses amounted to fewer than 17,000.

During this time the Chindits, now commanded by Wingate's successor, Major General Lentaigne, came under the operational control of Stilwell, together with a smaller but similarly trained American force, formally 5307 Composite Unit (Provisional), code named Galahad and dubbed Merrill's Marauders after their commander. On 17 May the Marauders, with a bold swoop, took Myitkyina airfield – a prime objective. But the Japanese defended the town itself fanatically, and it was not captured until August. The nearby town of Mogaung was also a key objective, which Stilwell demanded should be captured 'at all costs' by the Chindits.

With the coming of the monsoon, conditions in the jungle became appalling. In the first part of June Merrill's Marauders, now supported by 20,000 Chinese-

American troops, were making no progress against Myitkyina; so Stilwell called upon the Chindits to help. They should not have been used thus, in a normal infantry role, and the Chinese seemed never to be there when most needed. In repeated attacks on both Myitkyina and Mogaung the Chindits suffered terrible casualties. The word reached Slim, who went to see Stilwell hoping to restore mutual confidence between him and the Chindits. No use. But on 16 June Stilwell reached Kamaing, where, by an agreement made at Cairo the previous December, he would come directly under the Supreme Allied Commander. On 27 June, as Rooney narrates:

> after a final bloody onslaught in which the Chinese again refused to attack, the Japanese were driven out. 77 Brigade was reduced to 800 men, having suffered more than 50 per cent casualties in the battle for Mogaung.
>
> They had suffered enough, but the next day they had to endure another typically underhand blow from Stilwell. The world radio announced that the Chinese-American forces had captured Mogaung. Showing admirable restraint, Calvert signalled Stilwell: 'Understand Chinese have taken umbrage.' The Chindits enjoyed a moment of grim satisfaction when they heard that Stilwell's son, who was his Intelligence officer, announced that umbrage must be a very small village because he could not find it on the map.[24]

Mountbatten, having learned that the Chindits were being wiped out by battle casualties, tropical diseases and exposure, flew to see Stilwell, whose comments implied that they were malingering. Mountbatten organised an inspection of all the men by an Anglo-American medical team. On seeing their report he ordered Stilwell to evacuate the sick and wounded at once; and in view of Stilwell's obstructive attitude he sent senior officers to supervise the arrangements. It cannot be said that Slim, as 14th Army commander, fully shared Mountbatten's belief in the military value of long-range penetration groups. He would rather have had the additional brigades to bolster his superiority over the Japanese 15th Army around Imphal; nor did he make use of airborne troops. In making these judgements Slim was not, perhaps, at his best.

Ever since the end of April, when it had become evident that the Japanese main offensive had been halted, Mountbatten had been attempting to extract from the Chiefs of Staff a revised directive taking into account the expulsion of the Japanese from northern Burma. This he now felt sure would be achieved by the 14th Army and its supporting air forces by keeping up the pressure even after the arrival of the monsoon, and going over to the offensive the moment the Japanese 15th Army began to retreat. In the meantime SEAC headquarters were removed from Delhi to Kandy in Ceylon. The Supreme Commander provided separate headquarters for army group and air commands within a few miles of his own; but General Giffard and Air Chief Marshal Peirse preferred to remain in Delhi.

On 3 June Mountbatten received, after a wait of six months, a 'new' directive from the Chiefs of Staff. It enjoined him, following his own suggestion, to develop, maintain, broaden and protect the air route over the 'Hump' into China; but he was also instructed to press advantages against the enemy during the current monsoon season, and exploit the development of overland communications with China. All these operations were to be carried out with the forces already in the theatre. Having thus been deprived of any prospect, for the time being, of mounting an amphibious assault as an alternative to prolonged jungle warfare, Mountbatten was gratified, justifiably, to receive the following personal message, dated 10 June 1944:

> To-day we visited the British and American armies on the soil of France. We sailed through vast fleets of ships, with landing-craft of many types pouring more and more men, vehicles and stores ashore. We saw clearly the manoeuvre in process of rapid development. We have shared our secrets in common and helped each other all we could. We wish to tell you at this moment in your arduous campaign that we realise that much of this remarkable technique and therefore the success of the venture has its origins in developments effected by you and your staff of Combined Operations. (signed) Arnold, Brooke, Churchill, King, Marshall, Smuts.[25]

On 8 July Mutaguchi, beset by the monsoon and vigorously harried by the 14th Army, finally gave the order to withdraw from Assam; there was to be no respite for the Japanese, as far as SEAC was concerned, until they had been driven out of Burma. But, although their 15th Army had been defeated with enormous casualties, ten Japanese divisions remained in Burma; while in southern China a Japanese offensive was about to be launched, aimed at capturing the airfields from which General Chennault's B-29s were attacking Japanese shipping and supporting Chiang's armies. Advised by Stilwell, with Mountbatten's encouragement, Roosevelt had urged Chiang Kai-shek to order his Yunnan force to advance towards Burma across the River Salween. Concerned now lest they should lose possession of the oilfields in Burma, the Japanese were reacting strongly.

Against this background, Mountbatten and his staff at SEAC formulated two plans which, having flown to London early in August, he presented to the Chiefs of Staff. In his own words:

> CAPITAL was to be an advance by 14th Army, which now consisted only of IV and XXXIII Corps, since XV Corps had been put directly under 11 Army Group. They were to cross the Chindwin and deploy armour against the enemy in the Ye-u/Shwebo area, with a subsequent exploitation to Mandalay. Airborne troops were to seize Kalewa, whilst a second landing was made at the entrance to the Mandalay Plain. General Stilwell's Northern Combat Area Command and the Chinese Expeditionary Forces were to undertake a complementary advance to the South.

DRACULA was the recapture of the Rangoon area by a combined airborne and seaborne assault to cut the main Japanese lines of communication. If the enemy reacted strongly, our northern forces would be able to advance against reduced opposition, but if there was no strong reaction, the seaborne and airborne forces would be able to advance northwards in conjunction with other operations to open the road to China. For the latter operation, additional reserves would, of course, be required from the United Kingdom.[26]

As recorded by Martin Gilbert:

For three days in mid-August, Churchill and his senior advisers devoted their mental energies to an attempt to evolve a strategy for the war in the Far East. At issue were two conflicting claims, those of the Pacific and the Bay of Bengal theatres. . . .

'Rangoon itself was in itself an important objective,' he said, 'and its capture would open up possibilities of further operations such, for example, as an advance on Moulmein or Bangkok or to the Kra Isthmus or Malay Peninsula.' Britain's 'general strategy' in the Far East, Churchill felt, 'might be to recapture the many valuable possessions we had lost in the area'.[27]

At the final staff conference on Far East strategy on 9 August, Mountbatten's plans were approved, despite the initial misgivings of the Chiefs of Staff. Churchill's support had been decisive. It had to be accepted, however, that the additional resources needed for DRACULA could only be made available if Hitler were defeated by October, which at that time was thought quite possible. An earlier collapse of Germany might offer the possibility of switching the main amphibious assault from Rangoon towards Singapore. The 'greatest offer of naval assistance' would at the same time be made to the US Chiefs of Staff, 'it being impressed upon them', as the conclusions of the meeting noted, 'that it is our desire to share with them in the main operations against the mainland of Japan or Formosa [Taiwan]'.[28]

This reflected Mountbatten's view that the modern battleships, fleet carriers, fleet train and a proportion of cruisers and destroyers could not only be spared from the Eastern Fleet, but would be better employed in the Pacific as soon as the Japanese battlefleet had ceased to be based on Singapore. He did, however, ask to retain 'enough old battleships for bombardment, auxiliary carriers for air support', and SEAC's amphibious resources. The modern element formed the British Pacific Fleet, which left the SEAC theatre in January 1945 under the command of Admiral Sir Bruce Fraser to join the US Pacific Fleet. The remainder became the East Indies Fleet, command of which was assumed by Admiral Sir Arthur Power.

During Mountbatten's absence for these intensive discussions his deputy theatre commander, General Stilwell, took over. Neither by inclination nor capacity was he suited to the task. He was in any case soon to part company with Chiang Kai-shek, in what Mountbatten called 'a tremendous reshuffle in the higher appointments'.[29] This had begun with the relief of Admiral Somerville in command of the Eastern Fleet by Admiral Fraser. In the naval command structure Somerville had been responsible directly to the Admiralty; the advent of his naval junior as 'Supremo' had caused friction, although a modus vivendi had been achieved. As Captain Hans Hamilton recalled:

> From my point of view I was highly impressed when he [Mountbatten] visited *Illustrious* in Trincomalee (1944) and sent for me who was deep in the sweaty bilges. In my filthy overalls he gave me news of my father in Combined Ops and later rang him to say I was doing a good job (?) and was well. My father always spoke highly of him when both were working in Norfolk House.[30]

And after this occasion Mountbatten had written:

> 10 June 1944
> Dear Commander in Chief,
> . . . thank you very much indeed for the excellent arrangements which you ordered to be made for my visits to Trincomalee. I went aboard the *Illustrious*, *Atheling*, *Phoebe*, *Gambia* and *Van Galen* in the morning, and in the afternoon Saunders took me round the naval base . . .
>   Again all my thanks,
>   Yours ever,
>   (Sgd) Dickie[31]

Fraser took over on 23 August 1944 and thereafter harmony prevailed between the naval commander-in-chief and the supremo, and their respective staffs.

Mountbatten's air commander-in-chief, Air Chief Marshal Sir Richard Peirse, was due for relief at this time, and Portal, as Chief of the Air Staff, proposed that his term should be extended. Although not in sympathy with the concept of a Supreme Commander, Peirse had been in the main helpful in the implementation of his policy directives. Latterly, however, he had become enamoured of the wife of General Auchinleck, the Commander-in-Chief, India, which had adversely affected his attention to duty; this affair may also have accounted for his opposition to the transfer of SEAC headquarters to Kandy. For these reasons Mountbatten did not agree to his remaining in post. Tragically, Air Chief Marshal Sir Trafford Leigh-Mallory, appointed to relieve Peirse, was killed in an air crash en route to India. His place was taken by Air Chief Marshal Sir Keith Park, a New Zealander, who readily accepted his role in a three-service team under a supreme commander.

The army commander, General Giffard, unlike Slim, had allowed his *amour-propre*, as well as a somewhat pedantic adherence to conventional military wisdom, to weaken his loyalty to the Supreme Commander. He was scornful of the policy of continuing to fight during the monsoon; he was sceptical of the value of Ultra or Magic intelligence; he did not believe in addressing the troops; he was opposed to the move to Kandy; and he failed, when the Japanese threat to Imphal had become critical, to reinforce Slim promptly. But for Mountbatten's intervention, Somerville recorded, the battle would have been lost. The general who relieved Giffard in November was Sir Oliver Leese, who had acquired a fine reputation under Montgomery. He, like Keith Park, was content to use the headquarters provided for him at Kandy, and to assume the title of Allied Commander-in-Chief, Land Forces, South-East Asia (ALFSEA), utilising the 11th Army Group staff with the addition of a few American staff officers.

The departure of General Stilwell to a post in the USA was the occasion for a long-overdue reorganisation of the American commands in the China-Burma-India theatre, which closely affected Mountbatten. In the first place his extremely able principal administrative officer, General 'Speck' Wheeler, was appointed as Deputy Supreme Allied Commander; General Sultan, who had been Stilwell's deputy commander, now became Commander of the American Forces in India and Burma, and succeeded to the command of the Chinese armies in India and Burma; and General Al Wedemeyer, who was Mountbatten's deputy Chief of Staff, relieved Stilwell as Chief of Staff to the Generalissimo, and Commanding General of the US Forces in China. Finally, Lieutenant General Pownall, whose health had deteriorated, was relieved as Chief of Staff to the Supreme Commander by Lieutenant General Sir Frederick ('Boy') Browning.

Mountbatten now had a team of forward-thinking British and Allied commanders and senior staff officers of all three services upon whom he could rely, jointly and severally, both to help formulate his strategy and to carry it out.

The year 1945 opened well in SEAC. As long ago as the previous June Mountbatten had issued to Giffard at 11th Army Group a directive that included, after reopening the Dimapur–Imphal road and driving the Japanese from the Imphal plain back to the River Chindwin, 'preparations to exploit across the Chindwin'. In response to this instruction the elements of a Bailey bridge, which would be the longest in the world, were built in Britain, America and India, shipped to Calcutta, taken by rail to Dimapur, then transferred by truck to Kalewa. By mid-December bridgeheads over the Chindwin were secure. In the meantime it had become evident that the Japanese intended to withdraw beyond the Irrawaddy and make their stand at Mandalay.

Slim was determined not to let the Japanese fight a successful rearguard action all the way down through Burma and extricate their armies. He therefore devised a plan, approved by Mountbatten and named EXTENDED CAPITAL, whereby the opposing commander, General Kimura, would be deceived into believing that Slim's main attack would be launched against Mandalay from the north-west, while a powerful striking force would work its way south along the Myittha valley to attack from the westward the important road and rail junction and supply base at Meiktila, 50 miles south of Mandalay. It was a plan of classic simplicity – and it exemplified the dictum of Clausewitz: 'Everything is very simple in war, but the simplest thing is very difficult. These difficulties accumulate and produce a friction which no man can imagine exactly who has not seen war.'

Mountbatten had seen war, and in giving his approval to EXTENDED CAPITAL he was fully aware that its feasibility was subject to uninterrupted supply by air of the total requirements of the advancing 14th Army. He was therefore sorely tried when Wedemeyer telegraphed him soon after arriving in Chungking to say that the Japanese had advanced 500 miles from Yochow to Liuchow and were threatening either Chungking or the vital 'Hump' terminal at Kunming; he asked to be sent two Chinese divisions, three combat cargo squadrons, two troop carrier squadrons of the Air Commandos and some heavy bombers. He repeated this demand simultaneously to the Combined Chiefs of Staff. Having been so recently Deputy Chief of Staff to SACSEA, Wedemeyer was fully aware of the resources and commitments in that theatre. But his priorities were now different. Indeed, Mountbatten himself took the view that his own operations were directed towards helping China and that they would be in vain if China were forced out of the war. He therefore at once gave orders for the moves to start, hoping that by so quick a display of generosity he might be spared further depredations.

The effect of these moves was first to cause the cancellation of the airborne part of CAPITAL; secondly, to slow up the advance of both 14th Army and the Northern Combat Area Command forces for lack of aircraft; and thirdly to upset General Sultan's plans by the withdrawal of a large proportion of his forces. Mountbatten experienced yet another severe setback when Hitler induced his beaten armies to continue the fight into 1945, so that the promised LSTs, 6th Airborne Division, and British-Indian divisions engaged in Italy could not be released for redeployment to SEAC. In consequence DRACULA, the amphibious assault on Rangoon, had to be cancelled.

It was some consolation that on 22 January 1945 the Chinese troops who had been fighting in grim conditions along the upper Salween valley had joined up with General Sultan's NCAC divisions near Bhamo, thus reopening the land route from India to China. Mountbatten was able to signal to Churchill and Roosevelt: 'The first part of the orders I received at Quebec has been carried out. The land route to China is open.'[32]

On 3 February 1945 Mountbatten received a new directive from the Chiefs of Staff, instructing him to liberate Burma at the earliest date and, subject to this, liberate Malaya and open the Straits of Malacca. By keeping up the pressure on the Chiefs of Staff he managed to obtain the promise of an additional 145 transport aircraft, 40 of which were to be used by his civil affairs officer, the retired Air Marshal Sir Philip Joubert, for feeding the civil population. As these aircraft began to arrive in SEAC, the largest-scale air supply ever seen was built up. As Mountbatten described the operation:

> It was not just a question of auxiliary air supply, because 96 per cent of our supplies to the 14th Army went by air. In the course of this campaign we lifted 615,000 tons of supplies to the armies, three-quarters of it by the US Air Force and one-quarter by the Royal Air Force. 315,000 reinforcements were flown in, half by the British and half by the Americans. 110,000 casualties were flown out, three-quarters by the British and a quarter by the Americans. . . .
>
> We had not really got the aircraft to do this, at all events on paper. In fact, we had only about half the aircraft that were really required, but we made up the other half by the expedient of flying almost double the number of hours allowed for sustained operations. Normally this would be considered an extremely dangerous policy, but we had no alternative. Weary aircrews turned round and flew again through the Monsoon, and weary maintenance crews, instead of going to sleep, switched on their lamps and started overhauling another aircraft. This went on day after day, week after week, and month after month. Although there was the gravest risk that the whole air transport arrangements might break down, they could see the results of their supplies in the daily advance towards Rangoon and their morale was so high that they somehow managed to carry on. Nevertheless I do not recommend that any plans should be made which entail aircraft working at over-sustained rates. I cannot pay too high a tribute to all the Allied air forces for their magnificent achievement which I do not believe has been equalled in war.[33]

Without air supply on this unprecedented scale EXTENDED CAPITAL could never have been carried out. But its success depended also upon two other indispensable elements – deception and, ultimately, the sheer courage, determination and skill of the individual fighting man. Ronald Lewin held that:

> the way Slim mystified Kimura, the concealment of 6 Panzer Army's location before the Ardennes offensive, and the persuasion of the Germans at the time of D-Day that a phantom Army truly existed in SE England may perhaps be accounted the three most interesting examples of military deception in the Second World War.[34]

How the deception of Kimura was brought about may also be gleaned from Lewin. In *Ultra Goes to War* he reveals the appointment of a fictitious Wren officer to Mountbatten's SEAC staff at Kandy, whose 'reports' (to a double agent):

composed, of course, in London – went first to the Abwehr [German military intelligence] and then, via the Japanese military attaché in Berlin, to Tokyo. The Allies' ability to decipher signals from the Berlin embassy to Japan provided a unique check. . . .

[But] in war what matters most is the effective concentration of strength at the critical point. In the end the battle is the pay-off.[35]

On 16 February, a day after the spearhead of General Messervy's IV Corps crossed the Irrawaddy, Mountbatten visited the bridgehead at Nyaungu to see for himself what Slim called 'this all-important crossing . . . on which the whole fabric of my battleplan rested'.[36] And a week later, at Calcutta, the Supreme Commander held the conference which determined the final phase of the Burma campaign.

General Christison, advancing with XV Corps directly under ALFSEA in the Arakan, supported by the exiguous amphibious forces which remained in SEAC, had already seized Akyab and Ramree Island, so aircraft could keep up the supply of 14th Army as it advanced south. Hence Mountbatten and his commanders-in-chief fully supported Slim's contention that, following the destruction of the Japanese divisions in the battles round Meiktila and Mandalay, 14th Army should go for Rangoon. On 4 March Meiktila fell, and on 20 March Mandalay. This gave rise to Churchill's comment, in his announcement of this momentous event in the House of Commons: 'Thank God they have got a place whose name we can pronounce.'[37]

So began the operation known in Slim's headquarters as 'Sea or Bust'. In terms of time and space the governing factor was the advent of the monsoon, due on 15 May. By mid-April 14th Army was still 300 miles from Rangoon. To keep up the pace would be a formidable task dependent, as ever, upon uninterrupted air supply. This was yet again at risk.

Earlier in the year a serious threat of famine imposed upon Chiang Kai-shek the necessity to reconquer vast areas of paddy fields to produce enough rice. In the course of a visit to Chungking in March, accompanied by Edwina, at the invitation of Generalissimo and Madame Chiang Kai-shek, Mountbatten had maintained, and his wife established, a cordial relationship with them. But, with Wedemeyer's support, the Chinese leader now insisted that the entire Chinese force fighting in Burma should be withdrawn. Given the progress made by 14th Army this could just be accepted. But to be deprived of the US transport aircraft would have ruined the prospect of Rangoon being retaken before the monsoon.

Typically, Mountbatten flew to Calcutta to meet Wedemeyer, who was on his way to Washington, and then on to Chungking to see the Generalissimo. His plan, which they accepted, was for the American Mars Brigade (which had relieved Merrill's Marauders) to be flown out to act as instructors to the

Chinese, and for the Chinese divisions in Burma to be flown out by transport aircraft from the US 14th Air Force. The US aircraft in Burma would be allowed to remain there in support of 14th Army until Rangoon was retaken. During this period Wedemeyer chose to act as if he had been appointed as an Allied theatre commander, which was not the case, although the American Chiefs of Staff seemed to consider that it was. This foreshadowed the politico-military problems over French Indo-China with which Mountbatten would soon have to cope.

Even with 14th Army's momentum being sustained, Slim had agreed with Leese on 19 March that a seaborne assault on Rangoon should be mounted, as an insurance against the arrival of the monsoon before 14th Army could get there – in effect a modified DRACULA. Not only did Leese delay, unaccountably, the production of an updated plan, but according to Lewin:

> it was as late as 10 April that Mountbatten, alert to the seriousness of the situation, had to fly to Calcutta and personally countermand a refusal by Leese for the use in the operation of essential airborne troops.[38]

Slim's insurance policy justified the premium, namely his readiness to accept that DRACULA might beat EXTENDED CAPITAL. This, by a short head, it did. For on 2 May the monsoon came, nearly a fortnight early. Slim's leading division, General Cowan's famous 17th, was still at Pegu, 50 miles north of Rangoon. But on 1 May a parachute battalion secured the batteries commanding the Rangoon river, and 26th Division, covered by a fleet of two battleships, two aircraft carriers, four cruisers and five destroyers, landed – to take over a city occupied only by welcoming inhabitants.

It was an anticlimax, certainly, and Slim was denied a triumphal entry into the city on which he had set his sights so many gruelling months before. Nor could Mountbatten be present, having been laid low by a severe attack of amoebic dysentery, although his astonishing capacity for work kept him going. He wrote to Carton de Wiart:

> the doctors have just discovered that I have got amoebic dysentery and, although I am retaining command and working regularly at the King's Pavilion in bed, with Speck Wheeler and Boy Browning coming to see me every day, the fact remains that my treatment will not be finished until around 20 May.

He went on to apprise de Wiart at length of a report about a meeting of the US Ambassador to Chungking with the British Chiefs of Staff, ending:

> I have always said that the Chinese want the war taken away from them, and not a war in and through China. The conflict of interest between SEAC and the China

theatre in the use of the British India–Burma base, and in particular of shipping resources, is likely to increase in intensity in the coming months.

As I write this the news of the fall of Rangoon has come through. I am delighted it is all over, although the measure of its capture was rather an anti-climax. We are now making active preparations for the Malaya campaign, and with the deteriorating Japanese position I see no reason why we should not speed up operations to some extent. I have still every intention of getting Singapore before the end of the year.[39]

On 5 May Mountbatten's resilience was tested when his Commander-in-Chief, Land Forces, General Leese, came to see him with the suggestion that Slim was a tired man, with little experience of combined operations, who in any case deserved a less active job. Leese's intention was to remit the planning of ZIPPER, the assault landing in Malaya, to the commander of 14th Army, who would be force commander. He believed that General Christison was the man for the job, and accordingly proposed to apprise Slim of his decision and offer him command of a newly formed 12th Army with the task of garrisoning Burma. As Supreme Commander Mountbatten disagreed, and said that unless Slim desired, through fatigue or for any other reason, to be relieved in command of 14th Army he should remain. According to General Browning, who was present, it was made clear to Leese that on no account was Slim to be given the slightest indication that Mountbatten had lost confidence in him; subject to that, Slim might be 'sounded out'.

Despite this General Leese sent, that very day, a private signal to Alanbrooke, the Chief of the General Staff, seeking approval for his proposals. The acknowledgement was non-committal. Nevertheless, Leese next went to see General Christison and informed him that he was to be commander of 14th Army in place of Slim. Having thus misconstrued, either deliberately or through insensitivity, Mountbatten's limited permission to broach the subject with Slim, and taken unauthorised pre-emptive action, Leese went to see Slim and informed him of the proposal, if not the confirmed intention, to remove him from command of his victorious army. Sir William Slim was stunned, as well he might be. In all conscience he could not accept the preferred relegation to an inferior command. His only recourse would be to send in his papers.

Slim's conduct in this affair was impeccable. Although a lapsed Catholic, he had retained the elements of faith and respect for the integrity of the clergy. To his old friend the Reverend Dr Donald MacDonald, Staff Chaplain to 11th Army Group, he wrote on 14 May:

I was suddenly told by Oliver Leese that he was removing me from command of the 14th Army. It was a bit of a jar as I thought the 14th Army had done rather well. However, he is the man to decide. I have had to sack a number of chaps in my time,

and those I liked best were the ones who did not squeal. I have applied for my
bowler and am awaiting the result.[40]

It was not until 14 May that Mountbatten himself learned, in a signal from
Alanbrooke, what Leese had done. Faced with the facts, he sent for Leese and
told him that he had acted without authority, that the changes which he had
initiated were unacceptable, and that they must immediately be reversed.

To feel obliged to sack yet another commander-in-chief was not a welcome
prospect. But Oliver Leese had not come up to Mountbatten's expectations as
ALFSEA, and although Slim was prepared to continue to serve under him, and
Mountbatten made a case for keeping him on, Alanbrooke would not do so.
Early in July a letter from the Supreme Commander informed Leese that he
would be replaced as ALFSEA by Sir William Slim. According to Lewin:

> Auchinleck, Sir Keith Park for the RAF, Admiral Power for the Navy, and the
> American General Wheeler, the stalwart of SEAC, all volunteered their approval of
> the change.[41]

The report that Rangoon had fallen on 3 May was almost completely eclipsed by
the next day's news of the surrender to General Montgomery, on Luneberg
Heath, of Admiral Doenitz and all the German forces. Victory in Europe (VE)
Day, 8 May, was marked in SEAC by appropriate ceremonial; and the words of
the Prime Minister in his victory broadcast, when he spoke of the war in the Far
East, were balm in Gilead:

> But there is another foe who occupies large portions of the British Empire, a foe
> stained with cruelty and greed – the Japanese . . . and we must turn ourselves to
> fulfil our duty to our own countrymen, and to our gallant allies of the United States
> who were so foully and treacherously attacked by Japan. We will go hand in hand
> with them. Even if it is a hard struggle we will not be the ones who fail.[42]

Yet again, however, in regard to SEAC, Churchill willed the end but failed to will
the means. On 8 June P.J. Grigg, the Secretary of State for War, announced that
service overseas for soldiers in SEAC would be cut from three years eight months
to three years four months. Mountbatten had not been consulted and the Chiefs of
Staff supported his complaint that this would deprive him of many of the key men
who would have been taking part in Operation ZIPPER, the recapture of Singapore.
But if it was, as some suspected, an 'election dodge', it failed. Slim proved to have
been better informed than Churchill when he said to him, during leave in England,
'Well, Prime Minister, I know one thing, my army won't be voting for you.'[43]

While planning for ZIPPER went ahead, its date set back by a month
owing to the cut in available manpower, Mountbatten visited General

MacArthur in Manila. The two supremos enjoyed each other's company. Neither the conflicting political pressures to which Mountbatten had been subject, nor the corrosive inter-service rivalry which MacArthur lived with, affected their relations with each other. Neither could assume, at that stage, that atomic bombs would soon be at the disposal of their leaders. To bring about the earliest practicable defeat of Japan with the means at their disposal was their united purpose. MacArthur agreed that the boundaries of SEAC should be extended to include the Dutch East Indies, French Indo-China, Portuguese Timor and Borneo. This would enable him to concentrate his maximum force for the invasion of the Japanese mainland, essential to bring about victory.

The implications of these talks were too far-reaching to be dealt with by signal, and Mountbatten set off almost at once for Paris, where he hoped to sense General de Gaulle's attitude to the restoration of Indo-China to French rule. While there he was summoned to join Churchill at Potsdam, where, with President Truman and Stalin, he was attempting to settle the outlines of post-war Europe.

Having been informed, in guarded terms, of the intention to deploy atomic bombs against Japan early in August, all Mountbatten could do was to alert his Chief of Staff in equally guarded terms to be ready for a sudden collapse of the Japanese. When this happened on 15 August, following the dropping of the bombs on Hiroshima and Nagasaki, the most immediate question for SACSEA was 'should ZIPPER be cancelled?' Mountbatten decided that it should proceed.

The preliminary loading was already well under way, and although it might be possible to dispense with some of the powerful fleet that had been assembled, there was no guarantee that pockets of resistance among fanatical Japanese soldiery would not be met. There would certainly be a need for the rapid deployment of adequate military force to restore and maintain public order, liberate prisoners of war, and round up any scattered and demoralised Japanese who might let themselves be taken prisoner.

It was going to be a mammoth task, fraught with the need for on-the-spot political and administrative judgements in conditions of great complexity. It was fortunate indeed that on 16 August Slim, who had been promoted to general on 1 July, took up his appointment as ALFSEA. The extension of South-East Asia Command agreed with MacArthur had been confirmed at Potsdam, with minor additions. Mountbatten would be responsible for all the territory, including the Netherlands East Indies, south of a line drawn from the coast of Indo-China to the equator in Dutch New Guinea. The population of the area was about 128 million, and 750,000 uniformed Japanese were still at large among them. The most urgent task by far was to rescue the 125,000 Allied POWs and internees, all of whom had suffered inhuman treatment, many being near death from starvation, disease and injury.

On 19 August General MacArthur, as Supreme Commander Allied Powers, decreed that no landings or re-entry into Japanese-occupied territory were to take place until after the formal instrument of surrender had been signed in his presence, on board a US battleship in Tokyo Bay on 2 September. This would delay by nearly three weeks the start of bringing relief to the prisoners and internees; and would dislocate plans for the rapid and orderly reoccupation of Malaya and other territories in SACSEA's area of responsibility. Despite these predictable setbacks, the British Chiefs of Staff enjoined compliance with MacArthur's order. In order to take control of events Mountbatten convened a SEAC conference at Rangoon on 27 August. The Japanese were represented by their most readily available senior officers. On finding that they would do as they were told, Mountbatten decided that until he could take full control his authority would be exercised through the Japanese chain of command.

With the major task of rescuing the POWs in mind Mountbatten had already, with the help of Lord Ismay, enlisted the support of Edwina, who had arrived at Kandy on 23 August. As Superintendent-in-Chief of the St John Ambulance organisation she had accompanied Mountbatten on a visit to Chungking as guests of Generalissimo and Madame Chiang Kai-shek. Thereafter she had toured SEAC for several weeks, visiting and reporting on hospitals and other aspects of forces welfare. Once again she demonstrated her dedication, expertise and organising ability, and it was under her aegis that, unofficially, the parachuting of aid into POW camps began immediately.

ZIPPER had been planned as an opposed landing of two divisions and three follow-up divisions, with the ultimate purpose of retaking Singapore. Convoys were sailed from distant ports on both east and west coasts of the Indian sub-continent. Because it would be necessary to clear the approaches to, and harbour of, Singapore before ships could safely enter them, it was intended to take Penang, at the entrance to the Malacca Straits, as an advanced base. The delay posed by MacArthur created a problem for the assault force, already well on its way, because the landing craft were not stout enough to make headway against the south-west monsoon if they were turned back. However, by sheltering in the lee of the Nicobars it was possible to refuel and reprovision them from larger ships.

On 28 August the main body of the East Indies Fleet, under Vice-Admiral H.T.C. Walker, arrived off Penang and the minesweepers began work. On 2 September Admiral Walker accepted the surrender, on board his flagship, of the local Japanese commanders. Next day the Royal Marines of the fleet took over Penang, and Royal Marine detachments from two cruisers were landed at Sabang in Sumatra. It was on this day, 3 September, that the naval commander-in-chief, Admiral Sir Arthur Power, having proceeded ahead in a cruiser accompanying the minesweepers, entered Singapore; the next day a convoy arrived carrying the 5th Indian Division.

The main assault landings began at daybreak on 9 September, across beaches in the vicinity of Port Dickson and Port Swettenham, not far from Kuala Lumpur and over 100 miles north of Singapore. In the first three days 100,000 men were put ashore, but it cannot be said that all went well. Clandestine reconnaissance carried out beforehand by the Combined Operations Pilotage Parties (COPP) had failed to discover that soft mud lay below the apparently firm sand of certain beaches, so many of the heavier vehicles got stuck and eventually submerged. There were also communications breakdowns. General Slim, who as ALFSEA was the responsible force commander, was not proud of this operation. And Mountbatten, who had initiated the COPP when he was Chief of Combined Operations, was on this occasion less than well served by these brave and normally conscientious men. But he maintained that as the Japanese had no more than 130,000 troops in Malaya, of the 750,000 million in South-East Asia, ZIPPER would have succeeded even if it had been opposed. As was later established, both strategic and tactical surprise would have been achieved, principally because such an operation was not expected during the monsoon, which was not due to end until November.

In September Admiral the Lord Louis Mountbatten, resplendent in white uniform, accepted the surrender of General Itagaki in the Singapore Municipal Buildings. Unlike MacArthur, who had ruled that the surrender of swords was an archaic practice not to be enforced (particularly as officers might be unable to control their men after losing face):

> Mountbatten decided that loss of face was the prime consideration, and with his benediction Slim carried out the policy ruthlessly. All Japanese officers in the area of his command surrendered their swords to British officers, and the more senior divisional and army commanders did so in front of large parades of their own men.[44]

And in a letter to General Carton de Wiart dated 21 August 1945, besides commenting upon the relationship between Chiang Kai-shek and the Communists in China, Mountbatten expressed his dissatisfaction with the way 'the whole surrender' is being handled. In his view the 'war should have been continued until the Emperor arrived in Manila to surrender in person to MacArthur'.[45]

What Mountbatten described as his 'Post Surrender Tasks' occupy a place in history of profound significance for the transition from a mainly imperialist world order to one composed largely of independent nation states. For two months SEAC had two headquarters, one in Singapore and one in Kandy. During the early stages of the transition from war to peace both were indispensable.

The post-surrender tasks themselves fell into two main categories, although interaction between them was continuous. There was the rescue of the POWs and internees, plus the restoration and maintenance of public order; and there was the nurture, in each country in the area, of responsible and stable government. For these parallel aims to be achieved in reasonable time – and with every day that passed their achievement became more difficult – power had to be exercised: the power of legitimate authority to determine, in the first instance, to whom political authority should be devolved; and secondly, the extent to which the control of military aid to the civil power should be devolved also. Given that, pending the re-establishment of normal patterns of agriculture and trade, emergency measures were essential to provide food for starving millions, it is evident that had there not existed a politico-military Supreme Allied Commander, South-East Asia, it would have been necessary for the victorious governments to establish one on the day the Japanese agreed to surrender.

Not only is it inconceivable that Churchill, Truman, Stalin and Chiang Kai-shek would have agreed instantly upon the necessity; but the nationality of the holder of so great a combination of responsibility and authority would surely have been contentious. Then, just supposing that a British nominee had been called for, upon whom would the selectors' eye have fallen? A post-captain in the Royal Navy may have been, in Palmerston's day, the best man to act in Britain's best interest anywhere in the world; but in 1945 that world had changed out of all – or nearly all – recognition. It seems wildly improbable that Captain Lord Louis Mountbatten, even though marked out for early promotion to Rear Admiral, would have been put in charge of the rehabilitation of South-East Asia. But he was certainly the man for the job. Accustomed by now to the exercise of military command at the highest level, over sea, land and air forces, he was both by youth and temperament sympathetic to the political aspirations of the peoples he had helped to liberate from Japanese overlordship.

With up to 1,000 messages per day being handled by SEAC, providing or seeking information on a wide range of operational administrative, military and civil activities, from Cabinet minister to junior commander level, the paramount need was for staff work of the first order. This was what SEAC was manned, organised, equipped and trained to provide. And by its aid Mountbatten carried out the tasks with which he was confronted with high efficiency and remarkable dispatch.

While setting in train the earliest practicable rescue of POWs and internees, their welfare and prompt repatriation, the release to return home for demobilisation of the armed forces, and the procurement and distribution of food and other necessaries, Mountbatten persisted with his efforts to stabilise the political situation in Burma. For him, government with the consent of the governed was the aim. Not having been a colonial administrator, to whom the prospect of granting political independence to a subject people was at best a distant possibility, he sought to identify and gain the trust of individuals and groups who had the widest popular support.

In Burma he had ascertained that Aung San, who had initially led the Burmese National Army recruited and armed by the Japanese to help 'liberate' Burma from British rule, had long since deserted the Japanese, a fact confirmed by the breaking of their diplomatic ciphers. Mountbatten sought therefore to postpone the reimposition of indefinite direct rule. He believed that if a reasonable date were set, an independent Burma might emerge, content to remain within the British Commonwealth. But the old hands in Whitehall won the day and on 16 October, at the instance of the Cabinet, the pre-war governor of Burma, Sir Reginald Dorman-Smith, was reinstated. An opportunity was certainly missed to initiate the development of stable and liberal self-government in Burma; but as Aung San and most of his ministers were murdered, and Burma became independent under a regime of quasi-military dictatorship, that avenue has remained closed.

In Malaya and Singapore ethnic conflicts, compounded by Communist infiltration, produced a more complex situation, even, than that which prevailed in Burma. Once again, by wise measures of administration, Mountbatten maintained civil order and promoted the move towards political independence within the Commonwealth, which he believed to be the best way to accommodate the aspirations of the people with the preservation of public order and the promise of prosperity. Again the old hands, and some of his military advisers, were sceptical of his liberal attitude, and were particularly affronted by the consideration which he showed towards Pandit Nehru during a visit to Singapore in March 1946, when the large Indian element in the population greeted him with wild enthusiasm, in which the Mountbattens were included.

A fortnight later, on 1 April, at Mountbatten's prompting the Malayan Union was restored to civil government under Lord Killearn, who had been appointed Special Commissioner for South-East Asia, and a few weeks after that, again at Mountbatten's instance, Malcolm MacDonald took over as Governor-General of Malaya and Singapore. The role of SEAC was nearing its end.

Although Siam (Thailand) had been technically at war with Britain her royal ruler had changed sides early in 1945.[46] As an independent country, which Britain intended should remain so, she did not present any serious problem. Indo-China, on the other hand, was to prove most intractable. The Potsdam agreement had required Mountbatten to take over the country south of the 16th parallel when the Japanese surrendered; the territory north of that line was to be surrendered to Chiang Kai-shek. This arbitrary arrangement gave rise to troubles, which were to destroy the prospect of a united and independent Indo-China. Before the French could provide adequate military force to support the re-establishment of their colonial regime, Ho Chi Minh and his Viet Minh movement declared the independent Republic of Vietnam. Although not in sympathy with the French desire to reimpose colonial rule, Mountbatten, with the help of General Slim, managed to maintain order with the troops who had been sent there to round up the Japanese. He tried to persuade the French to make an accommodation with the Viet Minh, but failed to do so. On 4 March 1946, much to his relief, Indo-China ceased to be a part of SEAC.

His primary task in the Netherlands East Indies – already proclaimed an independent republic by the dynamic Dr Soekarno – was the rescue and rehabilitation of Allied POWs and internees. Mountbatten sent General Christison there with orders to impose martial law only in key areas. Political intelligence upon which to base measures to re-establish civil government was meagre – the most helpful information which came his way was from Edwina. When visiting the POW camps she had happened to meet Laurens van der Post who had spent two years in one of them, and who, being a man of rare intelligence allied to a liberal disposition, had correctly gauged the power and determination of the independence movement.

The Dutch government and its administrators exemplified, most stubbornly of all, the immediate post-war propensity of the European colonial authorities to have learned nothing and forgotten nothing, like the courtiers surrounding Louis XVI on the eve of the Revolution. Mountbatten managed to bring about the beginnings of an acceptance by the Dutch that there was no reasonable prospect of restoring the pre-war status, and prevailed upon Prince Bernhard of the Netherlands to send out a personal observer. It had been essential to replace the Indian troops as soon as possible by Dutchmen; but equally indispensable that their activities should be strictly limited to aiding a civil power no longer answerable to the Hague. In accordance with his usual practice, Mountbatten, still Supreme Commander, provided Christison with a clear directive and complete freedom to carry it out, while remaining fully prepared to accept responsibility for the consequences. His confidence was not misplaced. The outcome was the least unsatisfactory that could have been expected in a situation of immense complexity charged with political and ethnic dynamite; but the thwarted extremists of all parties chose to revile Mountbatten just the same.

No one was better qualified than the Supreme Commander to determine the date upon which it would be appropriate and prudent to wind up SEAC nor, one would have thought, to advise upon the structure of military command called for to succeed it. Not surprisingly, given the economy of force with which the Japanese in Burma had been defeated and the post-war tasks successfully accomplished, Mountbatten recommended to the British Chiefs of Staff that a combined headquarters for South-East Asia should be retained in Singapore, with a 'supremo' to be in overall command of all three services and give military advice to the civil authorities and British government. But when he left Singapore on 30 May 1946, having turned over command of SEAC to General Stopford, this arrangement held good only until November. Thereafter the Bourbons of the armed forces in Britain, each of whom had made his reputation by leading his own service in war, and upon whom no slur should therefore be cast, saw to it that SEAC should be replaced by a committee of single service commanders-in-chief. Thus was the clock retarded, not to be advanced until November 1962 when Admiral Sir David Luce was appointed the first unified commander-in-chief of the new Far East Command. By then Mountbatten had not only achieved the main ambition of his professional career by becoming First Sea Lord after reverting to naval service, but he had succeeded to the post for which his experience as a Supreme Commander had uniquely qualified him, namely Chief of the Defence Staff.

Carton de Wiart described Mountbatten well in saying that he was a 'Royal democrat'. A similar perception of his persona, added to first-hand knowledge of the political and diplomatic skills with which he had conducted post-surrender affairs in South-East Asia, no doubt inspired his selection by Clement Attlee to be the last Viceroy of India.

5

VICEROY AND GOVERNOR-GENERAL OF INDIA (1947–48)

I hated the decision to abandon India but I believe that that decision was wise and could not have been long postponed. It was not the Indian people nor Indian sentiment that made it impossible for the British to remain in India. It was the British people and British sentiment, strongly supported by the sentiment, based largely on ignorance, of their American cousins. The idea of the inhabitants of an island in Europe governing against their will an Asiatic population ten times more numerous than themselves is not acceptable to the modern mind.

Duff Cooper[1]

Chapter 5

To put it colloquially, if a change of bowling is desired it is not always necessary that there should be an elaborate explanation.

Clement Attlee, Prime Minister
House of Commons, 7 March 1947[2]

I am sorry for you, you have been given an impossible job. I have tried everything I know to solve the problem of handing over India to its people; and I can see no light.

Wavell to Mountbatten, March 1947[3]

What, then, was this job? And why was it impossible? In the imperishable words of Edmund Clerihew Bentley, 'Geography is about maps, but Biography is about chaps.'[4] Here we have both. Governing India, prior to 15 August 1947, amounted at the very least to maintaining law and order among upwards of 350 million people of different ethnic, religious and social groupings, throughout a subcontinent measuring about 2,000 miles from its northernmost border to its southern tip, and a similar distance from west to east. For comparison, the distance from the entrance to the Baltic to the Straits of Gibraltar, and from London to Istanbul, is 1,500 miles or so.

It is acknowledged by most historians that the assumption by Great Britain of responsibility for governing India was not part of any grand imperial design but the by-product of mercantile expansion, supported wherever necessary and feasible by the force of British arms. In 1765 Clive obtained for the British East India Company the title Bahadur (Honourable) as inheritor from the declining Mogul Empire of the right to rule. Then, following the final defeat of Napoleon and hence the elimination of French competition, the scope of Company administration rapidly increased until it encompassed the whole of India. But its incapacity to govern led to the Mutiny of 1857, and in 1858 responsibility was transferred from the Company to the Crown, represented constitutionally by a Cabinet minister, the Secretary of State for India.

Indian affairs thus became integral with domestic, foreign and colonial policy, at a time when the extension of the franchise and the power of the press were revolutionising politics. Democracy and the nation state were displacing aristocracy and empire. Liberal voices were echoing and re-echoing the sentiments expressed by Thomas Macaulay in the House of Commons on 10 June 1833:

> The destinies of our Indian Empire are covered with thick darkness. It is difficult to form any conjecture as to the fate reserved for a state which resembles no other in history. . . . It may be that the public mind of India may expand under our system till it has outgrown that system . . . that, having become instructed in European knowledge, they may, in some future age, demand European institutions. . . . Whenever it comes, it will be the proudest day in English history. . . . The sceptre may pass away from us.[5]

The trouble was that as the demand grew in coherence and urgency, the practical difficulties of handing over the sceptre increased pro rata. European institutions, evolved over centuries, once introduced fed the appetite for political freedom and independence. The crucial question now became, 'to whom, when, and under what conditions should the sceptre of sovereignty be handed over?'

Macaulay, in his prophetic oration, went on to say, 'Unforeseen accidents may derange our most profound schemes of policy'; but even he could hardly have forecast the emergence of Mohandas Karamchand Gandhi, who became, as Mahatma (sage), the most powerful Indian nationalist leader. Despite having fought for the rights of citizens of a British Crown colony (Natal), whatever their colour, he had urged his followers to help defend it against the Boers; and when he left in 1914 to return to India, the South African leader General Smuts called him a saintly man.

Gandhi's power to influence the destiny of the people of India became manifest in the aftermath of the First World War. During the war more than a million Indians, soldiers and non-combatants, had served overseas, suffering 100,000 battle casualties and 36,000 dead. And India had contributed much in treasure as well as blood. In all this Gandhi had acquiesced. But this ascetic, brown barrister of the Inner Temple possessed a potent infusion of radical ideas first encountered in the company of people such as George Bernard Shaw and Annie Besant, socialist vegetarians intellectually opposed to the onset of capitalist and industrial society, and convinced of the superiority of moral over materialist values. He had read Tolstoy avidly; he had studied comparative religion; and he had concluded that India and her peoples could never realise their true spiritual identity unless, through a nationalist political movement, the masses could render the continuance of British rule impossible.

Leading Liberals in Britain intended the policy to be one of 'increasing association of Indians in every branch of administration, and the gradual development of self-governing institutions, with a view to the progressive realisation of responsible government in India as an integral part of the Empire'.[6] But in the meantime, Gandhi seemed to have become aware of his own power to lead, and had revitalised the Congress party as a nationwide political force which, together with the Muslim League, would rapidly attain political independence for India. Thereafter, it was assumed, wise, benevolent, representative and skilful government would alleviate the misery of the half-starved and hopeless masses.

The Hindu–Muslim concord did not last long. Muslim nationalism soon gave way to a pan-Islamic tendency arising from the disintegration of the Turkish Empire. Hence anti-British activity, while increasing sporadically, remained uncoordinated. But the onset of national consciousness was perceived by the British authorities in India as the main threat, and in consequence the Rowlatt Acts were passed by the Supreme Legislative Council against the unanimous opposition of its Indian members. These Acts were in effect an extension into peacetime of the wartime emergency power to imprison without trial anyone accused of sedition. Gandhi called upon his countrymen to take sacred vows to disobey the Rowlatt Acts, and support for him began to build. He himself was arrested entering the Punjab and sent back to Bombay.

Then, on 13 April 1919, came the notorious Amritsar massacre when the general in charge of troops sent to aid the civil power caused his men to open fire upon a large crowd, killing about 400 civilians and wounding 1,200 more, including women and children. What was inexcusable in the action of the general, which was in any event a harshly excessive use of force in a badly misjudged situation, was his deliberate use of such force as exemplary punishment, rather than the minimum essential to maintain law and order.

In December 1919 the British government passed an Act designed to implement the spirit of Edward Montagu's 1917 promise of eventual self-government for India within the Empire. But it was too late. Gandhi was impelled to launch a multiple boycott campaign of nonviolent non-cooperation, given effect by the mystical magnetism of his leadership; a combination of religion and politics that ran counter to the concept of a modern, secular state, in which there would be no cause for communal strife. Not surprisingly, given that the Muslim faith is also basically theocratic, under Gandhi's leadership Muslims as well as Hindus supported the Indian National Congress party.

When the Prince of Wales visited India in 1921–22 for a durbar, Gandhi exercised his power to call strikes and boycotts. Mountbatten, acting for the second time as a personal aide to the Prince on a world tour, noted with concern the miserable conditions of life for the vast majority of the populace, and persuaded the Prince that he ought to meet Gandhi. Even the lower officials in the government of India were appalled at the prospect of the future King-Emperor making such an approach. Nor was young Mountbatten allowed, on that occasion, to meet the man who, a few years later, was to represent

Congress at a series of round-table conferences with the British government. In 1922 Gandhi was arrested, and held in prison until 1924.

While he was in gaol political activity in India increased, in response to the opportunities provided by the 1919 Government of India Act. It may be looked upon now as a period of transition from exercise of the British political process at regional level to self-government as a nation. But by 1927 dissatisfaction with the system known as 'dyarchy', by which elected ministers bore responsibility only for certain 'transferred' departments, became manifest. At Indian request the review after ten years provided for in the 1919 Act was brought forward two years. An Indian Statutory Commission, chaired by a Liberal, Sir John Simon, visited India; but as there were no Indian members it was boycotted by all parties. Its recommendations, when eventually they emerged, included the abolition of dyarchy at provincial level but not at the centre. However, by this time a round-table conference had been convened, to draw up a constitution for India as a final step to the granting of Dominion status.

In this regard the goalposts had once again been moved. For the outcome of an imperial conference held in 1926 had been an agreed statement that:

> Great Britain and the dominions were 'autonomous communities within the British Empire, equal in status, in no way subordinate one to another in any aspect of their external or domestic affairs, though united by a common allegiance to the Crown and freely associated as members of the British Commonwealth of Nations'.[7]

This radical proposition was embodied in the Statute of Westminster in 1931, and became the rubric to be utilised in due course in the transition of the British Empire into a free association of nation states.

When on 26 January 1930 Congress pledged itself to a declaration of independence, it had new-style Dominion status in mind. It was not surprising, therefore, that Congress stayed away from the first round-table conference, convened in London in November 1930. For what was to be put on the table was a federal structure to link British India with the 600 or so principalities, each of which was governed more or less capriciously by an hereditary ruler in direct and independent treaty relations with the British King-Emperor but under his suzerainty, the whole making up nearly half the territory of the subcontinent and about a fifth of its population. The British government was much concerned, also, with the well-being of the many millions of people of the lowest caste, known then as untouchables, but whom Gandhi called 'Harijan' – God's people.

Congress apart, the federal plan was well received in principle; there was even hope that Congress would accept it. The Viceroy, Lord Irwin, amazed his Conservative friends by persuading Gandhi to call off the current campaign of non-violence in return for the release of all political prisoners not guilty of violence. The Mahatma then came to London for a second round-table conference, at which he demanded Dominion status for India. This was refused, as the British government remained concerned that Muslims and other minorities might be disenfranchised. Gandhi therefore withdrew and resumed his non-cooperation campaign. As the final outcome of the round table conferences, Britain's Prime Minister, Ramsay MacDonald, issued a Communal Award which perpetuated the system of separate electorates and separate constituencies for all who might be considered minorities. Paradoxically, this offended against Gandhi's campaign to bring the Harijan, the untouchables, into the wider community; so once again he sought to bring about a change of policy by fasting.

After some delay, arising from the opposition of right-wing Conservatives led by Winston Churchill, the Government of India Act of 1935 was passed. It was based on an elaborate federal structure (never put fully into effect), and embodied a multiplicity of safeguards and reservations. Most significantly, and no doubt because it was seen as the launch pad for the full independence of India, no provision was included for a further constitutional review. The more socialist element of Congress, led by Jawaharlal Nehru, condemned the Act. Despite this, Congress took part in the elections under the new constitution in 1937 and, being relatively well organised, won an absolute majority of the seats in six provinces, enough to be able to form a ministry in the remainder, except for Bengal, where there had to be a coalition. In no province did the Muslim League gain a majority.

The structure and constitutional basis for the government of India with which Mountbatten would have to deal in 1947 were now in place; and the leaders with whom he would have to contend were already experienced and internationally known. Gandhi was the architect of Indian independence, by now an elder statesman, and the apostle of non-violence in the name of nationalism.

Gandhi's heir-apparent, Jawaharlal Nehru, was a Kashmiri brahmin, militant son of the moderate leader Motilal Nehru. Born in 1889, he was educated at Harrow and Trinity College, Cambridge, called to the Bar at the Inner Temple, and spent in all some seven years in England. Temperamentally, as he said of himself, he was 'a queer mixture of East and West'. Although an intellectual who in his earlier years accepted Marxist ideology, his nationalism was instinctive and overriding.

Gandhi saw in Nehru a potential for action, although the younger man's views differed in many ways from his own. Nehru, for example, viewed industrialisation and a centrally controlled economy as indispensable to India's future prosperity, rather than reliance upon cottage industry and local self-government. But both men were totally dedicated to the attainment of Indian independence, and both were imprisoned from time to time for leading

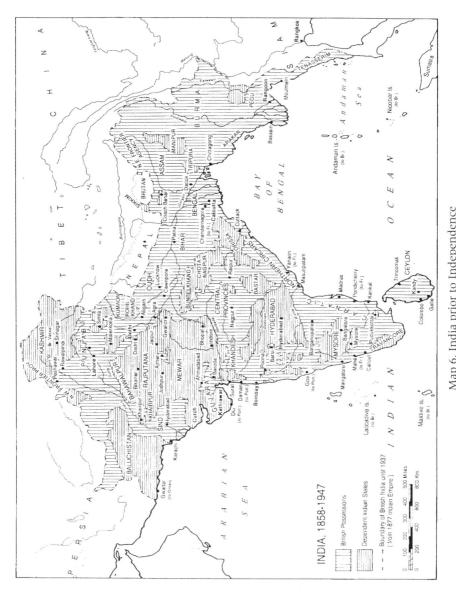

Map 6. India prior to Independence
(Showing the division between British possessions and dependent Indian states.)

non-cooperation movements. Neither, however, was a terrorist; and they personally neither feared nor hated the British.

The third powerful leader with whom Mountbatten would have to negotiate 'the handing over of India to its people' was Mohammed Ali Jinnah. Born in 1876, Jinnah had also been called to the Bar in London, being learned in English jurisprudence and a sharply intelligent observer of the British political process. Having become a barrister at the age of 19 with the support of his father, a prosperous Karachi merchant, he took the keenest interest in Indian affairs while paying frequent visits to the House of Commons, where Gladstone was leading his fourth administration. Jinnah was also active in the election campaign of the Parsee, Dadabhai Naoroji, who became the first Indian to sit in the House of Commons.

In 1896 Jinnah returned to Karachi. His father's firm was no longer prospering and he found it hard to make a living. His marriage was unhappy. His only interests were law and politics. In 1906 he attended the Calcutta session of the Indian National Congress at which the desire for Dominion status and eventual independence for India was recorded; and in 1913 he joined the India Home Rule League. Jinnah worked hard to establish and maintain political union between Hindus and Muslims, and remained throughout his life a firm believer in using constitutional methods to achieve political ends. But a break came in 1920 when he opposed Gandhi's non-cooperation tactics and resigned from both the Home Rule League and the National Congress. He attended the 1930–32 round-table conferences, providing a list of 14 points (an augury of presidential ambitions?) to be included in the future constitution of India, many of which were accepted. But Jinnah did not at that time fully represent the opinion of the Muslim League, which was divided over the extent to which specifically Muslim interests should prevail over the wider issues of national concern. Between 1930 and 1935 he remained in the UK, returning to India for the elections there in 1937.

The exclusion of Muslims by the Hindus from any participation in the government of the provinces brought about a serious deterioration of inter-communal relations. On the outbreak of war between Britain and Germany on 3 September 1939 the Viceroy, perhaps injudiciously, used his prerogative to declare that India was at war with Germany without first seeking the support of her political leaders. In consequence, although neither Gandhi nor Nehru was opposed in principle to going to war against Nazi Germany, the Working Committee of the All-India National Congress ordered all Congress provincial ministries to resign in protest. Whereupon Jinnah, emerging as the undoubted leader of the Muslims, called on them to observe a day of thanksgiving and promptly raised the level of Muslim demands.

In March 1940 the League passed a resolution proposing the formation in the north-west and east of 'independent states'. The press trumpeted this as a cry for 'Pakistan' (Land of the Pure) – a separate homeland for the Muslims of India. From that moment the prospect of transferring power to a united India, comprising the whole subcontinent, became progressively dimmer. Given that British policy remained firmly committed to unity, the final days of the Raj were bound to be fraught with conflict.

In the emergency of war it is not surprising that Gandhi, Nehru and many other Congress leaders were detained. While the Indian army remained loyal and fought bravely in North Africa, Italy and, after the Japanese attack on Pearl Harbor in December 1941, in Burma, the 'Quit India' movement gathered strength; and the more, by good leadership and energetic direction, the diversity of India's millions could be mobilised for war, the stronger grew the sense of nationhood and with it the imperative for political independence.

Early in 1942, when the Axis powers were confident of victory, Churchill and the War Cabinet sent Sir Stafford Cripps on a mission to India, empowered to offer its leaders self-government after the war. But, since Churchill had explicitly excluded India from the self-determination clause of the Atlantic Charter, Cripps's credibility was minimal and his mission failed. The determination of Congress to hold out for instant self-government may well have been strengthened by the sortie of a Japanese fast carrier force and subsidiary cruiser and destroyer force into the Indian Ocean and the Bay of Bengal between 31 March and 9 April. A small British carrier, two heavy cruisers and a destroyer were sunk by air attack; Colombo was bombarded; merchant shipping and troop transports were endangered. Public opinion in India could hardly fail to believe that the British Raj was all but finished.

The All-India Congress Committee concluded that a final 'Quit India' push would do the trick, and on 8 August it activated a 'mass struggle on non-violent lines' on the widest scale. This soon escalated into violence. Gandhi and the Congress leaders were immediately rearrested, bringing about widespread insurrection. Wavell, now Commander-in-Chief, India, had to use 57 battalions, 24 of which were drawn from the field army, to maintain a semblance of order; troop training and movements, stockpiling and airfield construction were all held up. In due course law and order were restored. Then, in October 1943, Wavell replaced Linlithgow as Viceroy, with a brief that reflected Churchill's reluctance to accept any relaxation of Britain's hold on India. In any case his first task was to provide food for the starving people of Bengal – on the day Wavell arrived Linlithgow warned him to expect 1–1.5 million deaths, and that would be getting off lightly. Japanese control of the rice-bowl regions, shortage of shipping, hoarding and Bengali maladministration all contributed to the disaster.

Wavell certainly did his best to cope with the famine; but by 11 August 1944 he could still add as a postscript to a letter to the CIGS, 'Our food problem is acute so please continue to support me.'[8] By this time Mountbatten and Slim, with indispensable air support, were driving the Japanese out of Burma, and in June 1945 Wavell called a conference of Indian leaders at Simla to discuss the formation of a politically representative executive council. He believed that a political settlement was best achieved while the war was still in progress and British authority correspondingly strong. Much to Churchill's relief – he remained staunchly opposed to granting independence to India – nothing came of the Simla conference, owing this time to Jinnah's intransigence as leader of the Muslim League.

There followed in rapid succession the dropping of the first atomic bomb, on Hiroshima on 6 August; the declaration of the final results of the general election in Britain on 9 August, with the consequent replacement of Churchill by Attlee as Prime Minister; and on that same day the dropping on Nagasaki of the second atomic bomb. Wavell, as Viceroy, did not inspire confidence in Attlee any more than he had in Churchill. In consequence, when he reported that serious disturbances were once again in prospect in India, yet another Cabinet mission was sent out. It was not helpful. As Lewin wrote in his biography of Wavell:

> in the final stages Gandhi withdrew Congress from co-operation in an interim government. Then Jinnah, sensing an advantage, quickly persuaded the Muslim League to accept the terms proposed, assuming that this would result in a Muslim-dominated government. Instead both Wavell and the Mission interpreted the texts as requiring them merely to institute a caretaker government and await fresh negotiations before anything was finalised. Thus Gandhi was left to gloat while Jinnah felt that he had been conned.[9]

At this time Mountbatten was closely and heavily engaged, as Supreme Commander, South-East Asia, in the rehabilitation of the countries in the region which had been occupied by the Japanese. The first of these was Burma, where he initiated policies that were to lead in due course to the transfer of pre-war colonial power to the emerging nations. Inevitably, Mountbatten was opposed by colonial administrators, men of high integrity but for the most part dedicated primarily to keeping order until, at some indefinite date, the subordinate peoples were deemed fit to govern themselves. What he saw clearly, and they did not, was that by the end of 1945, with the departure of the British and Commonwealth armed forces to demobilise, there was no power left to transfer. The best that could be done was to terminate the colonial, and in the case of India, the imperial, relationship by a given date, when a new nation would be born, to be governed with the consent of its people.

Late in 1946, by which time Mountbatten had been promoted to the substantive rank of rear admiral and appointed to command the First Cruiser Squadron, Attlee decided to replace Wavell with Mountbatten as

Viceroy of India, if he would accept the appointment. In his autobiography Attlee wrote:

> It was my own thought entirely to choose Mountbatten to negotiate India's independence. I knew his record in the war, and I decided he was the man to get good personal relations with the Indians, which he did. He and I agreed entirely. I told him I wanted a man to end the British Raj. He wanted a definite date to bring the Indians up to scratch of decision.[10]

As early as the summer of 1942, when Leo Amery, as Secretary of State for India, was looking for a new Viceroy, Mountbatten was on a list which eventually included a former Viceroy (Lord Halifax, when he was Lord Irwin), R.A. Butler, Sir John Anderson (a former governor of Bengal), Oliver Stanley, Oliver Lyttleton (later Lord Chandos), Lord Salisbury and Anthony Eden. But Churchill, having in mind India's contribution to the war effort rather than any further move towards self-government, preferred to elevate Wavell from Commander-in-Chief, India, which was his line of country, to Viceroy, which was not. Mountbatten himself was evidently aware that he might be asked at some stage to take on the job. According to Ziegler he wrote, early in 1945, to Edwina:

> I really want to go back to the Navy, as you know, and don't like the idea of governing . . . but if it ever became unavoidable I know that you would make the world's ideal Vicereine.[11]

In December 1946, while Mountbatten was preparing to go back to sea, Attlee asked him if he would take over from Wavell as Viceroy. Now a rear admiral, and relishing the prospect of commanding a cruiser squadron, Mountbatten first obtained the assurance of the First Sea Lord that, on completion of his task in India, he would be permitted to resume his sea command. He next satisfied himself that Attlee's intention was for a definite date in the near future to be set for the transfer of power, hopefully, to a government of all India, and he sought approval to recruit his own senior staff to be additional to, rather than replace, the existing administration in Delhi.

Major General Sir Hastings Ismay (later General the Lord Ismay), who had throughout the war represented Churchill on the Chiefs of Staff Committee in his capacity as Minister of Defence, had recently retired and was about to visit Australia and New Zealand with his wife, as guests of their respective Prime Ministers. A few weeks before they were due to embark, Mountbatten confided in Ismay that he had been asked to succeed Wavell as Viceroy, and that 'power in India should be transferred to Indian hands by June 1948 at the latest'. Just as Mountbatten's abilities and career qualified him beyond doubt to undertake

6. As the Chief of Combined Operations, Mountbatten inspects members of a Royal Navy Beach Party at HMS *Armadillo*, a shore station on the west coast of Scotland, 6 March 1943. (*IWM A 15107*)

7. Winston Churchill and Vice-Admiral Lord Louis Mountbatten stand at the gate of President Roosevelt's villa in Casablanca, Morocco, during the Allied conference in January 1943. It was agreed there that 'unconditional surrender' by the Axis powers was the sole objective. (*IWM A 14107*)

8. Mountbatten with the Combined Chiefs of Staff at the Quebec Conference at the Château Frontenac on 23 August 1943. Left to right: Mountbatten, Admiral of the Fleet Sir Dudley Pound, General Sir Alan Brooke, Air Chief Marshal Sir Charles Portal, Air Marshal L.S. Breadner, Field Marshal Sir John Dill, Lieutenant General Sir Hastings Ismay, Admiral E.J. King, General H.H. Arnold, Admiral W.D. Leahy, Lieutenant General K. Stuart, Vice-Admiral P.W. Nelles and General G.C. Marshall. (*IWM A 18826*)

4. Vice-Admiral Lord Louis Mountbatten in the grounds of Broadlands, his Hampshire home, in 1942. (*IWM F 492*)

5. Mountbatten (far right) watches a landing exercise on the beach at the Combined Operations Centre, Dundonald Camp, on 9 December 1942. (*IWM A 13228*)

2. Captain Lord Louis Mountbatten (2nd from left) with other officers on the bridge of the destroyer HMS *Kelvin* in September 1940. (*IWM A 661*)

3. The K-class destroyer HMS *Kelly*, leading the 5th Destroyer Flotilla, was commanded by Mountbatten throughout her brief wartime service with the Royal Navy. She was lost in action during the Battle of Crete on 23 May 1941. (*IWM A 2908*)

1. Earl Mountbatten photographed at his desk at the Admiralty in London on his appointment as First Sea Lord, in 1956. (*IWM D 76841*)

15. Mountbatten arrives on board the light cruiser HMS *Glasgow* at Malta to assume command of the Mediterranean Fleet, 16 May 1952. (*IWM A 32141*)

16. Mountbatten (right) outside the Ministry of Defence, London, on his retirement as Chief of Defence Staff in August 1965. With him is his successor in the post, Field Marshal Sir Richard Hull. (*IWM MH 28466*)

17. Earl and Countess Mountbatten, with the author, Commander Ian McGeoch (seated right), and Rear Admiral W.W. Davis, Flag Officer (Air) and second in command Mediterranean Fleet (far left), at the Phoenicia Hotel, Valetta, Malta, 17 December 1952. (*Angus McGeoch*)

13. Viceroy of India: Lord and Lady Mountbatten with Mahatma Gandhi, 1947. (*IWM IND 5298*)

14. Watched by Lady Mountbatten, Jawaharlal Nehru is sworn in as India's first Prime Minister by the outgoing Viceroy, Lord Mountbatten, 15 August 1947. (*IWM GOV 1929*)

11. Mountbatten with General Chiang Kai-shek, the Chinese Head of State (left) and Dr T.V. Soong (right). In the background are Captain R.V. Brockman, Lieutenant General F.A.M. Browning and General Carton de Wiart, VC (far right), at Chungking, China, April 1945. (*IWM SE 3547*)

12. Mountbatten reads the surrender terms to Japanese delegates in Singapore, 12 September 1945. (*IWM A 30492*)

9. Mountbatten as Supreme Allied Commander, South-East Asia, studies a map in his command car during a tour of inspection of the front line in Burma, 13–18 January 1945. Looking on is Lieutenant General Sir Oliver Leese, Commander of Allied Land Forces, South-East Asia. (*IWM SE 1404*)

10. Mountbatten addresses men of the 2nd Division near Sadaung, Burma, 20 January 1945. (*IWM SE 2203*)

this immensely difficult and delicate task, so were those of 'Pug' Ismay ideally suited to supporting him in it. Having joined an Indian cavalry regiment, survived the First World War, and qualified as a staff officer, he served for two years as military secretary to the Viceroy of India, Lord Willingdon; then, after a spell in the Intelligence Directorate of the War Office, had been appointed Deputy Secretary of the Committee of Imperial Defence, to become in due course Churchill's indispensable link with the Chiefs of Staff. By 1946 Ismay's knowledge of the levers of power and how to operate them was unsurpassed. After reflecting overnight, and encouraged by a loyal wife, this great public servant offered to accompany Mountbatten to India and was accorded the post of Chief of the Viceroy's Staff.

Captain (S) Ronald Brockman (later Vice-Admiral Sir Ronald Brockman), who had been Mountbatten's personal secretary since he was Chief of Combined Operations, remained with him in that capacity; and Sir Eric Miéville, who as private secretary to Lord Willingdon had been a colleague of Ismay, agreed to join the new team in the capacity of principal secretary. Also included were Lieutenant Colonel V.F. Erskine-Crum as conference secretary, and Alan Campbell-Johnson as press attaché. Among the experts, mainly members of the Indian Civil and Political Service who were already in post serving the Viceroy and Governor-General (to give the full title), were Mr (later Sir) George Abell, whose advice was particularly valuable, and John Christie.

So far, Mountbatten had not confirmed his acceptance of the viceroyalty. In effect, he wished to lay down his own terms of reference for what he would set out to achieve, and by what date; at the same time he sought what he later termed 'plenipotentiary powers', namely carte blanche to negotiate in what he conceived to be the best interests of the British government and King-Emperor. But it is evident, from the context and the assiduity with which he kept the Cabinet informed at every stage, that Mountbatten wished to follow the naval custom of making a signal to a senior officer 'Intend to proceed . . .' on the understanding that no reply would indicate approval to act accordingly. In particular he had been aghast at Wavell's supine attitude in seeking permission from the government in London to talk to Gandhi, even informally; this had, of course, been refused. It was made clear by Mountbatten, also, that he and his wife would hope to visit Indian leaders in their homes on occasion, unaccompanied by officials. The whole archaic panoply of viceregal protocol was to be swept away. At the same time, Mountbatten was never averse to colourful ceremonial when appropriate. Like Gladstone, he favoured splendour but not luxury – though from princely propensities rather than a high Anglican ethic.

There were divisions in Cabinet to be resolved before Mountbatten's appointment was made public, and the Conservatives would certainly be hostile. But the sense of urgency had been heightened by Wavell's warning that, as Attlee put it to the Cabinet on 24 December 1946, 'we shan't be able to hold India beyond March 1948, and possibly not for so long'. He also told them, on 31 December 1946, that the objective being 'to bring the principal communities in India to co-operate . . . the announcement of our intention to leave India by a specified date might have the effect of bringing the communities together',[12] and it would be well to derive whatever advantage possible from the early announcement of an action which would, in fact, be inevitable.

Cripps disagreed. He thought that an early announcement might prejudice the creation of a united India, discounting Jinnah's evident determination to get an independent Pakistan; and Ernest Bevin, the Foreign Secretary, for different reasons objected strongly to fixing a date for withdrawal:

> you cannot read the telegrams from Egypt and the Middle East nowadays without realising that not only is India going, but Malaya, Ceylon, and the Middle East is going with it, with a tremendous repercussion on the African territories. . . . We appear to be trying nothing but to scuttle out of it . . . and I am convinced that if you do that our Party . . . will lose when the public becomes aware of the policy of the Cabinet at this moment.[13]

Mountbatten helped to resolve this impasse by expressing dissatisfaction with the draft statement reflecting the Cabinet's vacillations which Attlee sent him on 8 February, commenting:

> The draft of the proposed statement, however, contains the phrase 'the middle of 1948'; a term which I still consider so wide as not to be in keeping with your declaration that any form of escape clause must be avoided. And the vagueness of this term is underlined by certain points which could easily be misinterpreted.[14]

Before the Prime Minister could finally make up his mind, the waters were further muddied by a telegram from Wavell calling for a delay in the announcement of a withdrawal date. Having written to Wavell on 31 January 1947 telling him, somewhat ungraciously, that a new Viceroy was to be appointed in time 'to take over at the end of February or early in March', Attlee was in grave danger of finding himself with no Viceroy and India on the brink of civil war. But the reduction in National Service from 18 months to a year had been accepted by the Chiefs of Staff on the assumption that troops would be withdrawn from India. This eliminated the possibility of holding India in the event of civil war. He therefore turned down Wavell's suggestion that the date of British withdrawal from India should be left to the new Viceroy to determine after he had had time to assess the situation for himself. Instead, he obtained Mountbatten's consent to the announcement in the House of Commons on 20 February 1947 that it was the government's intention to transfer power to 'responsible Indian hands' not later than June 1948, and that Mountbatten was to succeed Wavell as Viceroy; he would fly to Delhi on 20 March.

There would be a debate in the House of Commons on 6 March preceded, on 25 and 26 February, by a debate in the Lords on what amounted to a vote of censure put down by Lord Templewood (formerly Sir Samuel Hoare), the Secretary of State for India responsible for the India Act of 1935, which Churchill had bitterly opposed. It was comforting for Attlee, and exemplified the cross-party virtues of the hereditary House at its best, that Lord Halifax (the only former Viceroy to take part) concluded:

> I am not prepared to condemn what His Majesty's Government are doing unless I can honestly and confidently recommend a better solution. . . . I should be sorry if the only message from the House to India at this moment was one of condemnation, based on what I must fully recognise as very natural feelings of failure, frustration and foreboding.[15]

The motion was withdrawn.

Not so in the Commons, where the issue was fought to a division on strict party lines. In leading the attack, Churchill declared that the government had gone beyond the offer of Dominion status made under his aegis in 1942; he accused them of abandoning all responsibility for carrying out the earlier pledges to the minorities and depressed classes, as well as to the Indian States; and he deplored the departure from the necessity for agreement between the Muslim and Hindu communities implicit in the Cripps declaration of 1942. Then, having to everyone's surprise suggested that, as had been done in the case of Palestine, a solution should be sought by invoking the aid of the United Nations, Churchill's oration ended:

> It is with deep grief that I watch the clattering down of the British Empire with all its glories, and all the services it has rendered to mankind. . . . But at least, let us not add – by shameful flight, by a premature hurried scuttle – at least, let us not add to the pangs of sorrow so many of us feel, the taint and fear of shame.[16]

Attlee, winding up the debate, made an impressively earnest, persuasive speech, tinged with irony at Churchill's expense:

> we all have to recognise how little we know about India, and how soon that knowledge gets out of date. . . . I ended my time on the Simon Commission nearly 18 years ago. I therefore hesitate to be dogmatic or prophetic about what may happen in India. In this, I admit, I differ from the leader of the Opposition. I think his practical acquaintance with India ended some 50 years ago. He formed some strong opinions – I might almost say prejudices – then. They have remained with

him ever since . . . the essence of the Indian problem is to get Indian statesmen to understand what are the real problems they have to face. . . . A very grave fault of the reforms we have carried out over the years is that we have taught irresponsibility. All Indian politicians were permanently in opposition, and, speaking with long experience, it is not always good to be in opposition. . . . Anyone who has read the lives of the great men who have built up our rule in India and who did so much to make India united will know that all these great men looked to the fulfilment of our mission in India, and the placing of responsibility for their own lives in Indian hands.[17]

With the publication of his appointment Mountbatten and his special staff, headed by Ismay, were allotted rooms in the India Office and given facilities for studying the problems which would confront them when they got to India; and in particular, as Ismay put it, 'to bring ourselves up to date with the history of past efforts to devise a realistic and acceptable scheme for the transfer of power to Indian hands'.[18] There was the pressing matter, also, of proper compensation for the many members of the Indian services who would not wish, or might not be wanted, to continue in India after the British withdrawal. Wavell had already advised Mountbatten to have the responsibility for ensuring payment of adequate compensation accepted by HMG, and this was achieved, with a corresponding boost to the morale of those who, as Ismay said 'had borne the heat and burden of the day in India, and were about to lose their livelihood'.[19]

The Mountbattens, with their entourage, arrived in Delhi on 22 March 1947, and were met at the airport by the Wavells, who departed for the UK next day. On 24 March Rear Admiral the Viscount and the Viscountess Mountbatten were sworn in as Viceroy and Vicereine, resplendent in robes, orders and, in Edwina's case, a magnificent tiara and dazzling jewellery. He was not yet 47, and she a year younger. Their silver wedding would be celebrated in July. Now began, for both of them, the most intensive and demanding task of their hyperactive public lives.

In addition to the statement of government policy, and the principles in accordance with which the transfer of power to Indian hands was to be effected, which had accompanied the announcement of Mountbatten's appointment, the Prime Minister had written to him on 16 March:

My colleagues of the Cabinet Mission and I have discussed with you the general lines of your approach to the problems which will confront you in India. It will, I think, be useful to you to have on record the salient points which you should have in mind in dealing with the situation. . . .

It is the definite objective of His Majesty's Government to obtain a unitary Government for British India and the Indian States, if possible within the British

Commonwealth, through the medium of a Constituent Assembly, set up and run in accordance with the Cabinet Mission's plan. . . .

Since, however, this plan can only become operative in respect of British India by agreement between the major Parties, there can be no question of compelling either major Party to accept it.

If by 1 October you consider that there is no prospect of reaching a settlement on the basis of a unitary government for British India, either with or without the co-operation of the Indian States, you should report to His Majesty's Government on the steps which you consider should be taken for the handing over of power on the due date. . . .

The date fixed for the transfer of power is a flexible one to within one month; but you should aim at 1 June 1948 as the effective date for the transfer of power. . . .

You will no doubt inform Provincial Governors of the substance of this letter.[20]

No doubt. The letter included authorisation 'at such time as you think appropriate, to enter into negotiations with individual States for adjusting their relations with the Crown', and:

You will do your best to persuade the rulers of any Indian States in which political progress has been slow to progress rapidly towards some form of more democratic government in their States. You will also aid and assist the States in coming to fair and just arrangements with the leaders of British India as to their future relationships.[21]

In effect, what Mountbatten was being called upon to do was the equivalent of resolving peaceably in 14 months, in the subcontinent of India, problems which in the western world had arisen from the Reformation, the French Revolution, the Industrial Revolution, the rise of the nation state, the Russian Revolution and the collapse of the Hapsburg Empire, and which after four centuries of ceaseless conflict had left Europe partitioned, in a state which was soon to be termed 'Cold War'.

No wonder Mountbatten had sought from the British government what he later claimed to have received, namely 'plenipotentiary powers' to negotiate on their behalf the final and complete transfer of political sovereignty to Indian hands. Mountbatten recalled Nehru saying that, in contrast to former Viceroys, he talked as if he were making the decisions. But Attlee's letter of 16 March had set out clearly enough the scope of his remit – it was certainly comprehensive, and gave him discretion, as Ziegler put it, 'far wider than any Viceroy had known since the invention of the telegraph had brought Whitehall to within a few minutes of New Delhi'.[22]

Within a few days of his arrival in India Mountbatten was reporting to the British government:

The only conclusion that I have been able to come to is that unless I act quickly I may well find the real beginnings of a civil war on my hands . . . I am convinced that a fairly quick decision would be the only way to convert the Indian minds from their present emotionalism to stark realism and to counter the disastrous spread of strife.[23]

And this was supported by Ismay's experience:

I had thought before I left England that a period of 15 months was far too short a time in which to complete arrangements for the transfer of power. But I had not been three weeks in India before I was convinced that so far from being too short, it was too long. The principal reason for this change of mind was the realisation that communal bitterness had grown to incredible proportions since I was last in India. . . . This spirit of bitter animosity had been rampant throughout the country for several months, and there had been a fearful record of massacres . . . fighting was in progress . . . a hundred miles from Delhi, and there was tension everywhere. . . . Panic and a lust for revenge stalked the land. . . . In the past there had been a splendid police force to deal with disturbances of this kind, but they had ceased to be fully reliable from the moment that our impending departure from India had been announced.[24]

The all-Indian government set up in August 1946 had singularly failed. Nine of the members belonged to the Congress and five to the Muslim League. The only point on which the groups, who otherwise voted en bloc according to communal interest, were in agreement was that the British should quit India as soon as possible. As far as the machinery of government was concerned, by early 1947 British power had vanished. Ministers in charge of departments had simply appointed co-religionists when vacancies occurred, regardless of qualifications, and Ismay noted that by the time he arrived with Mountbatten 'there were only two British officers in the whole of the Secretariat of the Government of India – discounting the Army and Political Departments'.[25]

The task of assessing the opinions of as wide a cross section as possible of the Indian body politic continued non-stop. The Viceroy and Vicereine travelled widely throughout the subcontinent, meeting people and talking with them; Ismay, Miéville and Abell built upon their many years' experience of the Indian scene. Numerous alternative plans for effecting 'the transfer of power to Indian hands' were canvassed. Mountbatten himself spent many hours in private talks with Gandhi, whose intervention could still wreck any settlement which he was not prepared to accept; with Pandit Nehru, determined that the power should be transferred to his hands; and with Mr (as Mountbatten always called him) Jinnah, by now rock-like in his stand for the partition of political power between a Hindu India and a Muslim Pakistan.

Having established close personal relations with the Indian leaders, Mountbatten invited the governors of the provinces to Delhi for an exchange of views. All were agreed, both that a decision must be made as a matter of urgency, and that partition was inevitable. As to the business community, the sooner a settlement could be made, one way or the other, the better for them. There remained the honouring of Britain's obligation to the Princes, whose states covered 40 per cent of the subcontinent. But their destiny could not finally be determined until the political authority of British India had been transferred 'to Indian hands'.

Following reports of further unrest in the North-West Frontier Province, the Mountbattens visited Peshawar towards the end of April, to be greeted by a crowd of over 70,000, mostly Pathans and supporters of the Muslim League. Their mood was potentially dangerous. The situation was saved when the Viceroy and Vicereine, without ceremony and wearing bush shirts rather than the trappings of pomp and power, scrambled up a railway embankment and faced the mob, Mountbatten instinctively giving a naval salute, since no address was possible. The shouts of 'Pakistan Zindabad!' died away. But the Pathans had made their point. Richard Hough, in *Edwina*, records:

> Later, at the town of Kahuta in the Punjab, they were able to see what could happen when crowds like this got completely out of hand. A Moslem horde had swept through the town, burning, killing, raping the women before killing them. There was no one left alive, not a building standing, the sight was for Mountbatten confirmation of the urgent need to reach a settlement before massacres like this could be ascribed to British dilatoriness.[26]

By superhuman efforts the Viceroy and his outstandingly able and well-qualified staff had by the end of April devised a plan for the transfer of power, and on 3 May this was presented by Ismay and Abell to the India–Burma Committee of the Cabinet at 10 Downing Street. British India was to be partitioned into two independent sovereign states, one predominantly Hindu, to be called India, the other predominantly Muslim, to be called Pakistan. The provinces of the Punjab and Bengal, in which the populations were roughly equal Hindu and Muslim, were themselves to be partitioned, Western Bengal (including Calcutta) and the Eastern Punjab were to go to India, with Eastern Bengal and the Western Punjab going to Pakistan. Frontiers would be demarcated by a boundary commission comprising a British chairman and one Hindu and one Muslim as members.

The Cabinet Committee accepted the plan in essentials, but required a slightly revised version. It so happened that Nehru was with Mountbatten when the new version of the plan reached him. Believing that it was virtually the same as that to which Nehru had already agreed in principle, Mountbatten showed him the Cabinet's plan, whereupon Nehru declared that he had been deceived and rejected it. The Viceroy was thus faced with an impasse. But with the invaluable help of V.P. Menon, a man of much wisdom, political skill and integrity, as well as Miéville, a new draft plan was quickly produced. In return for conceding partition, Nehru obtained a firm foundation for his India as a nation state, secular in character, as opposed to a federation of more or less loosely attached states – 'Balkanisation', as he put it.

Even then, the key to final acceptance by all parties was the earliest practicable transfer of power to the new sovereign states, plus Dominion status, while Britain undertook to persuade the Princes to forgo their independence under British paramountcy and merge their states with one or other of the new powers. The plan included provisional arrangements for the division of the assets of British India, and the armed forces, equitably between India and Pakistan. On 19 May Mountbatten placed before Attlee and his colleagues this fresh plan which, he was able to assure them, had received the assent of both Congress and the Muslim League.

The Labour Cabinet having accepted the new plan, and given the Viceroy discretion to work out the details of its implementation, he next had to present it to the Leader of the Opposition, Churchill, whom he met with Anthony Eden, Sir John Anderson and Lord Salisbury on 20 May. Within 24 hours Churchill had agreed that, provided Mountbatten 'could achieve Dominion status for both Hindustan and Pakistan, the whole country would be behind us, and the Conservative Party would help to rush the legislation through'.[27] And to Jinnah, who for some reason (pan-Islamic pressures?) seemed to be disinclined to accept Dominion status, he sent a personal message 'pointing out the perils of hesitation', as Ziegler recorded. With the assurance of all-party support for his plan in the Commons, reinforced by an undertaking of the Law Officers of the Crown that the necessary legislation could be prepared within six or seven weeks, given a final decision on what was required, Mountbatten flew back to Delhi with Ismay. They arrived at about midnight on 31 May 1947.

At 10am on 2 June a meeting of crucial importance took place in the Viceroy's study. Soundings taken since his return from London had indicated reservations on all sides which, if not circumvented, could wreck the plan. Now Mountbatten's power as a person to gain the confidence of other extremely powerful men and lead them to a realistic and binding agreement became manifest as never before. Consider. There assembled were Nehru, President of the Congress Party, representing over 250 million Hindus; Jinnah, President of the All-India Muslim League, representing over 90 million Muslims; and Sardar Baldev Singh, representing over 5 million Sikhs. In support of Nehru were Sardar V. Patel and Kripalani; and with Jinnah were Liaqat Ali Khan and Sardar Rab Nishtar. Mountbatten by this time knew them all well – well enough to expect any of them to raise at the last moment some formidable objection. And in the background was Gandhi, still capable of stalling the whole process.

Mountbatten began the meeting by handing round copies of his plan, now in the form of an announcement which His Majesty's government proposed to make the following day. He then led a discussion, in his most persuasive manner, mingling a princely recognition of co-equal statesmen, conscious of their mutual responsibility at a decisive moment in the history of mankind, with the practical details of governing while transferring power. The concentrated, purposeful and self-confident exertions of the past ten weeks proved not to have been in vain. By the end of the meeting the plan had been accepted in principle by all the parties. Nehru, Jinnah and Baldev Singh had agreed to broadcast the next night on Indian radio to say that they themselves approved the plan, and were appealing to their followers to keep the peace and not resort to violence or bloodshed. Written agreement to the plan was promised no later than midnight by Kripalani on behalf of the Hindus, and Baldev Singh on behalf of the Sikhs. But Jinnah refused to commit the Muslim League on paper. Late in the evening Mountbatten and Ismay did their best to get him to do so, but had to settle for his grudging concession that Attlee might be advised that he could go ahead with his announcement about the plan in the House of Commons the following day.

In the meantime Mountbatten tackled Gandhi, who had denounced the very idea of partition and sought to impede it. It happened to be one of the Mahatma's days of silence, so the Viceroy was able to do all the talking. Thus favoured, he managed to convince Gandhi that the plan was really his idea, and that it was the only one possible.

On 3 June the same party reassembled in the Viceroy's study, this time with photographers in attendance. Stage management was essential to maintain the momentum. Mountbatten began by declaring that all three parties had notified him of their acceptance of the plan, albeit in each case with reservations. However, he went on, since none of these caveats would be acceptable to the other parties it seemed pointless to waste time discussing them. He therefore assumed that the plan was generally approved and could now be made public. Leaving no time for second thoughts he then handed round copies of a bulky document entitled 'Administrative Consequences of Partition', prepared by John Christie, his joint private secretary, aided by the rest of the staff. The effect upon the Indian leaders was salutary. The time had come to face the responsibilities that power entailed. And that meant dividing the assets of British India between the two new states.

That afternoon Attlee announced the plan in the House of Commons, and Churchill gave it his blessing. Ismay recalled:

In the evening the All-India radio was given over to the momentous news. Mountbatten spoke first. He was brief and simple. 'For more than a hundred years,

155

hundreds of millions of you have lived together, and this country has been administered as a single entity. . . . It has been impossible to obtain agreement . . . on any plan that would preserve the unity of India. But there can be no question of coercing any large areas in which one community has a majority to live against their will under a Government in which another community has a majority. The only alternative to coercion is Partition. . . . The whole plan may not be perfect; but, like all plans, its success will depend on the spirit of goodwill with which it is carried out.'[28]

When Mountbatten had finished, the plan was read out in detail, followed by speeches from Nehru, Jinnah and Baldev Singh. 'Who could have believed,' wrote Ismay, 'that such a degree of unanimity would be achieved in the space of 75 days? It was little short of a miracle.'[29]

On 4 June came the celebrated press conference at which Mountbatten, according to Ziegler:

Speaking without notes . . . spent three-quarters of an hour expounding the background and details of the plan, and then dealt with more than a hundred questions, ranging from rabid abuse to searching requests for amplification of the finer points. The Viceroy answered them all with courtesy, confidence and extreme quick-wittedness. Sometimes he was surprisingly frank, as when he was asked whether the States would be free to opt for independence as members of the Commonwealth. When paramountcy lapsed, he replied, the States could do as they wished, but they could not enter the Commonwealth as Dominions. Was he certain that Congress, the Muslim League and the Sikhs, deliberating at leisure and in full session, would honour the undertakings of their leaders?[30]

Patiently he explained that it was a risk he had accepted, and repeated his leitmotiv: it was the people of India who had demanded independence; it was they who had made partition inevitable; and it was they who now must make it work. Seemingly as a throwaway line he told the 300 or so journalists present that he expected the transfer of power to be about 15 August.

In the event, as a concession to the astrologers, to whom the auguries of that day were bad, Mountbatten convened a meeting of the Constituent Assembly for late in the evening of 14 August. That left just 75 days, during which, by a feat of administrative parthenogenesis unparalleled in history, two fully fledged sovereign states suddenly came into being where there had been but a single satrapy, albeit highly developed.

Without question the main, and potentially calamitous, effect on the Indian body politic of the British government's announcement on 20 February of 'independence by mid-1948' had been to undermine the morale of the police and other government servants. To whom, after independence, would they owe their allegiance? To whom would they have to look for their pay and promotion? With partition confirmed, and only about two months to go, this dilemma became acute. The spectre of civil war still stalked the land. Only the momentum of the vast Indian ship of state kept it going, like a supertanker when the engine stops.

With the countdown to Independence Day started, a Council of Ministers chaired by the Viceroy began putting into effect Christie's scheme for the division of assets and liabilities. Three main and separate concerns remained to be dealt with in the very short time available: the boundary commission, the armed forces, and the future of the Princely States.

It was agreed that Sir Cyril Radcliffe (later Viscount Radcliffe of Hampton Lacy), a distinguished member of the English Bar who had never been involved in politics, should be invited to chair two boundary commissions, one for the Punjab and the other for Bengal and Assam; the commissioners in each case were four High Court judges drawn from the different communities. As unanimity could hardly be expected, Radcliffe would have the casting vote. The terms of reference were not settled without heated discussion, but in the end a simple formula emanating from the Congress camp was adopted:

The Boundary Commission is instructed to demarcate the boundaries of the two parts of the Punjab on the basis of ascertaining the contiguous majority areas of Muslims and non-Muslims. In doing so, it will also take into account other factors.[31]

The commissioners, who 'were desired to arrive at a decision as soon as possible before 15 August', were constituted on 30 June and were already at work when Radcliffe arrived in India on 8 July:

Unable to attend the simultaneous sittings of both Commissions, he attended those of neither, but studied the daily record of their proceedings and all material submitted. His base was a house on the Viceregal estate in New Delhi, the Viceroy having decided that it would be improper for the Commission chairman to stay at Viceroy's House, where he might be thought to be under Viceregal influence. Indeed Lord Mountbatten was careful to keep personal contacts with Sir Cyril to a minimum, and to decline either to offer any interpretation of the terms of reference – which Sir Cyril certainly did not invite from anyone – or to make any third-party representations to the Commissions.[32]

Turning to the Indian army, that magnificent, infinitely loyal, highly efficient and courageous fighting force had recently been victorious over the Japanese under Mountbatten's supreme command. No wonder he did his utmost to keep it intact. In this he had the unequivocal support of the commander-in-chief, Field Marshal Sir Claude Auchinleck. Since most regiments were composed both of Hindus and Muslims, their differences submerged in a common loyalty to a regimental tradition, the Indian army was the embodiment of the all-India secular state which Nehru saw as successor to the British Raj; sadly, Jinnah would not accept any postponement whatsoever of the complete disbandment of the Indian armed forces and their reconstitution as the national forces of Pakistan and India. Ismay was desolated at the prospect and did his utmost on Mountbatten's behalf to keep the armed forces in being, with a gradual reorganisation on a communal basis if expedient:

> Jinnah was adamant. He said that he would refuse to take over power on 15 August unless he had an army of appropriate strength and predominantly Muslim composition under his control. There was nothing for it but to prepare a scheme for the immediate partition of the armed forces; and this was done in record time.[33]

As a former supremo, Mountbatten was more competent to judge the military factors in the situation than a politician, and better able than most military men, by virtue of his post-war SEAC experience, to gauge the political aspects. Having had to accept as second best the creation of two dominions to succeed the British Raj, rather than 'a unitary Government for British India and the Indian States', Mountbatten hoped he might become the first Governor-General of both India and Pakistan, thereby preserving at least a symbolic unity. Nehru, when inviting him on behalf of Congress to be the first Governor-General of India, said they would not take it amiss if he were to accept the same office in Pakistan. Ismay recalled:

> Mountbatten had replied that, subject to the King's approval, he would be honoured to be Governor-General of India for a limited period. Jinnah was opposed to the idea of a joint Governor-General for both Dominions, and thought that a better solution would be for Mountbatten to be a super-Governor-General or 'stakeholder'. Mountbatten had at once expressed grave doubts about the practicability of his remaining in any arbitral capacity. . . . It was not until the end of June that we learned . . . that Jinnah had decided to nominate himself as Governor-General, and to make Liaquat Ali Khan Prime Minister. In breaking the news to Mountbatten Mr Jinnah expressed the hope that it would make no difference to his acceptance of office as the first Governor-General of India, or to his being Chairman of a Joint Defence Council of the two countries.[34]

In regard to the future of the Princely States – the Indian States, as Attlee called them in his directive to Mountbatten – it was bad enough that there were to be two sovereign states with which 'fair and just relationships' must be established, but the fact that one of them would be Muslim and the other predominantly Hindu compounded the problem. Historically, the hereditary ruler of each of the 565 separate states was bound by a treaty entered into by a forebear with the Queen-Emperor according to which, under the rubric of paramountcy, the presence of a British Resident was accepted in return for a guarantee of independence. But the states ranged in size and power from the equivalent in population and extent of territory to a considerable European country down to a domain no larger than that of a Scottish laird; economically, the best were viable and forward-looking, but most were impoverished and backward; in common was autocratic governance, varying from comparatively enlightened to arbitrary, corrupt and cruel. In some cases also, a Muslim dynasty ruled over a Hindu populace, as in Hyderabad which, with 18 million people, was the largest of the states; but in Jammu and Kashmir, the second largest, a Hindu dynasty ruled a predominantly Muslim people. Both these rulers were to prove difficult to accommodate under the new dispensation.

For the rest, once again Mountbatten's phenomenal powers of persuasion and clarity of purpose achieved the aim of the British government, namely, that in transferring power to 'Indian hands' he would 'create an integrated India, which, while securing stability, will ensure friendship with Great Britain'.[35] Having organised an assembly of the Chamber of Princes on 25 July, attended by 25 major rulers and 74 state representatives, the Viceroy appeared before them, himself a princely figure in full rig, ablaze with orders and decorations. He proceeded to explain that each ruler had three options: first, complete independence, but without the guarantee of security and familial concern implicit in British paramountcy; secondly, two or more of the rulers could, in theory, band together to form larger entities, capable of independent existence; thirdly, each ruler could merge his state with either Hindustan or Pakistan, depending upon geography and other circumstances.

As to the first option, Mountbatten pointed out, not even the largest state could reasonably expect to remain secure in its independence without British support; as to the second, in the short time available before the British Raj came to an end the formation of new and larger polities would be impossible, and thereafter, without the paramountcy of Britain, impracticable. So, urged Mountbatten, 'let British influence, before it expires, help you to accede to one or other of the new Dominions on terms that are fair and just; what is more, your personal relationship with the King-Emperor will not be completely severed thereby'.[36]

In the event, by 15 August only the two largest states had not acceded to either India or Pakistan; for geographical reasons mainly to the former. The Nizam of Hyderabad was beset by Muslim extremists and holding out against accession to India; while the Maharaja of Kashmir, admittedly in a far more complex situation, seemed to have a hankering for independence but refused to discuss the matter. The Viceroy succeeded in obtaining from the Indian leaders an extension of two months for the Nizam to make up his mind; but the future of Kashmir continued to fester and remained, even in 1991, 'a disputed legacy', as Alastair Lamb termed it in his book *Kashmir*.[37]

Since the award of the Punjab Boundary Commission has been held by some to have prejudiced the free exercise by Maharaja Sir Hari Singh of Jammu and Kashmir of his option to join either Pakistan or India, or remain independent, it is necessary to examine the evidence. This must begin with the award itself, set out in a document dated 'New Delhi 12 August 1947' and signed 'Cyril Radcliffe'. Having named the other commissioners, the document then gives their terms of reference (see note 31). The work of the commission, which received 'numerous memoranda and representations', is then described, but:

> it became evident in the course of our discussions that the divergence of opinion between my colleagues was so wide that an agreed solution to the boundary problem was not to be obtained . . . differences of opinion as to the significance of the term 'other factors', which we were directed by our terms of reference to take into account, and as to the weight and value to be attached to those factors, made it impossible to arrive at any agreed line. In those circumstances my colleagues . . . assented to the conclusion that I must proceed to give my own decision.[38]

Radcliffe then states that the demarcation of the boundary line as detailed in Annexure A is to prevail if it should differ in any respect from that shown, for the purposes of illustration, on the map at Annexure B.

In view of allegations that Radcliffe changed his award in response to political considerations outside his terms of reference, his paragraph 8 is of special interest:

> Certain representations were addressed to the Commission on behalf of the States of Bikaner and Bahawalpur, both of which States were interested in canals whose headworks were situate in the Punjab Province. I have taken the view that an interest of this sort cannot weigh directly in the question before us as to the division of the Punjab between the Indian Union and Pakistan since the territorial division of the province does not affect the rights of private property, and I think that I am entitled to assume with confidence that any agreements that either of these States has made with the Provincial Government as to the sharing of water from these canals or otherwise will be respected by whatever Government hereafter assumes jurisdiction over the headworks concerned.[39]

Further evidence of Radcliffe's unimpeachable adherence to his terms of reference is to be found in paragraph 9:

> in my judgment the truly debatable ground in the end proved to lie in and around the area between the Beas and Sutlej rivers on the one hand, and the river Ravi on

the other. The fixing of a boundary in this area was further complicated by the existence of canal systems, so vital to the life of the Punjab but developed only under the conception of a single administration, and of systems of road and rail communication, which have been planned in the same way. There was also the stubborn geographical fact of the respective situations of Lahore and Amritsar, and the claims to each or both of these cities which each side vigorously maintained.[40]

Again, in paragraph 10:

I have come to the conclusion that it would be in the true interests of neither State to extend the territories of the West Punjab to a strip on the far side of the Sutlej and that there are factors such as the disruption of railway communications and water systems that ought in this instance to displace the primary claims of contiguous majorities.[41]

Paragraph 11 explains that it was not possible to preserve undivided the irrigation systems of the Upper Bari Doab Canal, although small adjustments to the Lahore district boundary were made to mitigate some of the consequences of this severance.

Radcliffe's final paragraph testifies to the integrity with which he made his award:

I am conscious too that the award cannot go far towards satisfying sentiments and aspirations deeply held on either side but directly in conflict as to their bearing on the placing of the boundary. If means are to be found to gratify to the full those sentiments and aspirations, I think that they must be found in political arrangements with which I am not concerned, and not in the decision of a boundary line drawn under the terms of reference of this Commission.[42]

It will be conceded, surely, by those who from the eve of Independence Day until the present have sought to prove that the Radcliffe Commission award was tainted by partisan political pressure exerted by the Viceroy, that the award, taken as a whole, reveals no hint of any such distortion. It is obvious, also, that the award is complex. We know from the report itself that after the public sittings the commission met at Simla for final discussions; and Sir Cyril Radcliffe was totally insulated by the Viceroy and his staff from last-minute efforts by parties on both sides of the divide to influence his judgement. Although his casting vote had continually to be utilised, none of Radcliffe's fellow commissioners resigned.

There was undoubtedly some disagreement between the Viceroy and Sir Cyril over the date on which the awards were to be announced. To resolve this Mountbatten met Radcliffe privately to discuss the matter:

He asked whether Sir Cyril could hold his reports until after 15 August. Sir Cyril replied firmly that he could not delay beyond 13 August at the very latest. The Viceroy agreed that the reports should be sent to his office on 13 August. He was leaving for Karachi that afternoon and would not have time to see them until he returned on the evening of 14 August, which would automatically delay publication until 15 August or later.

This was the plan that was followed. The Bengal report was delivered, but not read by the Viceroy, on the morning of 13 August, the Punjab report not until later in the day. Lord Mountbatten was therefore able to write to Pandit Nehru and Mr Jinnah that afternoon saying that all the reports had not been received before he left for Karachi, and calling a meeting at the Viceroy's House on 16 August to decide upon the timing of publication and the method of implementing the Partition Council's undertaking.[43]

In Karachi, on 14 August, Mountbatten drove with Jinnah through vast crowds celebrating the birth of Pakistan, and attended Jinnah's installation as its first Governor-General. Both men knew that somewhere amid the throng there lurked at least one man with a bomb. However, no attack took place, and, as cited by Ziegler from Mountbatten's diary:

> With an unusual display of emotion, Jinnah placed his hand on the Viceroy's knee when they reached their destination and thanked God that he had brought his visitor back alive. 'I retorted by pointing out how much more serious it would have been if he had been bumped off.'[44]

Back in Delhi that evening, the last Viceroy composed himself for the funeral rites of the British Raj and the birth rites of the Indian Union – Hindustan, as Churchill called it. In the Legislative Assembly, the Lokh-Sabha, where Mr Speaker, armed with the weighty tome of Erskine May's *Parliamentary Procedure*, recalled the Mother of Parliaments at Westminster, Pandit Nehru spoke: 'At the stroke of the midnight hour, when the world sleeps, India will awake to life and freedom.'

As Governor-General of the new Dominion, Mountbatten's role paralleled that of his cousin, George VI, as a constitutional head of state. Having himself been sworn in, it was his first duty to swear in the new ministers; thereafter, in Walter Bagehot's classic phrase, 'to advise, to encourage and to warn' them. Amid scenes of wild enthusiasm and rejoicing by hundreds of thousands of people who packed the streets of Delhi, Their Excellencies Rear Admiral the Viscount Mountbatten of Burma and his Viscountess attended one momentous and memorable occasion after another, including on that first afternoon a party for about 5,000 children:

> To end the day, 3,000 people came to an evening party at Government House. They stayed till 2am. Mountbatten can hardly have slept for more than 11 or 12 hours in

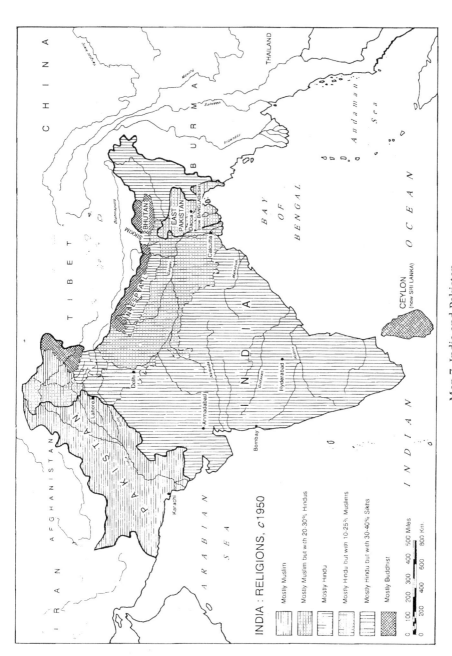

INDIA : RELIGIONS, c1950

Mostly Muslim

Mostly Muslim but with 20-30% Hindus

Mostly Hindu

Mostly Hindu but with 10-25% Muslims

Mostly Hindu but with 30-40% Sikhs

Mostly Buddhist

0   100   200   300   400   500 Miles
0   200   400   600   800 Km

Map 7. India and Pakistan
(As constituted on 15 August 1947, and showing the division between religions.)

the previous three nights, he had been the focus of unremitting public attention, he had made four major speeches, conducted negotiations of great importance, enjoyed hardly a moment of waking relaxation. Somehow he kept going, concealing his exhaustion, endlessly charming. At last it was over, India and Pakistan were well and truly free; the first part, at least, of his task was accomplished.[45]

From Attlee came a telegram of congratulations:

My warmest thanks to you on this day which sees successful achievement of a task of an unexampled difficulty. The continual skill displayed in meeting every difficulty has been amazing. Your short tenure of Viceroyalty has been one of the most memorable in a long list. In this I include Edwina, Ismay and other helpers.[46]

Ismay himself wrote:

I still can't believe that you have pulled it off. It is the greatest *personal* triumph for you and Edwina of modern times – far more so than winning a great battle or even a great campaign.[47]

For his own part, Mountbatten also had a tribute to pay. Enclosed with a copy of Attlee's telegram which he passed to Edwina was a note to:

the person who helped me most . . . surely no husband in history has had the proud privilege of transmitting a telegram of appreciation from the Prime Minister to his wife. I'm very proud to be that exception. . . . Thank you, my pet, with all my heart.[48]

Mountbatten was raised in rank from Viscount to Earl. Nehru and Patel paid many public tributes, the latter deploring the fact that his wisdom and guidance had not been made available 'at a much earlier date'. Most highly valued, probably, of all the eulogies was that by Walter Lippman in the *Washington Post*:

Perhaps Britain's finest hour is not in the past. Certainly this performance is not the work of a decadent people. This on the contrary is the work of political genius requiring the ripest wisdom and the freshest vigour, and it is done with an elegance and a style that will compel and receive an instinctive respect throughout the civilised world. Attlee and Mountbatten have done a service to all mankind by showing what statesmen can do, not with force and money, but with lucidity, resolution and sincerity.[49]

Next day, 16 August, the euphoria was sustained – just. Nehru and Sardar Patel for the Indian Union, Liaqat Ali Khan for Pakistan and Baldev for the Sikhs gathered in the council chamber of Government House to consider the Radcliffe awards. Their impartiality was reflected in the indignation showed by all parties to one or other aspect. It was agreed, even if under protest, that they should immediately be published.

Sadly, news from the Punjab and Bengal soon dispelled hopes of a peaceful transition. In Calcutta Gandhi proclaimed a fast unto death if the communities did not cease to slaughter each other. His power to create a public mood now brought diminished strife. But in the Punjab the mayhem was getting out of hand. Since the beginning of August there had been ferocious rioting in Lahore and Amritsar. Now, with partition a fact, about 2 million sorely aggrieved Sikhs, finding themselves domiciled in what was now an alien country with a repugnant religion, were on the march, formed with military precision into convoys of bullock carts escorted by heavily armed guards. Moving in the other direction were Muslims who had found themselves, suddenly, in a country now foreign to them. Altogether there were millions on the move.

Foreseeing civil strife on a fearful scale, a joint Indian–Pakistani force some 55,000 strong, known as the Punjab Boundary Force, under an Indian army officer of proven fighting ability, Major General T.W. Rees, was deployed where the worst trouble was expected. It was too little, too late. The scale of the conflict was too great. As the situation worsened, the two prime ministers, Nehru and Liaqat Ali Khan, sought to set an example of cooperation between communities by travelling in the same aeroplane to some of the principal trouble spots. According to Ismay:

> Their visits to Lahore in the West Punjab, and to Jullundur and Amritsar in the East Punjab, resulted in a marked improvement in the situation.[50]

Ismay himself had been brought low by an attack of dysentery just before Independence Day, which he had thus spent in acute discomfort. A few days later, fit enough to travel, he was ordered to go to Kashmir to convalesce. Mountbatten asked him, while he was there, to see if he could persuade the Maharaja to hold a referendum at once on the question of whether his people wished to accede to India or Pakistan. Over 70 per cent of his people were Muslims, but by no means all of them, it seems, would have opted to join Pakistan and lose the prospect of the more democratic government which accession to India promised. The Maharaja refused to discuss the matter, and his fence-sitting brought about and perpetuated the rift between India and Pakistan over Jammu and Kashmir, prompting Ismay to comment:

> We ought long ago to have used the paramount power which we possessed in order to reform the system of government in the more backward or reactionary states.[51]

Meanwhile, the frenzy of communal massacres, rape and looting continued to spread far beyond the boundary areas. As an example, one of Ismay's daughters, who had been staying with the Mountbattens in Simla, was in a train returning to Delhi with her fiancé, one of the ADCs, when, in a station only 20 miles from there, a bomb exploded, followed by a general attack on all Muslim passengers. 'Men, women and children were pulled out of the train by their Hindu fellow-travellers and butchered in the most brutal manner.'[52] This massacre was not attributable to dissatisfaction with boundary awards; it was a manifestation of the communal hatred which had itself brought about partition. As Nehru commented many years later (in the author's hearing): 'Had Kashmir acceded to Pakistan at that time, Hindus would have been killing Muslims all over India. My idea of a secular state would not have been realised.'

When Ismay got back to Delhi he found that the Muslim members of his domestic staff were 'frightened out of their wits' lest they should be set upon by their Hindu colleagues, who had to be called to order; and it was evident that communal bitterness was spreading to the armed forces:

> It was at this juncture that Mountbatten was able to render services to India and Pakistan, and indeed the whole British Commonwealth, which have never been fully realised. It was largely due to him that Delhi was saved from anarchy, and that the orgy of communal strife did not spread to the whole sub-continent. This is no reflection on the leaders of the two new Dominions. Nehru and Patel, Jinnah and Liaqat Ali Khan strove, with the utmost courage and resolution, to suppress the disorders, but none of them had the knowledge or experience to deal with a cataclysm of this kind.[53]

Because he enjoyed the absolute confidence of the Indian Cabinet, Mountbatten's advice as Governor-General was accepted and an emergency Cabinet Committee was immediately set up to deal with the crisis. At Nehru's invitation Mountbatten took the chair; members included Nehru, his Home Minister, Patel, his Minister of Defence, Baldev Singh, and a newly appointed Minister for Refugees, with other ministers being co-opted as required. Ismay's 'palatial office' became virtually an operational headquarters:

> Meanwhile Lady Mountbatten, in her own sphere, made us all immensely proud of British womanhood. She was utterly dedicated, completely indefatigable and uniquely experienced. Undaunted by fatigue, danger, disease or stench, or the most gruesome scenes, her errands of mercy took her to hospitals and refugee camps all day and every day, and a good deal of the night.[54]

As matters grew worse and worse the Punjab Boundary Force, with little support or encouragement either from local civil authorities or the new governments, proved unequal to the scale of the problem and was disbanded.

The vernacular press in India and Pakistan, while commenting freely on events, thanks to its liberal heritage from the Raj, unfortunately failed to hold facts sacred. The most blatant calumnies were given prominence in the most irresponsible manner. Nor did attacks upon the British cease now that they had 'left'. Sir Cyril Radcliffe, for example, whose services on the boundary commission had been given free of charge and at great personal sacrifice, was caricatured in both India and Pakistan carrying away enormous bribes from the other side. And communal hatred was fuelled almost to the point of spontaneous combustion into civil war by the publication of wildly exaggerated and often groundless stories of complicity by the opposing government in planned atrocities and warlike preparations.

Ismay himself was sent on a mission to see Jinnah in person and try to convince him that the Indian government was doing its utmost to succour refugees and protect the Muslims still within its borders. By conveying a note to this effect signed by Neogy, the Minister for Refugees, he succeeded in restoring some degree of confidence in the good faith of the Indian government. He also managed, during a short visit to England early in October, to persuade Sir George Cunningham to accept Jinnah's invitation to become governor of the North-West Frontier Province, a post from which he had recently retired after eight successful years; and he provided the British Cabinet and press with first-hand information to balance the less responsible reports from the Indian subcontinent.

By the end of October some degree of order had been restored – or one might say that the bloodlust had been to some extent assuaged – when news was received in Delhi that numerous frontier tribesmen were invading Kashmir. It transpired soon afterwards that the pusillanimous Maharaja had fled his capital, Srinagar, after signing a letter asking for accession to India. Mountbatten, as Governor-General, had no choice but to act on the advice of his government and accept it, but felt constitutionally able to stipulate that a plebiscite be held as soon as practicable to ascertain the wishes of the people of Jammu and Kashmir. This was a measure for which he had been pressing ever since the future of the Indian states had come under consideration.

Now, as chairman of the newly formed Defence Committee in Delhi, Mountbatten was able to mastermind a timely intervention by Indian airborne forces to counter the Pathan incursion and establish the security of Kashmir; but, despite his most strenuous efforts, he could not bring about a resolution of the dispute between India and Pakistan over Kashmir. As Ziegler summarises: 'Once again he had learned painfully that reason and goodwill could not always prevail when prejudice and national pride were ranged against them.'[55]

Not for the first time Mountbatten's advice to the British government was more soundly based than that being generated in Whitehall. His efforts to get the UN Security Council to send a force to stop the fighting were ultimately to bear fruit; but Nehru's preference was for a war of words in New York. This was fatal. The battle lines of the Cold War had by now been drawn up. The Americans and British saw Pakistan as a sounder bet than India in the anti-Communist stakes. In Attlee's personal opinion, Russia's aim was to prevent a settlement of the Kashmir issue, then bring about anarchy and chaos throughout the subcontinent; Mountbatten's response was that Russia would probably consider her interests better served by 'the emergence of a strong, stabilised India, activated by a deep feeling of gratitude and admiration towards Russia'.[56]

Given his determination to prevent war breaking out between India and Pakistan over Kashmir, and the influence he could exercise in Delhi as chairman of the Defence Committee, it was hard for Mountbatten to decide whether or not to return to England for the wedding of his nephew, Prince Philip, to Princess Elizabeth, the future queen and a not-too-remote cousin. It could be argued, as Edwina did with persistence, that to attend the wedding would be tantamount to deserting his post. But by this time her relationship with Nehru, even though platonic, which it surely was, had impaired her judgement. By departing from Delhi at a critical time, Mountbatten believed, he would help to restore public and governmental confidence that peace would be maintained; he would place the responsibility for this firmly where it belonged, in the hands of the Indian leaders; and as Governor-General he, with Edwina, would properly represent in a general way the link of the new Dominions with the Crown.

The royal wedding took place on 20 November 1947; by 24 November the Mountbattens were back in harness. In their few days' absence from India nothing much had changed. The Kashmir imbroglio simmered on, with the UN Security Council unhurriedly considering whether or not to send a commission – which eventually it did – to mediate between the two parties. But the preferred solution, partition, was never brought about. The business of Hyderabad also remained unfinished. The Nizam and his associates among the Muslim fanatics believed that India's preoccupation with Kashmir would enable them to keep Hyderabad independent more or less indefinitely, with their safety as a minority guaranteed by Pakistan. Mountbatten did manage to get an even-handed Instrument of Accession drafted, but it was never signed, and 14 months later Hyderabad was forcibly absorbed into the Indian state.

In the meantime the Mountbattens were preoccupied with gubernatorial duties – visits all over India to open hospitals, look at schools and universities, and inspect factories and power stations. They were also the guests of the Princes in the final scenes of the last act of their existence as hereditary potentates, whose fulsome speeches to a relative of the King-Emperor and ritual slaying of 'big game' were loyally offered and dutifully accepted. They were invited to Burma and received with affection and respect in that proudly independent but far from stable country. In competitive hospitality the

Mountbattens were not easily to be outdone. According to Ziegler, 'during their 15 months in India they had 7,605 guests to luncheon, 8,313 to dinner, 25,287 to garden-parties and other such receptions'.[57]

But before this marathon of proconsular hospitality came to an end, Mountbatten's 'firm but conciliatory manner' towards subordinates (which naval officers were enjoined by the King's Regulations and Admiralty Instructions to adopt) was once more called into play at the highest level. With independence and the division of the armed forces in India, the post of Commander-in-Chief, India, held by Field Marshal Auchinleck, had metamorphosed into that of Supreme Commander. Despite his transparent impartiality, Auchinleck was accused by Pakistan of favouring India in his administration. Paradoxically, premature closure of the now redundant Supreme Headquarters was seen by Pakistan as evidence of Mountbatten's pro-Indian bias. Yielding to events, Auchinleck resigned, with dignity and heartening words from Mountbatten, reinforced by the recommendation that he should be offered a peerage in recognition of his distinguished career in India.

Another matter of particular importance which Mountbatten resolved, again demonstrating his impartiality, was obtaining Gandhi's help to induce the Indian government to pay Pakistan the outstanding balance of cash owing as a result of partition, withheld in view of the Kashmir crisis. This outcome, arising from the mutual regard between the apostle of non-violence and the warrior-statesman, must have contributed to the genuine grief felt by Mountbatten when, on 30 January 1948, the Mahatma was shot dead while taking a prayer meeting at his temporary home in Delhi. Mountbatten, who had been riding with his daughters that afternoon, went at once to Gandhi's house on being given the news. As he entered he heard someone shout: 'It was a Muslim who did it!' Rounding on him he thundered, 'You fool! Don't you know it was a Hindu?' At that stage Mountbatten had no idea who the assassin had been; as it turned out, he was a Hindu fanatic who felt that Gandhi had betrayed his people. Presence of mind, coupled with luck – so crucial as to have overtones of destiny about it – must have prevented yet another and even more widespread bloodbath as Hindus wreaked vengeance on Muslims, guilty by association with the supposed slayer of Gandhi.

Sensing that Nehru and his Cabinet ministers were, unsurprisingly, so shocked and stunned with emotion that they needed rallying if they were to provide the leadership so urgently needed, Mountbatten once again somewhat exceeded his constitutional obligations and persuaded Nehru and Patel to broadcast jointly that evening to the nation. It had been Gandhi's emphatic wish that when he died he was to be cremated within 24 hours, as befitted an orthodox Hindu. A crowd of hundreds of thousands assembled for his funeral. The Governor-General with his family and staff were ushered with difficulty through the throng of people to join other dignitaries at the base of the funeral pyre. Once again, with typical presence of mind, Mountbatten took charge in a perilous situation. By urging the front three or four rows to sit down, they formed a barrier, less likely to be propelled on to the funeral pyre itself and immolated. Despite this, the weight of the vast crowd began to grow threateningly. At this point Mountbatten stood up and announced, 'We must go now'; then, linking arms with his party, managed to extract them safely from the imminent danger.

In accepting the invitation to become the first Governor-General of the Indian Union, Mountbatten had intimated that he would not wish to stay beyond April 1948. But pressure on him to stay longer increased, especially after the death of Gandhi, which Nehru felt left him without a special counsellor. The compromise reached was for the Mountbattens to depart towards the end of June, after the Constituent Assembly had finished its work. The actual date, 21 June, was determined by Mountbatten's wish, out of affection for his ageing mother, to be at home for his birthday on 25 June.

The Mountbattens' last days in office were marked by both formal and informal social occasions, recalling the splendour and emotional intensity of those which had marked Independence Day. In the midst of all the tributes and the assessments, the last Viceroy of India and first Governor-General of the Indian Union found time to write down, for the benefit of Nehru, Patel and his own successor-designate, Rajagopalachari, some notes which were the equivalent of Navy 'turn-over' notes from an outgoing flag officer to his relief. In this case the guidance Mountbatten offered may not have been exactly welcome, but it was not rejected.

Wavell had not concealed from Mountbatten that he was turning over to him a poisoned chalice: 'You have been given an impossible job . . . handing over India to its people.'[58] In his celebrated Lees-Knowle lecture at Cambridge in 1939 Wavell said: 'This is the first and true function of the leader, never to think the battle or the cause lost.' Did the youthful, princely rear admiral succeed where the famous field marshal had failed? Incontestably, Mountbatten succeeded. By operating within the Attlee guidelines, under the intense pressure of events, and by a combination of empathy, dynamism and a feeling for what was possible, he created, out of incipient total anarchy among one-fifth of the world's population, two new nation states, united as members of the British Commonwealth, at peace with each other and the rest of the world.

That was the job he was given to do. Whether he, or anyone else, could have achieved this without the accompanying mayhem and hideous internecine slaughter must remain a matter for speculation.

Andrew Roberts, claiming to speak for 'a new generation of historians', avers that 'Mountbatten's reputation must ultimately stand on his record as the last Viceroy of India, and that is now ripe for revision.'[59] But his own method (for example 'Lord Mountbatten and the perils of adrenalin') owes more to political comment than to historiography. Roberts, after exhaustive research and the use of 'private information' (sources withheld), opens his innings with the description of Mountbatten as:

> a mendacious, intellectually limited hustler, whose negligence and incompetence resulted in many unnecessary deaths – the numbers of which increased exponentially as his meteoric career progressed . . . promoted wildly above his abilities, with consistently disastrous consequences.[60]

He quotes with approval Montgomery's biographer, who wrote that, as Chief of Combined Operations, Mountbatten was 'a master of intrigue, jealousy and ineptitude'; and 'another historian' as saying 'there was about almost everything Mountbatten did an element of the makeshift, the insubstantial, the incomplete and the disingenuous'. Roberts himself is a painstaking exponent of the *suppressio veri* and the *suggestio falsi*. For instance, he quotes Montgomery's diary for April 1944 as noting that 'the situation (in South-East Asia) is very poor indeed', but does not reveal that Mountbatten at that time was closely engaged in helping Slim to win the Imphal–Kohima battle which turned the tide against the Japanese; and that, as Slim later wrote:

> Admiral Mountbatten at last was able to persuade the Combined Chiefs of Staff to accept an Allied Land Forces commander with an integrated Anglo-American Headquarters, ALFSEA.[61]

Moving on to India, Roberts states what 'logic' (his logic) should have told Mountbatten to do to avoid a cataclysm, and asserts that for not doing it he 'deserved to be court-martialled on return to London'. This is a travesty even in revisionist terms – it is not history.

Roberts has tried desperately to establish that Radcliffe altered his boundary award under pressure from Mountbatten, and fails to acknowledge that aspects of it which were pre-released had not been finalised; that last-minute changes accorded with Radcliffe's terms of reference; and that he himself was a man of such integrity that he would not, under any circumstances, have made a final award which he did not judge to be scrupulously fair, taking into account all the factors in the situation.

It is curious, also, that Roberts should have chosen to quote (although without a reference) the Indian writer Nirad Chaudhuri as being astounded that Mountbatten 'has been represented as a great statesman. If generalship were judged by the same criteria, Napoleon's greatest achievement should be his ordering the Retreat from Moscow.' For Chaudhuri, writing in 1980, also said:

In 1923 three spectral hatreds were skulking on the Indian political stage: the hatred of all Hindus for British rule; the same hatred on the part of the Muslims; and the mutual hatred of the Hindus and the Muslims, which was ineradicable. . . .

It was after independence that I became fully aware of the futility of the political moves between 1921 and 1947, and since then I have firmly held the view that the best date for transferring power to the Indians, as was done in 1947, was 1921.[62]

In a final denigratory sally with regard to India, Roberts makes what is, even by his standards, the astonishing claim that:

Mountbatten had gone out to India with five specific instructions from the British government. . . . In each and every one of these objectives, which he himself had helped to draft, Mountbatten failed.[63]

Let an experienced observer of Indian politics, H.V. Hodson, have the last word:

Lord Mountbatten's Governor-Generalship of independent India must be judged as a whole. Against the criticisms that have been levied, especially in Pakistan and in some circles in Britain, must be set his salvation of Delhi when its disorders threatened to bring chaos to India, his great and successful efforts to secure fairness for Pakistan in the division of assets, his support for every endeavour to lessen the Punjab disasters, his pressure for a peaceful solution in Kashmir, his untiring work for a compromise over Hyderabad, and his persistent steering of the new, untried government of India on a steady and moderate course.[64]

For a rear admiral aged just 48, it was a shore job somewhat above and beyond the call of duty. Now he could get back to sea.

6

CRUISER ADMIRAL, BOARD MEMBER, COMMANDER-IN-CHIEF AND FIRST SEA LORD (1948–59)

I don't think the later achievements of Dickie Mountbatten should ever be underestimated, in terms of the effectiveness with which he restored the navy to its proper place in the public consciousness – and in the priorities of politicians. Not all admirals could understand, as he could, that to persuade those who don't belong to the navy, a good deal of adroitness as well as bluff conviction is required. Mountbatten taught the navy a good deal.

Lord Carrington, First Lord of the Admiralty 1959–63[1]

I was thoroughly depressed by what Mountbatten told us, though beyond blowing his own trumpet full blast he told us very little.

One lesson we learnt from each war was never to scrap any ship, particularly small ones, until their bottoms fell out – TLs [Their Lordships] seem to have got rid of them as fast as they could.

I shall be very happy when the Navy is quit of M-blinking-B.

Lord Tovey, Admiral of the Fleet[2]

It was an administrative goal to economise and if the Services did not respond with ways and means Sandys could threaten to make cuts arbitrarily. Facing this threat it was the Sea Lords who suggested reductions in the reserve fleet, logistic facilities and reserve personnel forces. By careful study and planning these steps were effected without materially reducing the strength of the operational fleet. In the same manner it was the Admiralty which most forcefully called the lessons of Suez to Sandys's attention and recommended that mobile task forces would allow withdrawal from many of the overseas bases. In fact the Admiralty played a major part in changing Sandys's mind about the importance of limited war forces.

W.J. Crowe, Jr, Commander USN (later Admiral William J. Crowe Jr)[3]

Chapter 6

Reported to Naval Secretary, First Lord and First Sea Lord and said I wished only to go where they wished to send me.

Mountbatten, Diary, *25 June 1948*

On 2 January 1946, when still serving as Supreme Commander, South-East Asia, in the acting rank of admiral, Mountbatten had been promoted to the substantive rank of rear admiral, the youngest to hold that rank since Sir David Beatty in 1910 – and he, at 39, had been the youngest flag officer since Nelson. A condition of Mountbatten's acceptance of the post of Viceroy of India had been the First Sea Lord's undertaking to offer him further employment in the Navy when he had finished his task there.

The operational strength of the Royal Navy in mid-1948 was:

Battleships	1
Fleet aircraft carriers	nil
Light fleet carriers	3
Escort carriers	nil
Cruisers	10
Destroyers	23
Submarines	26[4]

Given the worldwide deployment of this exiguous force, the First Cruiser Squadron, consisting of four modern ships, was the best command available for a junior flag officer, and to this Mountbatten was appointed.

An officer serving as a lieutenant in the flagship HMS *Newcastle* recalled:

Admiral Mountbatten quickly made his presence felt, giving lectures to one and all on 'the transfer of power in India', having the Dockyard make improvements to the 'Cuddy' (including the mounting of badges of every unit of the 14th Army) and entertaining every officer in the Squadron to lunch. We embarked an extra Admiral's Assistant Secretary to cope with his enormous correspondence, including that with Mr Attlee (as a junior Rear Admiral!). . . . The countess set up home again at the

Villa Guardamangia with two impressive Indian bearers to set the tone. The wives in Malta, including mine, though naturally apprehensive, were quickly charmed and made at home by this remarkable Lady.

Up to that time, the four cruisers in the 1st CS had never been together in Malta – there always seemed to be a crisis somewhere to which one or other cruiser was sent, but within a short time, Mountbatten had us all there and led us to sea for spectacular 'Grid Iron' manoeuvres at high speed, gunnery and torpedo firings and Landing Party exercises in St Paul's Bay.

But the incident that stands out most in my memory occurred on the following Christmas Day. Mountbatten insisted that the Countess should accompany him on Christmas Rounds of the Messdecks. Whereupon our good Captain Stuart Paton said the Officers' wives might also accompany their husbands and off we all went. *Newcastle* was a very happy ship, the Messdecks were all decorated and the Lower Deck turned on the charm (plus much 'Sippers') as only they know how. It was a splendid occasion.[5]

Another aspect of Mountbatten's leadership was recorded by a naval chaplain who served with him at this time:

I had several long talks with him about churchgoing and the Church. . . . He felt that the abolition of compulsory church was a bad thing for the Navy and for a ship. He said that a whole Ship's Company at worship did something for them all and for the individuals. He was a great Church of England man and thought that the Established church was a tremendous asset to the whole nation.

. . . we anchored and remained (at Rhodes) for a few days. Countess Mountbatten and Lady Pamela had flown from Malta and they joined the Admiral for church. . . . Also present for this Service were the Consul's party and most of the English community.

This Service, which was to be quite remarkable, was held in perfect weather on the quarter deck. . . . The Royal Marines band were playing their voluntaries long before the Service commenced and, with their fine rendering of some well-known hymns, we were off to a good start. The Lesson read by the Captain described St Paul's voyage along this very coast. There was a great stillness during the Captain's reading of this Lesson, during prayers and during my sermon. The whole congregation seemed to be strangely moved and uplifted.[6]

The Commander-in-Chief, Mediterranean, at this time was Admiral Sir Arthur Power who, as C-in-C of the East Indies Fleet from November 1944 had been subordinate to Mountbatten, then Supreme Allied Commander, South-East Asia. Thanks to the qualities of both officers, the reversal of roles caused no friction, while the presence of HRH the Duke of Edinburgh in command of the frigate *Magpie* and his young wife, Princess Elizabeth, lent a special cachet to this naval epoch. It was, in retrospect, the golden evening of an association between Malta and the Royal Navy that had flourished since Nelson liberated the island from Napoleon.

In the spring of 1949 enough forces were available to justify a resumption of the customary Combined Fleet Exercises of the Home and Mediterranean Fleets. A midshipman in the Royal Canadian Navy, who was serving in the light fleet carrier HMS *Theseus*, in the BLUE force, recorded in his journal that Mountbatten, commanding RED, an inferior but faster force, outwitted BLUE by infiltrating 'agents' into BLUE's headquarters at Gibraltar, and disguising some of his destroyers as cruisers[7] – the sort of measures used in wartime which flag officers and their staffs should be trained to expect, but regarded by discomfited senior officers in peacetime as 'not quite cricket'.

The context of the 1949 combined fleet exercises was recognition of a new threat to the sea communications of the British Empire: that posed by the Soviet navy and air force as instruments of a Stalinist superstate bent upon world domination. A treaty of the utmost significance had already been drafted, and was about to be signed, whereby the American and British navies would find themselves the closest of allies rather than rivals:

On April 4, as Churchill was returning to Britain on board the *Queen Mary*, Ernest Bevin, in Washington, signed the North Atlantic Treaty. By this treaty, the United States and Canada joined with eight European countries in a defence organisation, the North Atlantic Treaty Organisation, soon to be known by its initials, NATO. Two days after the treaty was signed, Truman, in an informal talk to recently elected Members of Congress, said that he would 'not hesitate' to order the use of the atomic bomb if it were necessary for the welfare of the United States and if the fate of the democracies of the world were at stake. He added that he hoped and prayed it would never be necessary to do so; he considered that the signing of the North Atlantic Treaty would prevent the United States from having to make such a decision.[8]

In April 1950 Mountbatten, who had been promoted to vice-admiral in the previous June, became second in command of the Mediterranean Fleet, a post that had once been held by his father; but it was not to be for long. In May his term in command of the First Cruiser Squadron came to an end, and he left Malta to take up a new appointment as a member of the Board of Admiralty, known collectively in the Navy as Their Lordships, or TLs for short. The particular post which fell to Mountbatten was that of Fourth Sea Lord, with responsibility for the supply of naval stores of all kinds, from seamen's clothing to oil fuel. Typically, he soon found that there was an enormous amount to be done to eliminate waste arising from the post-war run down of the service; and, sensitive as always to the needs of the sailors, on discovering that service pay had not been reviewed since just after the war, he ensured that this was done and pressed for such a review to be carried out every two years. Aware, also, that few officers now had private means, he ensured that their pay was increased appropriately.

Mountbatten was determined not to prejudice his chances of going to the top of his profession by overplaying his hand. Over one matter, however, he felt strongly enough to take the initiative without informing even the First Sea Lord, namely the threat to the Navy's supply of oil fuel posed by the determination of Dr Mossadeq, leader of a radical government in Iran, to nationalise the Anglo-Iranian Oil Company. The handling of this crisis reflected little credit on successive British governments. The general election in October 1951 substituted a Conservative administration, headed by the ageing Winston Churchill, for a Labour government brought down by the conflicting financial demands of the National Health Service and rearmament arising from the Korean War. Neither the First Lord of the Admiralty, Labour's Lord Hall, nor his Conservative successor, Jim Thomas, could bring the Cabinet round to Mountbatten's way of thinking, clearly expressed both in writing and verbally, that to make empty (as they would be) military gestures in a vain effort to bolster prestige was futile. A better policy would be to surrender British national ownership in return for indirect control of the assets and a commercially determined stake in the enterprise – half a barrel would, in effect, be better than no oil.

This recognition of the necessity to accommodate the aspirations of nationalist, ethnic and religious forces in the post-war world, thus gaining advantage in the global confrontation with Soviet imperialism, brought upon Mountbatten's head the vituperation of social and political opinion-formers in western Europe and the USA. He himself recorded having advanced such views when dining with Churchill on board the *Queen Mary* at Southampton on New Year's Eve 1951, and being snubbed (though not sufficiently, according to Ismay) for his pains.[9] He believed that as a public servant he was equally responsible to whichever party was in power for advice on matters of prime concern to the nation, and particularly those of international relations, war and peace. It was a stance born of his inherited respect for the role of constitutional monarchy, sustained by his royal forebears Prince Albert and Queen Victoria, which located the sovereign above and outside politics, as head of state paramount over his or her subjects, yet in the last resort accountable to and even dismissable by them.

Having wrestled successfully as Fourth Sea Lord with what Sir John Lang, Permanent Secretary of the Admiralty and the Samuel Pepys of the day, termed 'the nuts and bolts' of the Royal Navy, Mountbatten was now professionally qualified to command one of the main fleets. Timing, as much as anything, seems to have determined his appointment in May 1952 to relieve Admiral Sir John Edelsten as Commander-in-Chief, Mediterranean, once again in the rank of acting admiral. It was the perfect opportunity, away from the political pressures and inter-service rivalry of Whitehall, to hold this command of Britain's finest fleet in historic waters; to reassert, while it was still practicable, the Navy's unique capacity to support British diplomacy; to make himself known to a new generation of young officers and men; and to build up their morale and efficiency by good administration, providing a well-balanced annual programme of weapons training, tactical exercises, cruises with foreign port visits, competitive games and sport.

Vice-Admiral Sir Hector MacLean, who as a captain commanded the Third Destroyer Squadron at the time, remembered visits paid by Mountbatten to his destroyers. In each case a more or less standard speech was embellished by topical and ship-specific references based on preliminary research by an officer on the commander-in-chief's staff. The effect upon the morale of the fleet was good. But Mountbatten was capable also of insisting on a high standard of discipline, behaviour and efficiency. Admiral MacLean recalled an occasion when, in the course of the fleet regatta at Navarino (now Pilos, in southern Greece), many of the sailors went over the side for a swim without the usual safety precautions being taken. The commanding officers present were required by Mountbatten to assemble on board the flagship next morning and received an extremely stern rebuke.[10]

Scuba-diving and spear-fishing, at which Mountbatten soon excelled, competed with polo as his main recreation, and these occupations filled in whatever spare time he had between visits to foreign dignitaries and heads of state, including the King and Queen of Greece, President Nasser of Egypt, Marshal Tito of Yugoslavia, and the Emperor Haile Selassie of Ethiopia. In his conversations, which he was meticulous in reporting to the British ambassador concerned, he did sometimes stray into the realms of British policy, jealously guarded by the Foreign Office as its preserve. But it was with his own head of government, Winston Churchill, that he held the longest and most intimate exchange of views. The fleet flagship, HMS *Glasgow*, was on a visit to Villefranche, where the Prime Minister was enjoying a painting holiday at Lord Beaverbrook's villa:

> Churchill at once invited the Mountbattens to dine at La Capponcina. After the women had left the table, Churchill and Mountbatten remained alone. 'With tears in his eyes,' Mountbatten wrote to his daughter, 'he kept repeating how much he loved me, that he had quite forgotten and forgiven me about India, that I had had a wonderful career and was on the threshold of an even finer career, the country needed me, etc. Quite embarrassing.'[11]

The main lines of British defence policy for the 1950s had been set out by the Chiefs of Staff in a paper they produced at Churchill's instigation early in 1952. First in priority was to counter Soviet aggression, and for this reliance would be placed principally upon the nuclear deterrent provided by the USA, backed up by Britain's own nuclear force. NATO would provide the command structure and conventional military forces in the European theatre necessary, as Lord Ismay, its first Secretary-General, is said (perhaps apocryphally) to have remarked: 'to keep the Americans in, the Russians out and the Germans down'.[12]

Outside the NATO area Britain's imperial and Commonwealth commitments, still extensive despite the independence of India and Pakistan and the loss of Ceylon and Burma, would call for countermeasures to the threat of Communist subversion and the growing power of 'Red' China. At this stage the atom bomb was regarded, in strategic terms, as 'usable'. If deterrence were to fail, therefore, a nuclear exchange would quickly decide the outcome, a NATO 'victory' being assured, owing to the advent of tactical nuclear weapons to compensate for the huge margin of superiority in conventional land and air forces deployed by the Soviet Union in the west.

The scenario envisaged deprived the Navy of a major role upon which to predicate its size and shape, and hence the appropriate allocation of resources to it. The best the Sea Lords could do was insist that provision be made for 'broken-backed' warfare, which might well continue after the nuclear exchanges had devastated the participants without breaking the enemy's will and capacity to fight. Churchill, having berated Mountbatten for daring to suggest that Britain should not place her destiny entirely in the hands of the Americans, a few days later 'attacked with heat' NATO's decision to give the command of the Atlantic to an American:

Turning to naval matters, Churchill 'declared', as the American note of the discussion recorded, 'that he was not convinced of the need for a Supreme Commander in the Atlantic. He had lived through two world wars without any such arrangement. He insisted that he was not speaking lightly for, indeed, the Atlantic supply line was of vital importance to the UK and if naval affairs in the Atlantic were mismanaged, the UK "would die".' This was 'not true' in the case of the United States, Churchill added, 'which later would still be in a position to land its armies in Europe'.

Churchill then asked the first Sea Lord, Sir Rhoderick McGrigor, to present the case for a British naval commander for the Atlantic. There followed what Colville recalled as 'an embarrassing incident', as the Admiral 'went red in the face, large drops of perspiration appeared on his brow and he was too overawed to do more than stutter a few disjointed words'.[13] At that moment, Field Marshal Slim 'stepped into the breach and presented the naval case coolly and calmly. It was a magnificent tour de force by the representative of another service.' The Americans did not agree, however, to the British proposal; three months later, when the Atlantic Command was formally set up it was under an American Admiral, Lyndon McCormick.[14]

Admiral McGrigor, albeit better briefed, was equally unsuccessful when he went to Washington in November 1952 to argue for the Allied naval forces in the Mediterranean to be commanded by a British officer, responsible direct to the Supreme Allied Commander, Europe. But the American Sixth Fleet, based in Naples, included a carrier strike force equipped with nuclear-armed aircraft, which in all circumstances would remain under US command and control even if the responsible admiral, an American, was also the NATO Commander-in-Chief, South. It was decided to set up Allied Forces, Mediterranean, with operational headquarters at Malta, commanded by the British Commander-in-Chief, Mediterranean, with the NATO title CINCAFMED.

Mountbatten was promoted to admiral on 27 January 1953, in time for the main naval event of that year, the Coronation Review of the Fleet at Spithead by the Queen on 15 June. Royal Navy ships present numbered over 200, drawn from the Home, Mediterranean and Reserve Fleets and Home Commands, with representatives of the navies of Australia, Canada, Ceylon, India, New Zealand and Pakistan. There were also present warships from 16 foreign countries, Royal Fleet Auxiliaries, and ships of the British Merchant Navy and fishing fleets.

Given that the post of First Sea Lord would become vacant towards the end of 1954 it was not too soon, when the Navy's elder statesmen foregathered at the Coronation Review, for the names of possible successors to be canvassed. The word went round that old Winston, having forgiven Mountbatten for bringing independence to India, had once again cooled towards him. Among the Admirals of the Fleet Lord Cunningham said, 'Dickie has great gifts but he lacks judgement. It would never do',[15] and Lord Tovey was even less supportive.

In the meantime Mountbatten was busy creating a harmonious and effective NATO maritime force in the Mediterranean, using his by now well-known tact and energy, and he provided the naval resources which searched for, found and recovered the wreckage of a Comet airliner which crashed into the sea near Elba. As a result, the reason for the loss of the aircraft was discovered, enabling a design change, crucial for safety, to be made.

Mindful always of the morale factor, Mountbatten decided that the Mediterranean Fleet should have its own broadcasting service. Reception of the general BBC Overseas Service was poor in the ships, and their receiving sets were not suitable in any case. Perhaps not entirely by accident, the fleet electrical officer was the brilliant J.D.M. ('Dafty') Robinson (later Captain J.D.M. Robinson), whose technical skill and ingenuity back in 1932 had, at Mountbatten's instigation, enabled the late King George V's Christmas message to the Empire to be broadcast to the fleet. Once again, this time with the wholehearted cooperation of Rediffusion Malta, recently set up, a remarkable success was achieved. Before long the Mediterranean Fleet Broadcasting Service (MFBS), managed by Bill Lapper, an assistant secretary detailed for the task, was in operation. As he recalled:

Soon we were getting letters and postcards from all over the world, with requests for the Fleet. . . . We soon began to realise that our music programmes were too stuffy. The 'Top Twenty' was what was wanted. . . . We became more ambitious, with Outside Broadcasts – I think our greatest technical achievement was the broadcasting of a running commentary from 500 miles away from Malta, retransmitted by Rediffusion and VHF, when the Fleet met the Queen on her return from the Commonwealth Tour.[16]

The royal yacht *Britannia*, on her maiden voyage, embarked the Queen and the Duke of Edinburgh at Tobruk on 1 May 1954. Mountbatten took his fleet to meet the *Britannia* and carried out a majestic manoeuvre at high speed, taking his ships breathtakingly close past the royal yacht, to the immense delight of the Queen and Admiral of the Fleet, the Duke of Edinburgh. The ship-handling, even after several rehearsals, tested the nerve of those in command, but the demonstration of their skill was good for the morale of their ships' companies, as well as those of the Navy's shore establishments, and gladdened the people of Malta. As Lapper recorded:

I played the tape of the broadcast of the Fleet meeting the Queen to both Lord and Lady Louis in the Drawing Room at Admiralty House shortly after the occasion was over. Both had their boxes beside them, Lady Louis curled up in a chair. It was, in spite of all the gossip about the past, a picture of perfect domesticity.[17]

Meanwhile, back in Whitehall and the London clubs, opinion began to crystallise in favour of Mountbatten as First Sea Lord in succession to Sir Rhoderick McGrigor. By now Edwina, secure in her new identity as an energetic, wise and compassionate administrator, had ceased to be jealous and scornful of her husband's naval successes, and wrote to Ismay:

It would be heartbreaking if Dickie's remarkable personality and outstanding ability was to be wasted in these next *vital* years in a back yard.[18]

But there can be little doubt of the decisive intervention, as far as professional opinion was concerned, of Rear Admiral Manley Power, who had earned Sir Andrew Cunningham's fullest confidence in the war and now got him to accept the fact that only Mountbatten could save the Navy from being sunk by the combined forces of the RAF and the Army, supported by worried politicians conscious of Britain's critically strained economy.

On 15 September 1954 McGrigor wrote to Mountbatten:

I want you to come here with your drive and powers of persuasion, experience and influence, to keep the Navy on its feet in the nuclear age, to give it a new look where necessary, and to keep up the confidence of the Service. I am sure you are the best man to do it, and it is essential for the good of the Navy and the Country that you should relieve me.[19]

Even then, the Prime Minister's consent had to be obtained and Churchill, somewhat maliciously exercising the power of which retirement was about to deprive him, vacillated. As a consequence, which may in the end have been intentional, it was not until Trafalgar Day, 21 October 1954, that Mountbatten received the intimation that HM the Queen had graciously approved his appointment as First Sea Lord.

When the day came, on 10 December, for Mountbatten to haul down his flag as Commander-in-Chief, Mediterranean, he relinquished also the post of CINCAFMED. Fittingly, the traditional galley's crew of senior officers to pull him away from his flagship was composed on this occasion of six admirals, each representing one of the nations whose forces had been under his command. There were, of course, numerous farewell receptions and parties; the Army and the RAF as well as the Royal Navy and the Royal Marines paraded guards and bands; the Malta breakwaters were crowded with cheering people; and at sea HMS *Surprise*, with Mountbatten embarked, was saluted by the fleet. But all this would have been accorded, although perhaps with less vibrant enthusiasm, to any departing C-in-C in the past. Captain Lapper recalls the unique Mountbatten touch:

> When he left the Mediterranean Fleet, he broadcast a farewell message live from the studio. When he had finished, I played the Sargent arrangement of 'Rule Britannia'. He and I were alone in the studio. Remembering all the great matters with which he had been concerned, I was much moved and I think he was too.[20]

On 18 April 1955 Louis Mountbatten, now Admiral the Earl of Burma, assumed the chair in the Admiralty which his father had occupied as First Sea Lord in 1912. Like him, he was master of his profession. But the Royal Navy was no longer the greatest in the world; nor was it in good shape. In a letter to his son-in-law, a few months before, Mountbatten had written:

> I hope the mess will have reached its nadir before I take over – as in Combined Ops, SEAC and India – then one has that comforting feeling that it can't get worse.[21]

At least his colleagues on the Board, still known collectively as TLs, were a strong group. The naval members had virtually selected themselves for promotion by outstanding service in the Second World War. Most were experienced staff officers as well as commanders, though few had passed the naval staff course, a qualification still held by many senior officers to be superfluous. But, especially given membership of NATO, war plans could no longer be neglected or, as in old Fisher's day, be kept in the First Sea Lord's head; and there was a need to articulate effectively, in the Chiefs of Staff Committee, the naval aspects of defence policy.

Because the Admiralty, unlike the War Office and the Air Ministry, acted as an operational authority, the advent of a new First Sea Lord seldom went unnoticed by the naval staff or in the fleet. But in Whitehall leadership of a special kind was needed, and this was what Mountbatten could provide. Vice-Admiral Sir Hector MacLean, who had been Director of Plans under Mountbatten's predecessor, remembered that whereas McGrigor had on at least one occasion failed to make any comment whatsoever at a meeting of the Chiefs of Staff, and in general seemed to be somewhat ineffective in maintaining the Navy's position, Mountbatten spoke confidently when required; but the fears of the other Chiefs that he would ride roughshod over them were not justified in the event.[22]

Following his practice when assuming a new command, whether an ancient destroyer or the Mediterranean Fleet, Mountbatten lost no time in making himself known to his subordinates and getting to know them. For Commander La Neice (later Rear Admiral Peter La Neice) the most memorable event of 1955 was Mountbatten's appointment:

> Not only was his presence immediately felt but he actually came round and met every single member of the Naval Staff. He then went to Bath to meet the Technical departments; this caused concern with one Engineer Officer who had been there so long working in civilian clothes that he was unable to find his uniform! One of Mountbatten's calls at Bath was on the Ship Design section, with whom I had been working closely. He asked to see the latest designs and was shown the gun-armed ships. 'What about the guided missile ships?' he asked. To most people in Bath at that time this was close to heresy; however, to his undying credit the Chief Constructor concerned calmly produced from his desk a sketch design of a guided missile destroyer which he had completed 'privately'. There and then the design was approved in principle. No further argument; our long battle with Bath was over.[23]

For too long, it appears, 'the trumpet' had been giving 'an uncertain sound'. No more. The new First Sea Lord had already visualised, while Commander-in-Chief, Mediterranean, a new model Navy which would give the British taxpayer the best value for money in the coming decades. Constantly in touch with key people in Britain, the Commonwealth and the USA, plus his additional contacts made as a major NATO commander, Mountbatten was seized of the cardinal factors affecting British defence policy in general, and the part that the Navy should play in it.

Against the background of superpower confrontation, and the containment of Asian Communist expansion in Korea, the British Empire was dismantling itself in much the same absent-minded manner in which it had been created. The Commonwealth of autonomous states united by the Crown was, however, growing as former colonies achieved independence and their security remained a British concern. American policy, rooted in anti-colonial sentiment, and prior to apprehending the threat of Sino-Soviet Communist expansion, had been to accept as inevitable, even desirable, the collapse of British power. By 1955, however, US government initiatives had brought into being the CENTO and SEATO pacts, aimed at extending the NATO security cordon across the southern borders of the Soviet Union and China. Now American policy sought to strengthen, rather than weaken, British power east of Suez.

Unfortunately, Britain's economy could no longer sustain the scale of defence expenditure arising from the Brussels Treaty commitment to keep the equivalent of four divisions and a tactical air force on the continent, while maintaining a strategic nuclear deterrent plus an adequate naval force in the Atlantic, and a post-imperial defence capability. As Phillip Darby pointed out:

> The root problem lay in the weakness of political thinking about the ends of policy and about Britain's position in the post-war world. So long as imperial considerations retained their hold on the official mind, there was a sufficient sense of purpose and direction to obscure the need for fundamental questioning.[24]

Mountbatten had the advantage over his predecessor as First Sea Lord and Chief of the Naval Staff of having experienced at first hand, and held responsibility for, management of the various components of national power – political, military and economic – in the post-war rehabilitation of South-East Asia; and as the last Viceroy had assisted at the emergence of two new nation states. His second advantage derived from his experience of, and responsibility for, the use in war of land, sea and air forces in combination, both as Chief of Combined Operations and as Supreme Commander, South-East Asia. A third advantage was a capacity to understand and apply technical innovation. Perhaps the greatest advantage he enjoyed, however, at this particular juncture, was being able, during three months' leave prior to taking up his appointment, to 'prepare himself for the battle'.

What he was to be up against, both as First Sea Lord concerned specifically with the Navy, and as Chief of Naval Staff corporately responsible with the other Chiefs of Staff for defence policy as a whole, was foreshadowed in the Prime Minister's personal guidelines to Selwyn Lloyd, his Minister for Defence:

> The main threat to our position and influence in the world is now political and economic rather than military. . . . Effort must now be transferred from military preparations to the maintenance and improvement of our political and economic position.[25]

Some key figures illustrate the effect of this edict upon the allocation of resources for defence:

Year	UK defence expenditure as percentage of gross national product (GNP)	Manpower in services (000s)
During Sir Rhoderick McGrigor's term as First Sea Lord		
1952	9.8	872.0
1954	9.2	838.9
During Mountbatten's term as First Sea Lord		
1955	7.9	802.9
1958	6.7	615.0
During Mountbatten's term as Chief of Defence Staff		
1959	6.4	566.1
1964	5.9	422.8[26]

Although the Navy, like the RAF, is capital-intensive, whereas the Army is relatively labour-intensive, it was shortage of manpower which presented Mountbatten with the most immediate problem when he took office. Nowadays it is an effort to recall that in the mid-1950s there was full employment in the civil economy – more jobs than people to fill them, in fact. So recruitment to the armed forces was inadequate, and in the Navy far too few ratings were re-engaging for further service. The naval staff had already begun to grapple with this adverse trend as an element in the 'Way Ahead' studies of major policy reforms initiated by the Director of Plans, Captain Hector MacLean; although, as he pointed out, 'Mountbatten invariably took the credit for any successful and important initiative in policy, even though an idea may have originated with a member of his Staff.'[27] Maybe so. But it is the top man who must determine the priority to be accorded to competing initiatives, and provide the drive to get things done; and the more effective the top man is perceived to be by the governing elites, the greater his capacity to get results – nothing succeeds like success.

At least Captain MacLean and his colleagues had the satisfaction of seeing their ideas given powerful impetus by the incoming First Sea Lord, with the indispensable support of the formidable Permanent Secretary, Sir John Lang. This unsmiling, omnicompetent administrator, who had served in the ranks of the Royal Marines and made his way almost to the top of the Civil Service, was apt to assume an air of authority over what he termed the 'uniformed branch' of the Navy which irritated its people. However, during Mountbatten's term as Fourth Sea Lord Lang formed a high opinion of his capacity, which bore fruit in his agreement that the 'Way Ahead' Committee to enquire into 'The Structure and Supporting Organisation of the Naval Service' should consist of the Naval Lords and himself only, the political members of the Board of Admiralty being excluded. This was a significant innovation, designed to expedite business, which it certainly did.

On 20 June 1955 the first meeting of the 'Way Ahead' Committee was convened. An executive working party chaired by the Assistant Chief of Naval Staff was set up to work direct to the First Sea Lord, forming subcommittees as required. Rear Admiral La Neice remembers being co-opted:

> One evening when I was working late I was summoned, as the only member of the Division remaining, to a high-level meeting where, at a stroke, we abolished a large proportion of the more obsolete ships of the Reserve Fleet.[28]

During the next couple of years, by such drastic but well-considered measures, the infrastructure of the Navy was brought into line with the shape and size of the active fleet so that it could be as powerful, balanced, and flexible as manpower and money permitted.

As yet, the central organisation for defence had not evolved from the shape it was given in 1946. The three service ministries existed independently, each dedicated solely to the well-being of the service which it administered, with its own minister as political head and its own links with the Treasury, Foreign Office, arms and equipment firms, and on occasion with 10 Downing Street. Inter-service competition for the largest possible share of the diminishing defence vote was fierce. But there were ground rules, formulated by the Chiefs of Staff in conclave, then submitted for approval through the Minister of Defence to the Defence Committee of the Cabinet, over which the Prime Minister presided. These 'rules', in 1955, took the form not of specific British interests to be defended and the grand strategy to be adopted, but of the priority to be accorded to the four roles envisaged for the armed forces:

> Contributing to the Allied capability to deter attack by nuclear weapons.
> Prosecuting the Cold War.
> Engaging in Limited War.
> Fighting in Global War if nuclear deterrence should fail to prevent it.[29]

Given that the nuclear deterrent was at that time provided by the RAF's V-bomber force, to be superseded in due course by a land-based strategic missile, Blue Streak; and that the Army was committed to major deployment in western Europe with the battle-tank as its main armament; it followed that the Navy would have primary responsibility in regard to both Cold War and limited war, as well as an alliance commitment in global war. These considerations, plus the advent of rocket-propelled guided missiles and nuclear-powered submarines, governed the shape and size of the fleet being planned by the naval staff at this time, for which Mountbatten had to obtain the necessary backing from his fellow Chiefs of Staff, the Minister of Defence, and ultimately the Cabinet. This was an arduous and continuing process.

Having enthused the naval staff and set the Admiralty machine as a whole moving at its best speed in the same direction, Mountbatten began to build upon his personal acquaintance with political and military, mainly naval, leaders throughout the Commonwealth and in the USA. He was aware that on 17 January 1955 the submarine USS *Nautilus* had made the historic signal 'Underway on nuclear power'. So, following a hectic visit to Canada ('with barely time to pee, let alone wash my hands', for which he blamed his own 'lack of adequate supervision'), he visited the USA to call on the Chief of Naval Operations, Admiral Arleigh Burke, renowned in the service as 'Thirty-one Knot' Burke.

On 20 June that year Congress had ratified the US/UK Military Atomic Co-operation Agreement, which stated, *inter alia*, that 'the USA may exchange with the UK such atomic information as the USA considers necessary for the development of the UK's defence plans'. It remained to be seen how, and by whom, the discretion as to what was disclosed would be exercised.

At this point the dominating personality of Admiral Hyman Rickover, USN, emerged to 'call the shots'. Captain J.O. Coote, RN, who was serving in Washington at the time as submarine specialist on the British Joint Services Mission, recorded:

My contribution to the First Sea Lord's (proposed) trip (in the first nuclear-powered submarine) was to prepare him for a meeting with Admiral Hyman Rickover. It seemed to me like briefing a Romanov to meet Rasputin.

. . . despite a frustrating and friendless naval career, towards the end of it Rickover had emerged as the single-minded, single-handed progenitor of the nuclear-powered submarine. . . . The USN Submarine Force freely admits that, but for him, *Nautilus* would not be at sea today.[30]

It was almost certainly owing to Rickover's intervention behind the scenes that, to the evident embarrassment of Arleigh Burke, on the day when Mountbatten was to have embarked in the *Nautilus*, the trip was cancelled. In Mountbatten's words:

On 4 November 1955 I was flown to Key West from Washington in order to go to sea in the first submarine designed hydrodynamically for high speed when fully submerged, USS *Albacore* (owing to nuclear security restrictions still in force I could not then be embarked in the nuclear-powered USS *Nautilus*). On return to harbour, Admiral Burke telephoned his office in Washington. He then drove me to the airfield for my return flight and during the journey expressed great indignation. He said that he wished to be friends with the US Air Force and had offered to go shares in their new IRBM, *Thor*, if they would change the fuel from liquid to solid, so that it could be fired from submerged submarines. They had categorically refused. He had then and there given the order to start work at once on a solid fuel IRBM to be mounted in a new class of large nuclear submarine.

I said 'Since the USAF does not support you, would you accept support from the RN?' I then offered to send a hand-picked RN officer, with missile experience, to join his special team. He accepted, and thereafter the First Sea Lord had his own representative in the Polaris project. This stood us in very good stead when we obtained help over our own Polaris submarines at the Nassau Conference between President Kennedy and Prime Minister Macmillan.[31]

Shortly thereafter Mountbatten initiated a personal correspondence with the American Chief of Naval Operations, whose letters, circulated only to members of the Admiralty Board, senior members of the Secretariat, the Director of Plans, and the Deputy Controller (R&D), were known as the 'Dear Dickie' file. In due course this 'private line' proved to be of inestimable value in expediting the procurement of nuclear-powered submarines for the Royal Navy; and in the initiation and timely completion of the British Polaris project when circumstances dictated that it should form the follow-on British contribution to the west's strategic nuclear deterrent.

In June 1956 the US government agreed 'to give the British data on the Nuclear submarine *Nautilus*, including information on nuclear propulsion reactors'.[32] The Flag Officer, Submarines, had since 1955 been advising the Board of Admiralty 'as forcibly as protocol permitted' that future submarines must be nuclear-powered.[33]

In 1956, therefore, work was begun on Britain's first nuclear-powered submarine, to be named HMS *Dreadnought*. A *Dreadnought* Project Team (DPT) was formed, at Mountbatten's instigation, to design and build a submarine very similar to USS *Skipjack*, the first operational boat to combine the *Albacore* shape with nuclear propulsion. The *Dreadnought* was to be powered with a British-designed and built reactor plant; to lead the DPT Mountbatten chose a senior member of the Royal Corps of Naval Constructors, Mr (later Sir) Rowland Baker, who had first come to his notice when he was Chief of Combined Operations as the dynamic designer and builder of landing craft.

No provision had been made in the relevant naval estimates for significant expenditure on a nuclear submarine project. In a typical coup, which Mountbatten delighted in describing, he produced, at a Defence Committee Meeting when this item was on the agenda, a model of the *Dreadnought* which could be taken apart to reveal its revolutionary features. The Chancellor of the Exchequer, Derick Heathcoat-Amory, whom he knew to be a naval officer *manqué*, was duly intrigued, and when called to order by the Prime Minister merely asked 'How much do you need, First Sea Lord?' On being told 'Twenty-five million', he affirmed that he would find the money somehow.[34]

While still Commander-in-Chief, Mediterranean, Mountbatten, with the Cs-in-C of the other fleets and stations, had been brought into the deliberations of the Mansergh Committee on the future structure of the Navy's officer corps. The author recalls being questioned by him one day on how seaman officers could be provided with a satisfactory career when a much reduced fleet would offer correspondingly fewer sea jobs – the opportunities to gain seagoing experience would be limited, and to command ships and submarines even more so. It had been recognised, also, that the Board's decision in 1925 to deprive engineer officers of executive status had been a profound error, mitigated only by the loyalty to the service and integrity of the officers concerned. This was to be redressed.

The outcome of the Mansergh Committee's recommendation was promulgated in a message signed by the entire Board, designated Admiralty Fleet Order (AFO) 1/56. Executive status was restored to engineer and supply officers but, in the rank of commander and above, eligibility for operational command and staff duties was to be restricted to a number of officers, determined in relation to the size and shape of the fleet. These would be selected for promotion to a 'Post List', reviving the notion of the post-captains of Nelson's day. The remainder of the full-career officers were to form a 'General List' with good career prospects, not excluding promotion to flag rank. But selection for the Post List on promotion from commander to captain was to be, on average, at an earlier age, conferring a corresponding career advantage.

As might have been expected, the two lists were immediately dubbed 'Wet' and 'Dry' respectively, and much discontent was evinced among the seaman officers affected by the new ruling. Many fine officers, whose seamanship and operational aptitude had been demonstrated, were desolated to find themselves, on promotion, condemned to desk jobs; and of these a goodly number accepted early retirement with a gratuity in compensation – a 'golden bowler'. A decade or so later it proved practicable to abolish the 'Wet' and 'Dry' lists in favour of selective appointing and individual career management. But the whole episode was badly handled, for which Mountbatten must be held ultimately responsible.

Early in 1956 Mountbatten devoted himself to explaining naval policy – the 'Way Ahead', the ships, submarines and naval aircraft of the future, the conditions of service – to the fleet at home, in the Mediterranean, the East Indies and the Far East; and he visited Australia, New Zealand, India, Pakistan, Burma, Ceylon and Singapore, taking in the Monte Bello Islands, where preparations were being made to test the H-bomb. His theme in every country was that, if war came, the survival of the British Commonwealth in its present form would depend upon the strength of the Navy.

The advent of the thermo-nuclear weapon had not changed the need for navies or their primary role. Russia, with the world's second most powerful navy and the greatest submarine fleet ever, had accelerated shipbuilding in recent years. Clearly Russia had recognised that if war came, massive land and air forces and the thermo-nuclear bomb would not be enough: she would also have to be able to dispute the command of the seas. 'A potential enemy' would certainly try to starve the UK and disrupt the British Commonwealth's sea lanes after the exchange of thermo-nuclear bombs had petered out. For what other purpose would 'a potential enemy' build so vast a fleet? The terrific strength of 'a potential enemy' could bring us to our knees after the initial phase if our navies were not ready to meet the threat.

These generalised warnings were augmented according to circumstances. In Canberra, for example, Mountbatten pointed out that 20 million tons of freight entered and left Australia annually by sea. The equivalent freight moved by air amounted to 2,000 tons, or one ten-thousandth of that moved by sea. A successful submarine blockade backed by naval surface and maritime air action could thus have disastrous effects on the course of the war after the first week or two unless the convoys could be adequately protected. Australia could neither help in the general defence of the British Commonwealth nor look after her own sea defence sufficiently far forward unless she could send and support forces by sea. Carrier-borne aircraft would have a vital part to play in the war at sea. The aircraft carrier was virtually a mobile airfield, which would certainly escape damage by being at sea during the period of the nuclear bombings. Thereafter it would provide the airfield wherever it was wanted, and, in the case of Australia, that would mean forward away from the coasts.

It would be a mistake to believe that Mountbatten was addressing only his immediate audience. He was sure that his words would be reported in the British press (they were) and help to mobilise public and parliamentary opinion in support of the Navy in the coming battle for resources. He was acutely aware that the Prime Minister, Anthony Eden, was determined to cut defence spending drastically as soon as he could and, moreover, that in his view the Navy was now the least important of the services.

While Mountbatten was on his Commonwealth tour, events in the Middle East were moving towards a crisis. On 1 March 1956 King Hussein of Jordan dismissed at 24-hours' notice General Glubb, who had served in Jordan since 1931, commanded its army, the Arab Legion, since 1939, and become Hussein's Chief of General Staff. It is enlightening to review the situation as seen by the under-secretary in the Foreign Office directly responsible for Middle East policy, Mr (later Sir Evelyn) Shuckburgh, as recorded at the time:

1 March

There was very little work today, and after lunch with Sir Norman Kipping, head of the FBI et al. . . . I was preparing to go off early. . . . Michael came in with a telegram saying that King Hussein has sacked General Glubb. . . .[35]

2 March

The Glubb crisis occupied everybody's time all day. I had to go nevertheless to the Chiefs of Staff, to talk about Israel, the impossibility of going to war with the Arabs if they aggress, and the question of re-disposing our forces so as to get round what they call the 'air barrier'. . . . Mountbatten and the new CAS – Air Chief Marshal Sir Dermot Boyle – pressed me to produce a statement showing 'our policy in the ME' which they both professed to think must be stateable. . . . When I told Kirkpatrick this he gave me a quotation from Palmerston to use next time this happens: 'When people ask one what is one's policy, the only answer is that we mean to do what may seem to be best upon each occasion as it arises, making the interests of one's country the guiding principle.'

13 March

The King of Jordan is to meet the King of Iraq and has refused to go and see Nasser in Cairo. But we are working ourselves up against Nasser and deciding the time has come to overthrow him (if we can) or isolate him. Unfortunately the PM has refused with violence and indignation to look at the paper which Nutting sent him last night, outlining a long-term policy for dealing with the Tripartite Declaration, Palestine, Baghdad Pact, etc., and weaning Saud from Nasser. He cannot bear long-term thoughts. . . .[36]

15 March

We have now got to a state where each telegram that comes in causes Ministers to meet, telephone one another, draft replies and curse everybody. Not only does each of our telegrams contradict the one before, but each paragraph in each telegram contradicts the paragraph before. . . .

16 March

I supped with Martyn and Pinkie, and Myra came round after supper so that I could dictate to her a Cabinet paper on future Middle East policy (how to do down Nasser). . . .

10 April

I applied last week . . . for the job of Civilian Instructor at the IDC. . . .

13 April

These days are deep in concern about the future of the Middle East . . . and they all show up the same grim truth – that Western Europe is dependent on the oil, and that Nasser can stop it coming if he wants to, by closing the Canal or the pipelines. . . .

20 June
Today I left the FO. . . . It looks as if Nasser were now completely under Communist influence, and he is playing a role amongst the Great Powers for which there is no justification in the strength of his country. . . . We have decided (with the help of the Americans) that we are not going to build the Aswan Dam. . . .

The Egyptian national day, Monday 18 June, was to celebrate the evacuation of Suez. It was built up into a frenzy of anti-British feeling. . . . Obviously my policy and efforts to save relations with Egypt have all been wrong.[37]

On 19 July the Americans backed out of a loan promised to help fund the building of a high dam at Aswan, and at once Britain followed suit. Whereupon Nasser who, with President Tito of Yugoslavia and Prime Minister Nehru of India, had been concerting a Third World grouping (no doubt with the object of playing both sides against the middle in the Cold War), and was under pressure to halt the blockade of Israeli shipping in the Gulf of Aqaba, decided to nationalise the Suez Canal. Without consulting the Arab League or other Arab allies he announced this to the world on 26 July, anticipating by 13 years the expiry of the Suez Canal concession granted by the Khedive Ismail in 1866.

The moment he heard of Nasser's action Anthony Eden summoned Mountbatten and General Templer, the CIGS, to 10 Downing Street where, as it happened, King Feisal of Iraq, on a state visit to England, was dining that evening. With him were his uncle, Crown Prince Abdullah, and Nuri es-Said, Prime Minister of Iraq, Britain's oldest ally in the Arab world.[38] Present also was Air Chief Marshal Sir Dermot Boyle, Chief of the Air Staff. The Arabs did not conceal their chagrin at Nasser's failure to confide in them before taking action with such grave political and economic implications for the Arab world. Eden was left with the conviction that he would have the backing of Iraq, and probably other Arab states, in taking strong measures, and if need be using force to oust Nasser. But, according to Anthony Nutting, then Minister of State for Foreign Affairs (he later resigned over Suez):

In the light of subsequent events, it is only fair to Nuri's memory to say that he later told me that he had warned Eden to resist any temptation to ally himself with Israel, or with France, in order to bring Nasser to heel, since any such alliance would have dire results for Anglo-Arab relations.[39]

Britain's intelligence services had given no warning that Nasser might seize the Suez Canal. Hence not even the vestige of a contingency plan existed as a brief for the Chiefs of Staff, faced as they were with an extremely angry and highly wrought Prime Minister.

A new appointment, Chairman of the Chiefs of Staff Committee and Chief of Staff to the Minister of Defence, had recently been created, but its first incumbent, Air Chief Marshal Sir William Dickson, was unfit for duty on 26 July owing to illness, and remained so throughout most of the Suez crisis. In consequence chairmanship of the CoS Committee reverted to Mountbatten, as its longest-standing member. The Downing Street emergency meeting was, in any case, informal. Having heard Eden's review of the situation the Chiefs of Staff were asked individually what immediate military action could be taken. As the fleet was assembled at Malta, Mountbatten said a force could be sailed forthwith, calling at Cyprus to embark the two Royal Marine Commandos stationed there; with air support from carriers, the Royal Marines could achieve a surprise landing within a few days, seize Port Said, and secure the first 25 miles of the causeway along the canal.

Sir Dermot Boyle reckoned that at least three weeks would be required to deploy a significant force of RAF Canberras to Cyprus; and Sir Gerald Templer, the last of whose troops had evacuated the Canal Zone, by agreement with Nasser, six weeks before, held that to put ashore a lightly armed force, to be met by Egyptian tanks, would be fatal; it would be essential to mount a Normandy-style invasion. Mountbatten did not press for the Navy and Royal Marines to go it alone. Without an up-to-date intelligence appreciation, let alone a clearly articulated political aim for the operation, it would have been irresponsible to make a firm recommendation for action. In the event, the Prime Minister told the Chiefs of Staff to prepare plans for a 'full-scale invasion'.

Having set the military machine in motion, Eden turned to his prospective allies to concert economic and military measures against Nasser. Within a few days Egypt's sterling balances and assets had been frozen by Britain, France and the USA; in Britain 20,000 reservists had been called up, and naval, army and air force reinforcements were on their way to the eastern Mediterranean. Military talks with France were in train, and the USA was kept fully informed. But it became evident that, in assessing the military balance in the region, any American forces should be excluded. Nor could the USA be expected to countenance the employment 'out of area' of British and French NATO-assigned forces. On the other hand, modern Soviet aircraft, and 'volunteers' to fly them, were being acquired by Egypt, while Israel was being furnished with tanks and modern aircraft by France.

In terms of politico-military geography, the theatre of operations formed the land bridge connecting Europe, Asia and Africa; three of the world's religions, Judaism, Christianity and Islam, originated there; it contained the world's largest oil reserves; the Arab world had refused to recognise the state of Israel; and the Suez Canal was a utility of prime international importance, especially to western economies. It was impossible for the Chiefs of Staff to make a sensible plan for a 'full-scale invasion' without a clear directive from the Prime Minister about the political aim he wished to achieve. Was the purpose of the military intervention to 'topple' Colonel Nasser, now President as well as Prime Minister of Egypt, and compared by Anthony Eden with Mussolini – 'his object was to be a Caesar from the Gulf to the Atlantic, and kick us out of it all'?[40] Or should the purpose be, rather, to back up diplomacy with force to ensure the continued operation of the canal as an international utility?

When Mountbatten, as acting chairman of the Chiefs of Staff, tried to get clearer guidance from the Prime Minister, he was told not to venture opinions on political matters. This put him in a dilemma. It was incumbent upon him to use his utmost energy and skill, with his colleagues, to produce a sound military plan to achieve what seemed to be required: namely, to seize the Suez Canal against whatever opposition might be encountered. But, as planning progressed, it became evident that Operation MUSKETEER, as it was named, would involve heavy bombing and bombardment prior to the landings, with the inevitable consequence of heavy civilian casualties. Morality and compassion apart, the effect would be to mobilise world opinion against the aggressors. And to expect our servicemen to inflict such horrors on a populace with whom we were not even at war would be outrageous. As Rear Admiral Manley Power, the Flag Officer, Aircraft Carriers, wrote privately to Mountbatten:

> Our pilots are trained for war, not for indiscriminate killing. They will, of course, do what they are told to do however repugnant it may be. But I wish to state most emphatically that I do not consider it either right or fair that they should be used in a manner which can only earn the obloquy of our own people and of the whole world.[41]

As the weeks went on, the contention of Britain and France that the Egyptians could not run the canal became harder to sustain as the world's shipping continued to use it 'without let or hindrance'. In an attempt to act as honest broker the USA organised a conference of the original signatories of the Constantinople Convention, together with other principal maritime nations and users of the canal. Egypt was of course excluded. Not surprisingly the outcome – agreement by the 18 nations represented that Egypt should hand over the running of the canal to them – was not acceptable to Nasser.

Mountbatten was well aware that in giving his opinion on the political aspects of the confrontation he was stepping out of line, but he remained convinced that:

> our trump card is the reasonable, constructive offer, backed by as many nations as we can collect and one that the Americans, as well as the countries of Asia . . . could not conceivably condemn as being 'imperialistic'.[42]

He was prevented by the First Lord (Cilcennin) and the Minister of Defence (Monckton) from placing these views formally before the Prime Minister. But to his fellow Chiefs of Staff he felt free to open his mind. In response to an earlier call from Templer for 'resolute military action in the military sphere', Mountbatten replied:

> If we were fighting a visible enemy who was trying to dominate the Middle East by force of arms I should back you to the limit. . . . But there is no such enemy. . . . The Middle East is about ideas, emotions, loyalties. You and I belong to a people which will not have ideas which we don't believe in thrust down our throats by bayonets or other force. Why should we assume that this process will work with other peoples? . . .
>
> You cannot, I suggest, fight ideas with troops and weapons. The ideas and the problems they create are still there when you withdraw the troops. What effect . . . would it have on our troops? Can the British way of life, which you and I believe must be preserved at all costs, survive if we use our young men to repudiate one of its basic principles – the right to self-determination – as permanent occupation troops?[43]

As chairman pro tem of the Chiefs of Staff, Mountbatten felt bound to ask the Prime Minister for guidance as to military action after the Canal Zone had been forcibly reoccupied. He pointed out that if Nasser was deposed a successor would have to be found and kept in power. The occupation of Egypt would tie down a large number of troops which, at the moment, were not available. Such representations got short shrift from Eden, whose main and unvarying concern was to find an excuse for using armed force to take over the canal. A number of provocative measures, such as withholding the canal dues of British and French ships, were introduced, but without effect. The canal continued to be correctly operated.

The mismatch between political intention and military action was becoming more and more evident. Mountbatten could barely be restrained from tendering his resignation, even by the combined advice of the First Lord and the Minister of Defence. The latter pointed out that such action would be tantamount to refusal by a serving officer to carry out his orders. But he was at least able to get approval for a modification of the MUSKETEER plan which would reduce the threat to civilian lives and property. The fact remained that instead of a constructive partnership between diplomatic activity and military pressure, Eden continued to seek a *casus belli*. The Foreign Office was discouraged from the study of long-term commitments in the Middle East. The USA urged negotiation, but in vain.

Eden had long since lost the capacity to conduct policy in a rational way. Instead, seeing himself cast in the heroic mould of Winston Churchill, he wrote to Eisenhower that:

Nasser's plan included the expansion of his power until he could, in effect, hold the Western world to ransom. If this were so, then Britain's duty would be plain: 'We have many times led Europe in the fight for freedom. It would be an ignoble end to our long history if we tamely accepted to perish by degrees.'[44]

Intoxicated by his own rhetoric, Eden refused to follow up signs that Egypt might negotiate on the basis of a six-point draft resolution tabled by Britain and France at the UN Security Council on 13 October. Instead, on 14 October, he accepted with gleeful excitement a French proposal to collude with them by inviting the Israelis to attack Egypt. Then, having given the Israeli forces enough time to seize all or most of Sinai, and thus gain control of the Gulf of Aqaba, Britain and France would order 'both sides' to withdraw their forces from the Canal Zone to save the canal from damage in the fighting. The most stringent precautions were taken by Eden to conceal this plot, even from most of his Cabinet colleagues; if the Chiefs of Staff were informed, their position must have been almost impossible to sustain.

Certainly Mountbatten had already done his best to make Eden see sense, while in some miraculous way keeping from even his closest subordinates in the armed forces any hint of his profound opposition to the operation on which they were soon to be launched. In company with the rest of the world, the soldiers, sailors and airmen taking part in Operation MUSKETEER heard on 29 October that Israeli forces had crossed into Sinai and begun their attack on Egypt. But they did not know that the Anglo-French ultimatum to Egypt and Israel to stop fighting, issued on 30 October, had been drawn up five days previously. Nor were they aware, when British aircraft bombed Egyptian airfields that evening and the next day, of the direct aid thus given to Israel in pre-empting air attack by Egypt in response to her aggression. 'The Egyptians were "the enemy", weren't they? Now we could rely on air superiority for the landings. Look out, Colonel Nasser, here we come.' But later that day the futility of MUSKETEER was exposed when the Egyptians sank a 320ft-long vessel, the *Akka*, near Lake Timsah, thus blocking the canal. In all, within a day or two of the Anglo-French intervention, a total of 47 block-ships were sunk in the canal, thus putting it out of action for many months.

For the previous fortnight the American government had been denied by their British and French allies any information about their plan to occupy the Canal Zone by force on the pretext of separating the embattled Israeli and Egyptian forces. It was not surprising that on learning of their ultimatum President Eisenhower should have at once telephoned the British Prime Minister. By a mischance his call was taken by William Clark, Eden's press adviser, who, before he could reveal his identity, heard the President say, 'Anthony, you must have gone out of your mind.'[45]

Eisenhower's conduct of affairs at this juncture was, in the best officer-like tradition, 'firm but conciliatory'. Within two days, under American leadership, the UN General Assembly passed a ceasefire resolution. But the MUSKETEER force continued to steam towards Port Said. In four days it would be there, to follow up the paratroops. The American Sixth Fleet cruised nearby, rather too close at times, intent on observing every movement of the Anglo-French force. In London Mountbatten, who on 22 October had been made an Admiral of the Fleet, wrote to Eden, his friend of so many years standing, now Prime Minister:

> I am writing to appeal to you to accept the resolution of the overwhelming majority of the United Nations to cease military operations and beg you to turn back the assault convoy before it is too late, as I feel that the actual landing of troops can only spread the war with untold misery and worldwide repercussions.
>
> You can imagine how hard it is for me to break with all service custom and write direct to you in this way, but I feel so desperate about what is happening that my conscience would not allow me to do otherwise.[46]

The Prime Minister telephoned his thanks to Mountbatten for writing so frankly, but refused to turn back the assault convoy. Turning to the First Lord, now Lord Hailsham, a couple of days later, the First Sea Lord was met with the constitutional advice that if anything should happen which impaired the honour of the Navy, it was for the First Lord to resign; whereupon Mountbatten sought, and obtained, a written order from the First Lord to remain at his post until further orders. This was confirmed next day by the Prime Minister.

In the meantime, even as Mountbatten was writing to Eden, on 2 November the French Prime Minister outlined to the American ambassador in Paris the whole story of French collusion in the Suez crisis step by step, including the fact that the British were involved.

On 3 November Syrian saboteurs blew up most of the British oil pipelines running through their country from Iraq to the Mediterranean. That same day the Soviet Union launched 200,000 troops and 4,000 tanks into Hungary 'to help the Hungarian people crush the black forces of reaction and counter-revolution'. By 4 November Israel had occupied nearly all the Sinai Peninsula and all the Gaza Strip. But still the Anglo-French assault force sailed on. As seen by President Eisenhower:

> The twin problems of Hungary and Suez now became more acute and in addition created an anomalous situation. In Europe we were aligned with Britain and France in our opposition to the brutal Soviet invasion of Hungary; in the Middle East we were against the entry of British–French armed forces in Egypt.[47]

From a military point of view, marching to the aid of Hungary was quite impracticable. But it was doubly disconcerting for the President to get a letter from the Russian premier, Nikolai Bulganin, proposing that the USA and the

Soviet Union join forces, march into Egypt, and put an end to the fighting lest it should develop into a third world war.

Despite the UN's adoption of a Canadian resolution calling for the creation of a UN force within 48 hours, an Afro-Asian resolution calling for a ceasefire within 12 hours, and the acceptance by Egypt of the ceasefire resolution of 2 November, Eden refused to order a halt. Throughout 5 November the attack on Port Said continued. Operation MUSKETEER went ahead with few hitches. A particularly successful innovation was the use of carrier-borne helicopters to land a Royal Marine Commando. During 6 November the leading British troops raced south, and were more than halfway to Ismailia by midnight when they received unequivocal orders to proceed no further. Both Israel and Egypt had agreed to cease fire, so Eden and his French fellows in collusion were left no option but to declare an Anglo-French ceasefire.

As Anthony Nutting wrote, not without a certain *schadenfreude*:

> To say the least, it was an extraordinary situation. For, in truth, we had achieved none of the objectives, whether pretended or real, with which we had set out on this sorry adventure. We had not separated the combatants; they had separated themselves. We had not protected the Canal; it was blocked. We had not safeguarded British lives and property, but had subjected them to the gravest hazards. Nor had we achieved our real aim of seizing control of the Canal. Least of all had we toppled Nasser from his throne.[48]

It was certainly 'no end of a lesson'. But had the lesson been 'read, marked, learned and inwardly digested'?

In 1953, Commander-in-Chief, Mediterranean, Mountbatten had been rebuked by the First Lord of the day because in some of his conversations with foreign statesmen he had 'approached rather too closely the dividing line between legitimate naval interests and foreign policy'. Thirty years later the Permanent Under-Secretary of State, Foreign and Commonwealth Office, gave a lecture on 'The Relationship Between Foreign and Defence Policy'. It is instructive to see what he said:

> There is still a tendency in some quarters to suggest that defence policy is the handmaiden of foreign policy and to present the Armed Forces as the executors of a policy determined by the Foreign and Commonwealth Office. . . .
>
> Rather than characterise a particular commitment as either a foreign or defence policy requirement, it makes much more sense to see it as a commitment undertaken in the national interest in which there are both foreign and defence considerations.[49]

Yes, indeed. But what about economic considerations? According to Eisenhower, Eden said that he arrived at the ceasefire decision at Suez:

because he had accomplished the British purpose: to separate the combatants and prevent the spread of the war. He also mentioned a great drain in British gold and dollar reserves, which had fallen by $57 million in September, $84 million in October, and $279 million in November – an amount equal to 15 per cent of the British reserves' total. The cost of war was not irrelevant.[50]

The President might have recalled, by the same token, that it was the withdrawal by the USA of the promise of a loan to help build the Aswan High Dam which had impelled Nasser to nationalise the canal; he needed the money, and Egypt had no oil.

It comes back to that golden precept for action of any kind, 'the selection and maintenance of the aim'. At the level of national security policy, 'the preservation of the state against both external and internal threats to its integrity and political independence', the factors affecting the aim are politico-military-economic. But the rules for selecting it are immutable: its attainment must further the higher purpose, and be feasible with the resources and time available, given the prevailing and relevant circumstances. 'Suez' was a fiasco because Eden's off-the-cuff, seat-of-the-pants aim was to use armed force to cut Nasser down to size. At the same time he was trying to persuade a young Arab leader from Libya, to whom he was giving lunch at 10 Downing Street, that 'armies, navies and air forces are out of date and nobody ought to want them'.[51]

It was fortunate that Mountbatten perceived the true aim to be the preservation of the canal as an international utility. When Harold Macmillan, Chancellor of the Exchequer, heard that the canal had been blocked and asked why he had not been told that this could happen ('We can't afford to have the Canal blocked; it would be ruinous for our trade'), Mountbatten said:

From 30 July onwards I have put it in writing, at every possible opportunity I've said loud and clear that they will block the Canal, they'll block the Canal, they'll block the Canal. . . . From the very moment I saw you were going ahead, I mobilised the Navy's salvage resources as for war.[52]

But it was not until all the British and French forces had been removed from Egypt that the Royal Navy's skill and resources were permitted to carry out the task of clearing the canal, and then only under UN control.

Sir Evelyn Shuckburgh had taken up his appointment at the Imperial Defence College by this time, and his diary records:

1 November [1956]
Mountbatten [First Sea Lord] came to lecture this morning, and could not conceal from us the fact that he, too, profoundly disapproves of the policy. He said that he had spoken against it up to the limit of what is possible, and was surprised that he

was still in his job. . . . Mountbatten told us that our Canberras were intercepted at 47,000 feet by Egyptian fighters, greatly to their surprise. Perhaps Russian or Czech pilots; but they did no damage. He also said that French ships are actively co-operating with the Israelis in the Sinai battle, while we are trying to pretend we've nothing to do with them.[53]

5 December
Now that our withdrawal 'without delay' from Suez has been announced . . . all the Services feel that they have been betrayed, and that we shall never be able to show any independence as a nation again. A long letter from Admiral 'Lofty' Power, who has been on the operation, and who describes it as 'conceived in deceit and arrested in pusillanimity'. Petrol is up by one and sixpence.[54]

On 9 January Harold Macmillan replaced Anthony Eden as Prime Minister. In his first television address to the nation he emphasised the need for defence economies; to show that he meant business he appointed Duncan Sandys as Minister of Defence, who lost no time in publicly declaring that Britain was spending more money on defence than she could reasonably afford. Then, on 24 January, Macmillan announced that in order to secure a substantial reduction in defence expenditure he had authorised Sandys to give decisions on 'all matters of policy affecting the size, shape, organisation and disposition of the Armed Forces, their equipment and supply (including defence research and development) and their pay and conditions of service'.[55] At the same time the chairman of the Chiefs of Staff Committee was appointed Chief of Staff to the Minister of Defence.

Sandys came to the Ministry of Defence having made up his mind how defence expenditure should be drastically reduced. He would begin by ending conscription – National Service. Out of a total of all-regular armed forces manpower the Navy would be limited to 80,000. The defence budget must be reduced from nearly 10 per cent of GNP to less than 5 per cent. It is a commonplace that no means exists of calculating the correct level of expenditure on defence at any juncture. The figure arrived at is bound to be determined by political skill in combining elements of professional advice into a coherent whole which can stand up to critical analysis.

From the point of view of the Chiefs of Staff, whose chairman was now Mountbatten, it was first necessary to formulate an agreed position on defence tasks, and this emerged as having three main elements:

1. A contribution to the Alliance sufficient to maintain its cohesion and deterrent effectiveness.
2. Reinforcement capacity.
3. Overseas presence.

Into this context the particular capabilities of the Navy were woven. A marker had already been put down, with unanimous acceptance by the Chiefs of Staff and Sandys, that:

> in the strategic circumstances with which we are faced, the carrier is the most flexible and valuable unit of the Fleet and that, if economies in Naval forces have to be made, these ships should be the last to be reduced.[56]

With them, a balanced fleet could be maintained, suited to Britain's needs and resources:

> To maintain the stability of the Commonwealth and Empire in the Cold War and to ensure peaceful conditions for the trade on which we depend.
> To bring immediate support by sea and air in the event of the United Kingdom being engaged in limited war.
> To assist in maintaining the unity of NATO in peacetime and to contribute to its quota of naval forces in global war.[57]

In a word, flexibility. On this basis Mountbatten argued convincingly that, given the Army's commitment to the central front in Europe; the RAF's dedication to mounting the strategic nuclear deterrent; and a limited war role for the Navy, the Admiralty's manpower total must not be less than 72,500 naval personnel and 7,500 Royal Marines.

Consistent with his enquiring and fertile mind, Mountbatten now envisaged a future fleet comprising a number of carrier groups, each with a carrier and supporting destroyers and frigates with afloat support; in addition there would be Commando carriers equipped with helicopters, following the success with which these had been used in the Suez operation. And he recommended the development, in conjunction with the RAF, of the NA39, the 'Buccaneer' – a carrier-operable aircraft designed to follow a low–high–low flight plan to give maximum range with the ability to penetrate below hostile radar coverage and deliver a nuclear weapon. At the same time he was aware that VTOL (vertical take-off and landing) aircraft might eventually be embarked in a missile-armed small carrier. He therefore cancelled the project to build guided-missile cruisers, so as to make the best use of the strictly limited funds now available.

Since 1955 Mountbatten had been keeping in touch, through semi-official personal letters, with Admiral Arleigh Burke, the American Chief of Naval Operations. At the heart of their correspondence was the impact upon sea warfare and nuclear deterrence of the application of nuclear power to submarine propulsion. Thanks to this valuable professional and personal relationship, USS *Nautilus* was permitted to visit Portland on 11 October 1957 and embark Sandys and Mountbatten for a five-hour trip to sea. Significantly, it was just a week after the Soviet Union had fired into orbit the world's first man-made satellite, named *Sputnik*, the Russian for 'travelling companion'.

The US Navy had already embarked on the development of a solid-fuel, nuclear-armed ballistic missile which could be fired from a submerged submarine – Polaris. The programme was now accelerated to achieve:

1. By December 1959 an operable 1,200-mile range missile.
2. By early 1962 an operational capability of two Polaris submarines and a third three months later.
3. By mid-1963 a missile of the performance specifications previously set up as a goal for 1965 (1,500-mile range).

For the time being Mountbatten kept this information to himself. He knew that any move to transfer responsibility for mounting the strategic nuclear deterrent from the RAF to the Navy would inevitably destroy the modus vivendi between the services.

A more immediate, and less controversial, requirement was to add impetus to the *Dreadnought* project. By now, Mountbatten had met the redoubtable and prickly Rickover. No doubt his genuine and knowledgeable enthusiasm for technical innovation, and his proven capacity to get things done, had communicated itself to 'My dear Rick', as his letters to him now began. It was at this time, also, that Mountbatten instructed Rear Admiral Le Fanu to prepare a plan for a British Polaris project in case the need for it should arise – as in due course it did, following the failure of the American Skybolt development.

Captain J.O. Coote recorded:

In March 1958, Rickover visited Britain. He arrived at the Ministry of Defence while there was a meeting going on of the top-level UK Nuclear Advisory Committee to consider a gloomy progress report of the British-designed propulsion system for HMS *Dreadnought*. Suddenly Mountbatten entered the room with his guest from Washington at his side. He announced that the two of them had just shaken hands on a deal to install a complete *Skipjack* propulsion unit in our first nuclear submarine. . . .

By 1958, I was still in my second year as Operations Officer to the Home Fleet and CinCEastLant. . . . Without any warning or explanation, a signal reached the flagship from the Admiralty offering us operational control of the *Nautilus* for a week's operational evaluation against our ASW [anti-submarine warfare] forces. The exercise was code-named 'Rum Tub' and took place in October 1958. It pitched Commander William Anderson and his crew against our top submarines, frigates, and airborne forces. It culminated in a spectacular event in the North-West Approaches, when the *Nautilus* successfully acted as an integral part of the anti-submarine screen for the carrier *Bulwark*, maintaining her station and tactical involvement by UQC [underwater telephone] and sonar without the slightest difficulty. It was a devastating demonstration of her potential, which changed our thinking for ever.[58]

It was now the accepted view of the Admiralty Board that:

the advent of such vessels must change the strategy and tactics of naval warfare. . . . If the Royal Navy did not acquire these submarines it would cease to count as a naval force in world affairs.[59]

Captain Coote, in his otherwise comprehensive report, made no reference to Admiral Rickover's demand that he should personally select the captain and key officers for the *Dreadnought*, as he had always done for the US Navy's nuclear submarines. Mountbatten resisted this gambit and persuaded Rickover to provide the *Skipjack* design, which was more advanced than the *Skate* design originally offered. But he certainly ensured that Rickover was given red-carpet treatment when he visited the UK, including an interview with the Prime Minister. The relationship thus created enabled Britain to complete the *Dreadnought* two or three years earlier than otherwise, and saved the country millions of pounds in research and development.

On 22 May 1958 Mountbatten was formally offered the post of Chief of the Defence Staff. This he accepted, to take effect in July the following year. During his final year as First Sea Lord his main concern, in addition to adapting the Navy to the age of nuclear weapons and propulsion, missiles guided and ballistic, and the electronic revolution, was to offset the inevitable cuts in service manpower by making the most effective use of the drastically reduced numbers remaining.

The primary aim of the 'Way Ahead' review had been achieved, namely that nearly 7,000 uniformed personnel had been made available to man the ships; unfortunately, that equated with the reduction in naval manpower decreed in the 1958–59 naval estimates. But, as the head of the Naval Historical Branch pointed out:

The most impressive real economy was, however, the reduction in civilian staff – no fewer than 13,500 UK personnel and 10,000 men employed abroad. . . . The effect on Service personnel was less severe: the General List was pruned by 1,900, each of whom seems to have been happy with his 'Golden Bowler', and the 950 senior ratings who became redundant were rewarded appropriately. Such largesse certainly impressed those who remained: times were reputed to be hard but pay was increased regularly, conditions of service had steadily improved under Mountbatten and he had convinced everyone of the Royal Navy's vital role in Sandys's dream of the future of defence.[60]

As to making the best use of available manpower, Mountbatten turned to industry and the other services for guidance. On 4 July 1958 he opened the Royal Naval School of Work Study:

> We of course have had for some ten years the Naval Motion Study Unit and the Organisation and Methods Branch in the Admiralty. . . . Work Study by itself really is new in the Navy; it's less than a year ago that we got cracking. But even in that short time it's proved itself. . . .
>
> ICI have trained several of our officers with great success. They have allowed this school to be modelled on their own . . . and so on behalf of the Navy I say 'Thank you very much indeed.' Then I would like to thank the RAF and the Army, who are ahead of us in this matter. They started work-study first.[61]

These innovative preoccupations, and the continued in-fighting with Duncan Sandys, did not curtail Mountbatten's exacting programme of visits and inspections. Captain D.G. Robertson, who joined his staff as a lieutenant in March 1953 when Mountbatten became CINCAFMED, accompanied him when he became First Sea Lord, and from March 1955 for over two years was one of his two assistant secretaries:

> It was an interesting time as it included both Suez and the early stages of Defence reorganisation. I saw a lot of Mountbatten at that time as my home in Bishop's Waltham was not far from Broadlands – if he wanted a shoulder to cry on at the weekend mine was the nearest!
>
> [An] incident which caused me some amusement occurred on a very hot Saturday evening in the summer of 1957. As often happened, Mountbatten boarded the same train to Winchester and invited me to join him in the dining car. He had been inspecting some unit in the London area and was in uniform. However he wanted to travel incognito and wore his Burberry throughout the meal. A horde of waiters buzzing around – A little more duck, My Lord' – did not appear to shake his confidence in his disguise. . . .
>
> On a more serious note there was a side of Mountbatten's character which seems to have escaped the attention of biographers and TV producers. Mountbatten had an astonishing capacity for courtesy and an astonishing willingness to apologise.[62]

Nor did Mountbatten lose touch with the day-to-day operations of the Navy, as the author, then commanding the Third Submarine Squadron based in the Clyde, can attest from personal experience.

An outgoing First Sea Lord usually has a decisive influence on the choice of his successor. But the Prime Minister and, as yet in 1958, the First Lord of the Admiralty formed their own opinion, based on personal acquaintance and soundings taken among senior serving flag officers and the Admirals of the

Fleet. The two obvious contenders were Admirals Sir Guy Grantham and Sir Charles Lambe. Both were professionally outstanding, having proved their abilities in challenging assignments in the Second World War both in command at sea and as Director of Plans on the naval staff.

Grantham, a submarine specialist, had been a cruiser captain; Lambe, a torpedo specialist, had commanded a fleet aircraft carrier. But Lambe had been a close personal friend of Mountbatten since they were naval cadets, and had many times during their careers given him sound, if not always palatable, advice; he had benefited from Mountbatten's royal connections and been a member of his polo team, although he was also a fine musician and had many other cultural interests which Mountbatten did not share.

What both candidates had in common was a love of the Navy, a warm humanity, and rock-like integrity. But Lambe enjoyed the overriding advantage of having served with Mountbatten as Second Sea Lord during the previous two hectic years of reforms. Lambe it was to be. The Navy would have been equally happy if Grantham had been chosen.

7

CHIEF OF THE DEFENCE STAFF (1959–65)

The selection of the objective . . . represents perhaps the greatest weakness of British diplomatic organisation. The British as a nation have never been good at long-term planning. They live from day to day, deciding questions as they come up sensibly enough, but never foreseeing what questions will come up or considering where they ultimately want to go. The Foreign Office is very like this.

Sir William Hayter[1]

Speaking in the House of Lords in March 1962, Viscount Montgomery summed up the strategic scene with characteristic pungency: 'The Atlantic is safe; Europe is safe; the Mediterranean is safe: the potential danger spots lie elsewhere, in the Near East, the Middle East and in Africa. It is to those areas that we should direct our gaze.'

Phillip Darby[2]

Great Britain has lost an Empire and has not yet found a role.

Dean Acheson[3]

The more we can instil sound ideas on naval war and the practical possibilities of joint action between the two Services into the minds of rising military men, the better.

Rear Admiral Prince Louis of Battenberg, 16 November 1904[4]

Chapter 7

> I personally am all for a Minister of Defence in certain conditions . . .
> which are to do away with the First Lord, Secretary for War and
> Secretary for Air, and let one Minister do the lot, with the Naval, Military
> and Air officers chiefs in their own Departments without another civilian
> over them.
>
> *Admiral of the Fleet Earl Beatty, 11 March 1926*[5]

Mountbatten began work as Chief of the Defence Staff on 16 July 1959;
Duncan Sandys was still Minister of Defence. But the whole period from
1957, when Mountbatten became Chairman of the Chiefs of Staff Committee,
until he stood down in 1965 has come to be known in Whitehall as 'the
Mountbatten era'. By that date the reform of the political direction of the armed
forces desired by Lord Beatty had been brought about, mainly by Mountbatten's
tireless, and not always popular, efforts.

As long ago as 1890 a Royal Commission, enquiring into 'the Civil and
Professional Administration of the Naval and Military Departments', had been
advised by Field Marshal Lord Wolseley that a Minister of Defence should be
appointed to oversee the two service departments. And in 1917 Lord Haldane,
tasked to look into the post-war machinery of government, considered, but
again rejected, the establishment of a Ministry of Defence. As before, the
political view was that in war, policy and strategy would be formulated by the
War Cabinet, chaired by the Prime Minister, supported by service ministers and
advised by service chiefs. In peacetime, the cost of a Ministry of Defence
merely to oversee the activities of the three service ministries could not
possibly be justified.

Alternatively, if one Minister of Defence, with his ministry, were to take the
place of the Admiralty, the War Office and the Air Ministry, with their ministers,
not only would his workload and that of his ministry be much too great, but his
power might rival that of the Prime Minister. Besides, what civilian minister
could possibly know enough about military matters to cope effectively with the
responsibility? And to appoint an admiral, general or air chief marshal to so
powerful a post as Minister of Defence would be to prejudice gravely the

ascendancy of the civil over the military power so painfully established after the Civil War.

An episode in the aftermath of the First World War did, however, precipitate an important reform. In the summer of 1922, during the Chanak crisis when there could have been war with Kemal's Turkish nationalists, the Prime Minister (Lloyd George), was presented by the First Sea Lord, the Chief of the Imperial General Staff and the Chief of the Air Staff with 'contradictory plans, which lacked any semblance of coordination and showed clearly how little things had changed since the disastrous Gallipoli landings in 1915'.[6] A special sub-committee of the Committee of Imperial Defence (CID) was therefore set up 'to enquire into the Questions of National and Imperial Defence'. In the chair was the Marquis of Salisbury; members included the Chancellor of the Exchequer, the First Lord of the Admiralty, and the Secretaries of State for Foreign Affairs, Colonies, War, India and Air.

In addition to reaffirming the need for an independent air force, the Salisbury Committee recommended that:

> each of the three Chiefs of Staff will have an individual and collective responsibility for advising on defence policy as a whole, the three constituting, as it were, a Super-Chief of a War Staff in Commission.[7]

In amplification, the Chiefs were to be responsible for keeping:

> the defence situation as a whole constantly under review so as to ensure that defence preparations and plans and the expenditure thereupon are co-ordinated and framed to meet policy, that full information as to the changing naval, military and air situation may always be available to the Committee of Defence, and that resolutions as to the requisite action thereupon may be submitted for its consideration.[8]

The Chiefs of Staff Committee met for the first time formally on 17 July 1923. It was to prove an enduring element in the machinery of government but, far from developing the culture of fully interdependent sea, land and air forces, and advising government accordingly, the CoS Committee tended to become the forum in which each service articulated its independent role, in the conditions prevailing, as part of its campaign to secure the largest possible share of whatever resources the Treasury proposed to allocate to defence expenditure.

It soon became evident that the continued existence of three service ministries, each headed by a Cabinet minister with a political reputation at stake, merely raised to a higher level the inter-service battles being fought out in the CoS Committee. Between the wars, with Germany rearming and the political threat posed by the Berlin–Rome–Tokyo Axis, the three service ministries battled on, desperately trying to repair the country's defences in the face of public indifference, political faith in collective security, and Treasury concern for the economy – but without a firm Cabinet lead combining diplomatic, economic and military elements into a coherent defence policy.

In the hope of providing this the Prime Minister, Stanley Baldwin, in March 1936 appointed Sir Thomas Inskip, a former Attorney-General, as Minister for the Co-ordination of Defence. By 1937 Inskip had obtained from the Cabinet new strategic guidelines for the Chiefs of Staff. Their priorities, overriding the independent role of each service, were to be: the defence of the UK, since if it fell the Empire would fall with it; the defence of sea communications worldwide; the defence of overseas territories; and finally, very much in fourth place, a 'field force' to deploy in support of an ally. All very well, but in the timescale of recruitment, equipment with modern arms and training, both too late and half-baked. As a result, each service pursued with renewed hope and enthusiasm its preparations to play its own independent role, despite the unifying intent of the strategic guidelines, and in each case compounded the error by failure to determine correctly the way in which its role should be carried out.

By the eve of war, their minds concentrated by its imminence, the Chiefs of Staff were beginning to work together through the Vice Chiefs (later termed by Caspar John 'the Vice Squad'), supported by the recently formed Joint Planning and Joint Intelligence Committees. But the bleak history of the Norwegian campaign, coupled with the early success of the U-boat offensive against shipping and the mining of coastal waters, testified to the failure of both Prime Ministerial leadership and service cooperation at the levels of strategy and the conduct of operations.

When Winston Churchill became Prime Minister on 10 May 1940, he assumed also the portfolio of Minister of Defence. Thus, when all was nearly lost, an authority was created with the power – and in this particular case, the strategic insight and experience – to direct the war effort with a singleness of purpose and drive which had been completely lacking in the inter-war years. At last the great issues of grand strategy were thought through, aims clearly established, and courses of action selected, to be resolutely followed up, with a high premium placed upon the interdependence of the sea, land and air components of fighting power.

Even Churchill, however, was not able to make good quickly enough the deficiencies of the single-service culture. Following the series of calamitous setbacks suffered by British arms in 1940, 1941 and early 1942, there appeared in *The Times* a leading article headed 'A Great General Staff'. It said:

The creation of a Minister for the Co-ordination of Defence . . . did not fundamentally affect the relation between the Services or the authority of their respective chiefs. The new Minister had no ministry, no clearly defined functions or power, and, above all, no single professional adviser qualified to speak in the name of the fighting services as a whole. . . .

The conviction that something is fundamentally lacking in the co-ordination of the three fighting services has steadily gained ground throughout the present war. . . . The misplaced reluctance of the two senior services at an earlier stage to recognise the equal claims of the air force has been answered by excessive insistence on the autonomy of the RAF. Wherever the fault may lie – and it may more fairly be attributed to the system than to any one service – lack of air support has accounted for a succession of naval and military disasters. . . . A new combined organisation at the top would give a fresh impetus to co-operation.[9]

The Times went on to support a proposal that a Combined General Staff be formed, modelled on the Prussian-type Great General Staff (OKW – *Oberkommando der Wehrmacht*), having no executive responsibility for the conduct of the operations which it plans, hence at variance with the British system of making the heads of the services individually and collectively responsible both for tendering military advice and for carrying out the decisions of the Prime Minister and his War Cabinet. But even the OKW could not win the war for Hitler. Unfortunately, the interdependence of the British services brought about by the 'grim arbitrament of war' was seldom accepted wholeheartedly; it was ignored by Bomber Command, for example, whose singleminded pursuit of maximum numbers in bombing industrial areas deprived Coastal Command of the handful of very long range (VLR) aircraft without which the mid-Atlantic gap in air support for convoys could not be covered.

As the war progressed the sheer scale and complexity of the campaigns, and the formidable directing power of the Allied political leaders, brought about the tri-service theatre commands of Eisenhower, MacArthur and Mountbatten. In achieving victory in war the fundamental interdependence of the three arms – sea, land and air – was proved. When peace came an attempt was made, in the UK at any rate, to preserve and nurture the combined arms ethos, for example by establishing the Joint Services Staff College at Latimer in 1947. As it happened, the Chiefs of Staff at this juncture were Admiral Sir John Cunningham, Field Marshal Lord Montgomery and Marshal of the RAF, Lord Tedder, of whom the authors of *The Chiefs* recorded: 'At no period before or since has there been such bitterness and personal animosity in the Chiefs of Staff Committee.'[10] It would be a mistake to attribute this sad state of affairs solely to the incompatibility of individuals. All three were professional leaders of mainly citizen forces, and had proven themselves in war. Abrasive and opinionated they may have been, but they had pulled together when kept on course by a dominating statesman at the helm. What should be borne in mind is the highly developed sense of single-service responsibility underlying the views of a senior commander in any of the armed forces.

Ever since he was a fledgling officer – as watchkeeper in a warship, or commanding a platoon, or leading a flight of aircraft – the commanding officer has had to 'say to one go, and he goeth', perhaps to his death; and he has learned the overriding importance of high morale in the fighting power of the men under his command. He knows, also, that the main constituents of high morale are belief in the cause for which one is fighting, trust in the competence of one's leader, and confidence in one's weapons, equipment and training.

Whether in peace or war, the officer's promotion has been by selection, at several stages, in the face of strong competition, on the basis of his performance in his current appointment as judged by his commanding officer. But the commanding officer is also required to state whether or not his subordinate would do well in the higher ranks of the service. In the nature of things, that judgement ensures that the officers who have the best chance of reaching the top of their particular service are the ones who have demonstrated their dedication to its well-being as an institution, autonomous and independent of any other; to its capacity to fulfil its role; but above all to its particular ethos.

As a matter of principle in the organisation of human beings for concerted action, responsibility should be matched by the authority needed for its effective discharge. Where the action may involve the commitment of armed forces to battle and the conduct of their operations, with the fate of the nation dependent upon the outcome, the responsibility is correspondingly great and the authority called for equally so. The professional sailors, soldiers and airmen to whom such responsibility and authority are entrusted tend to have selected themselves in the course of a career of outstanding excellence embracing every aspect of their service, in the sense of 'knowing something about everything', including its role in relation to those of the other services, and 'everything about something' pertaining to it, for example, anti-submarine warfare, tank warfare, or ground attack. But they have probably absorbed, also, the potentially divisive and quasi-divine dogmas of sea power, land power and air power, respectively.

Such men were the Chiefs of Staff, so called despite their personal responsibility for every aspect of their service, and executive authority over each member of it, conferred upon them by the Crown. Is it surprising that men wielding such power, even though it be constitutionally limited, do not readily agree to political decisions which in their view will impair the capacity of their service to achieve victory in battle; and that, as Ronald Lewin so memorably remarked, 'is the pay-off'?

Why should such men be expected to see themselves as mere staff officers, however exalted? Are they to be content with the role of expert witness, conferred upon them by clever young bureaucrats skilled in the paper warfare of Whitehall? Must they accept the seemingly wilful ignorance of Westminster in matters affecting armed force as a factor in the relations between states, yet acknowledge the subordination of the military to the political authority in the realm?

213

The Sandys–Mountbatten White Paper of July 1958 reflected the confrontation between a minister of great determination, with a cut-and-dried defence policy which he wished to impose on the services, and the Chiefs of Staff, equally determined to ensure that, in bringing about a reduction in defence expenditure as a whole, which they acknowledged to be inevitable, each service retained its core capability. The outcome was a real, if small, advance towards achieving:

> the task of reshaping and reorganising the Armed Forces in accordance with current strategic needs and in the light of the economic capacity of the country.[11]

In the first place, the subordination of the service ministers to the Minister of Defence was codified – they were no longer to be members of the Cabinet; secondly, the Minister of Defence was required, as a matter of duty, 'to take . . . all practicable steps to secure the most efficient and economical performance of functions common to two or more of the Services';[12] and thirdly, a new post of Chief of the Defence Staff was created. This was the innovation most feared by the Chiefs of Staff (the First Sea Lord excepted). But it followed from paragraph 10 of the White Paper:

> The Minister of Defence is ministerially responsible to the Prime Minister for the execution of military operations approved by the Cabinet or the Defence Committee.[13]

As principal military adviser to the Minister of Defence, the Chief of the Defence Staff could hardly be expected to issue 'Operational orders hitherto issued jointly in the name of the Chiefs of Staff Committee', even as 'Chairman of the Chiefs of Staff Committee', without the support of a tri-service staff capable of producing them. The dilemma was made manifest in paragraph 19 of the White Paper:

> The Joint Planning Staff, in their collective capacity, are directly responsible to the Chief of the Defence Staff as Chairman of the Chiefs of Staff Committee. He is entitled to call on the respective Chiefs of Staff to make available, to assist him in the discharge of his functions, the services of the Naval, General and Air Staffs, who are together regarded as forming a Joint Defence Staff. For the study of inter-Service problems these Staffs are responsible, through the Chiefs of Staff of their respective Services, to the Chiefs of Staff Committee and through its Chairman to the Minister of Defence.[14]

At this level of defence policy formulation and execution, virtually every plan, whether long term or operational, involves more than one of the services, and usually all three. To have isolated 'inter-service problems' therefore, as having to be dealt with through the Chiefs of Staff of their respective services, was a guarantee of single-service autonomy.

This matter was put to the test within weeks of Mountbatten becoming Chief of the Defence Staff. The air staff, taking account of the Middle East air barrier and looking ahead to the time when the African air route might be closed, had proposed the establishment of a chain of island staging posts reaching to Australia. One of these, on the island of Gan in the Maldives, had already been established, and in August 1959 a local political disturbance threatened its security. The situation was restored in short order by the naval, army and air commanders-in-chief in whose respective 'parishes' Gan was located, acting in concert, but the Ministry of Defence was neither consulted nor informed about the operations. Hence Mountbatten, soon after being made responsible as Chief of the Defence Staff for issuing the orders for 'operations approved by the Cabinet or Defence Committee', had to explain to a surprised and angry Prime Minister what had been going on. This provoked from Macmillan the mock-patrician comment that 'The only shooting he would permit this August was grouse.'[15]

Even as First Sea Lord, Mountbatten had tried to persuade his fellow Chiefs of Staff, and the senior commanders of all three services, that the appointment of a supreme commander in each theatre, proven in war to be essential, should be perpetuated on a small scale in peacetime. But having rejected this advice in 1947, they were no more disposed to accept it in March 1959 when Admiral Sir Gerald Gladstone, the naval commander-in-chief at Hong Kong, turned the proposal down flat. However, with the Prime Minister and Minister of Defence firmly on his side as a consequence of the Gan episode, Mountbatten was able to set up tri-service HQs with a single commander-in-chief in Cyprus (1 May 1960), Aden (1 March 1961) and, at long last, Singapore (28 November 1962). Sadly, in the process he incurred the declared enmity of General Sir Richard Hull who had been General Officer Commanding in the Far East and, like Admiral Gladstone, believed that a united theatre command was unnecessary.

Resolutely convinced as he had been for nearly 20 years that the three armed services must be regarded, and see themselves, as three prongs of a single defence trident, it was obvious to Mountbatten that as Chief of Defence Staff he must have a Director of Defence Plans who would be responsible directly to him. Needless to say this was regarded by the Chief of the Air Staff, in particular, as yet another uncalled-for accretion of power by 'the Centre', and he opposed it. The CIGS (Festing, who had commanded the 36th Indian Division in Burma under Mountbatten's supreme command) was not against the proposal, and the First Sea Lord, Charles Lambe, suggested that the scheme be given a year's trial to resolve the issue. That was agreed. Not content with this augmentation of his authority as CDS, however, Mountbatten also tried to establish the post as the only one to carry 'five star' rank; but that had to await the radical reconstruction of the central organisation for defence which he had in mind.

Air Commodore Rosier (later Air Chief Marshal Sir Frederick Rosier), who was appointed as Director of Plans to the CDS and Chairman of the Joint Planning Committee in September 1959, had been serving until then as the Director of Air Plans in the Air Ministry. He was therefore particularly well qualified to preside over the most crucial aspect of defence planning: Britain's nuclear deterrent policy. L.W. Martin had this to say about the new post of Director of Plans to the CDS:

> There was some question as to whether this development would strengthen or weaken the Minister of Defence in relation to the professional military, and the answer would depend on how the undoubtedly reinforced CDS employed his new instrument. Within the service ministries there were also some misgivings as to whether the new office would not be used to prejudice the work of the joint planning teams in directions favoured by the CDS. In practice, however, Mountbatten has apparently taken great pains to see that all sources of ideas are tapped and are known to be tapped. Before meetings of the Plans Committee to consider the drafts which planning teams have produced in consultation with the services and the Foreign, Colonial and Commonwealth Relations Offices, the independent Chairman secures other neutral views from the military, scientific and civil staffs in the Ministry of Defence. . . . Moreover, the CDS has the habit of very freely bringing in interested parties, particularly from the Civil Service . . . to avoid any appearance of a closed military shop. . . .
>
> As a result of all this, those involved in joint planning now feel that there is a freer flow of ideas, a more trustful atmosphere and a better blend of a variety of views and interests than at any time since 1945.[16]

A more recent academic study confirms that:

> The historical record, so far as it is open for scholars, shows just how much more work was carried out by Mountbatten as CDS than by his predecessor. It is already apparent that the range of subjects taken by the CoS Committee was very wide, and that important issues were constantly addressed.[17]

In the autumn of 1959 Mountbatten visited the USA. It so happened that Professor Solly Zuckerman, whom he had recruited to his Combined Operations staff in 1942, with J.D. Bernal and Geoffrey Pyke as scientific advisers, was 'spending a few months at the Californian Institute of Technology', as he put it.[18] Together they went to see the huge, heavily protected underground silos in which the Americans had emplaced their Titan intercontinental ballistic missiles. In Britain a project was under way, using technology made available following the Anglo-US Missile Agreement of February 1950, to design and build a 2,500-mile range ballistic missile, Blue Streak, which would carry a British nuclear warhead and replace the V-bombers in due course. Having seen Titan, Mountbatten was confirmed in his view that a static, liquid-fuelled, unprotected system such as Blue Streak, located in the relatively small, populous British Isles, would be neither militarily nor politically credible.

Returning to the UK he had to report to a new Minister of Defence, Harold Watkinson, an industrialist who at once set out to achieve, as he wrote in his memoirs:

> a reorganisation of Britain's conventional forces under firm businesslike direction, coupled with a policy which would speed up their reaction time and create a mobile force with a poised capacity to operate from land or sea bases. . . . This seemed to me a more important priority in 1959 than overmuch argument about nuclear philosophical heresies of one kind or another.[19]

The comfortable words of this elder statesman may be described, with a nod to Wordsworth, as 'commotion remembered in tranquillity'. It was fortunate for him that he was served by a CDS who, following the departure of Duncan Sandys to the Ministry of Aviation, 'began a rapid and adept campaign to soothe ruffled feelings all round'[20] in the Ministry of Defence, while encouraging the new minister to follow the paths of conventional defence righteousness. Thus coached, Watkinson 'set the tone of the new regime' as Darby put it, saying in a speech at Greenwich in January 1960:

> It would be wrong for us to seek to shelter in our defence policy too much under the shadow of the major nuclear deterrent. This means that we must see that we have well-balanced forces, equipped with the best and most modern weapons that are available.[21]

All very well, but it wasn't going to be easy to reconcile the conflicting demands of the three services for conventional weapons while containing the defence budget, even if the incubus of the nuclear deterrent could be diminished and given permanent shape. The most immediate and complex of these problems was what to do about Blue Streak, billed as the national nuclear deterrent of the future.

Mountbatten, backed by Zuckerman, who was now chief scientific adviser to the Ministry of Defence, had little difficulty in persuading Watkinson that it would be a futile waste of money, as well as positively dangerous, to persist with Blue Streak. When still First Sea Lord, the CDS had received a 'Dear Dickie' letter from the US Chief of Naval Operations:

It is a never-ending source of wonder that people in general do not fully understand the significance of having ballistic missiles at sea in ships instead of in fixed bases on land. In the United States there is commencing to be recognition of the important advantages, including, particularly, costs, relative invulnerability, the lack of magnet effect as a target, and the certainty of operations regardless of what the enemy does.

Whether land-based systems are located in the United Kingdom, the United States or for that matter in any other nation in the free world, it appears axiomatic that the enemy will know their exact geographical location and this, in my opinion, is where the great defect of land-based IRBMs lies. If possessing this knowledge, the Soviet believes that he is capable of destroying these sites before they can react to his attack, then deterrence has failed, regardless of whether or not the Soviets are correct in the belief that they could destroy all the missiles before they could be launched. If the deterrence fails to deter, the arguments of the proponents of land-based systems, that they can achieve some degree of invulnerability by hardening, dispersal, holes-in-the-ground, etc., become academic because the general war will have commenced.[22]

The argument could not have been more convincingly stated. And the letter was accompanied by a poster depicting an aircraft carrier, a destroyer and a submarine in company, with the surrounding slogan:

> MOVE DETERRENTS OUT TO SEA
> WHERE THE REAL ESTATE IS FREE
> AND WHERE THEY ARE FAR AWAY FROM ME

Admiral Burke's letter, dated 28 February 1959, included an indication that if the UK were to participate in a Polaris programme after the expensive R&D phases had been completed, the cost of the submarine-based system to the UK would compare favourably with that of other systems.

In the event, Blue Streak was abandoned in February 1960, and the £60 million already spent on the project written off. To replace it, one of three airborne systems might be selected: the USAF ballistic missile system, Skybolt, modified to fit the RAF's V-bombers; a ram-jet missile, Pandora, with which the RAF's TSR2 (tactical strike reconnaissance) aircraft could be equipped; or the continued development of a stand-off bomb for the RAF, Blue Steel. Alternatively the seaborne system, Polaris, which had already passed its first flight test, might be acquired. Mountbatten was not at this stage prepared to press for Polaris; given that favourable reports were being received from the USAF and its manufacturers about Skybolt's progress, it made economic sense to procure it and thus prolong the active life of the V-force. Polaris might come later.

In March 1960 Macmillan met President Eisenhower at Camp David, primarily to discuss a proposed nuclear test ban treaty:

[Macmillan] came back with an exchange of letters, in which Eisenhower agreed that Britain could buy Skybolt; and, in return, the Americans could use the Holy Loch in Scotland as a United States nuclear submarine base. No formal undertaking was given by Eisenhower to provide Polaris if the Skybolt development were to fail, but Macmillan felt confident that the Americans would be willing to do so in that event.[23]

This was an outcome satisfactory to Mountbatten. Sadly, he could take little pleasure in it. In the midst of all his exertions he had been poleaxed by the sudden death of his wife.

Edwina, despite a clear warning from her doctor that unless she gave up her intensely active public life she would kill herself, had left home in January for a Far Eastern tour on behalf of the St John Ambulance Brigade. Arriving in Jesselton, North Borneo, on 20 February, she at once began her round of inspections. Unusually, she soon showed signs of tiredness. A few hours later she was dead. In the early hours of 21 February Mountbatten was woken in his London flat by the telephone. Poignantly, on hearing the indistinct words 'Lady Mountbatten', he assumed when the line cleared that it was his wife telephoning and asked 'Edwina, darling, is that you?' But it was the acting governor of North Borneo.

Thus, only the death of one of them ended the turbulent marriage of two of the most high-powered and colourful people to enliven public life in the first half of the 20th century – a marriage which could certainly have broken down several times in earlier years. But Dickie's eminence on the world stage was taken as a challenge by Edwina, and in middle life she began to respond to his stature as a sailor-statesman. As their private lives became more stable in maturity, they found a common purpose in public service of notable distinction with Edwina seeking, in carrying out her own responsibilities, to outdo her husband – 'How many speeches did you make today, Dickie?' – 'At least five' – 'Oh, I made seven!' And time and again Mountbatten sought Edwina's advice or opinion on the great matters with which he was so absorbed. After her death he grew listless. He had loved her. His daughters knew it. They, with their husbands and children, did not fail him in their affection, but the void remained – and it ached, even though the Cole Porter lyric 'I'll always be true to you, Darlin', in my fashion . . .' echoed the faithlessness of Edwina in her glittering and self-indulgent youth.

In May 1960 Mountbatten received another personal blow when his most valued and oldest friend, Charles Lambe, was forced by ill health to give up the post of First Sea Lord. His place was taken by Admiral Sir Caspar John, a naval aviator with a keen brain, acerbic tongue and bohemian propensities (his father was the celebrated artist Augustus John), who had served both Mountbatten and Lambe well as the Vice Chief of Naval Staff. Three months later Charles Lambe died.

By this time Mountbatten had come to terms with the loss of Edwina, to the extent that he was working longer hours than ever, travelling widely to represent the British defence interest at NATO, Commonwealth and American gatherings, but never neglecting his beloved Navy. A typical recollection comes from Captain R.D. Franks:

> In 1960, when . . . I was captain of [the aircraft carrier] *Bulwark* for the first commission with the helicopters and a commando, [Mountbatten] visited us in Malta and dined in the Ward Room, mess dress. It turned out that his valet had omitted to pack his gold striped trousers. Major crisis! Signals right left and centre.
> But I think the visit went well.

In due course, from 'The Chief of the Defence Staff (Paris), 3 April 1960', came:

> I am writing to thank you very much indeed for all your kindness and hospitality to Brockman and myself during our short stay in *Bulwark*.
> I am writing a line to the Commander to thank him for the magnificent dinner in the wardroom.
> It was a great thrill to me to see the ship I had always dreamed about, as an actual reality. I think you have a thrilling task ahead of you in creating the technique of Commando Carrier operations, and I am glad that it is you who is going to do this.[24]

Within 15 months HMS *Bulwark* and her Commando were in action. The intervening period had seen not only the Skybolt agreement in the military field, but the dramatic effect of Harold Macmillan's epoch-making 'winds of change' speech, delivered in South Africa in February 1960. Already the strategic outlook worldwide had evolved into the nuclear stalemate, dubbed 'Mutual Assured Destruction' (in July 1960 the USS *George Washington* achieved the first launch of a Polaris missile from a submerged submarine); and a split in Sino-Soviet relations had been observed, so the risk of world war between the capitalist and Marxist–Leninist camps was thought to have lessened.

In Africa the Belgians had given independence to the Congo, and the unscrambling of empires continued at a gathering pace. In East Africa the belief that independence was still decades away was losing credibility in the face of nationalist opposition, yet the development of a military base in Kenya continued, together with that at Singapore. It was not an easy or rapid process to 'turn that Imperial wagon around'. But whereas the main post-imperial task for Britain's armed forces would be to help maintain public order and defend the newly independent states in East Africa and South-East Asia, her most immediate interest lay in maintaining access, on fair terms, to the oil of the Persian Gulf. It was here that the politico-economic situation was most complex.

Between 1957 and 1961 Kuwait alone supplied about 50 per cent of Britain's oil needs, and most of our remaining oil imports came from the same region. With the ongoing Arab–Israeli confrontation as background, Egypt, without oil of its own, formed a union with Syria, and an anti-western regime had seized power in Iraq. It was therefore deemed prudent to renegotiate the Treaty of 1899 with Kuwait, and this was announced in the House of Commons on 19 June 1961. Whereupon General Kassem, the Iraqi Prime Minister, revived an old claim that Kuwait was an inseparable part of Iraq. Rejecting Kuwait's claim to independence he pronounced the Ruler of Kuwait to be merely its district governor, within the Basra province of Iraq. Troop movements towards the Kuwait border lent force to Kassem's words. In the morning of 30 June the Ruler of Kuwait made a formal request for British assistance:

> By next evening (1 July) Brigadier Horsfield, commanding 24th Infantry Brigade, had the equivalent of half a brigade with tank and air support on the Mutlah Ridge, blocking the direct route to Kuwait city, and by the end of the week he had a force of five battalions with tank, artillery, air and naval gunfire support ready to oppose the Iraqis. Thus, an effective force had been assembled in a very short time, and the Government, advised by the Chiefs under Mountbatten's leadership, had taken the right political and military decisions.[25]

It had been a useful if somewhat fraught debut for the new Ministry of Defence Operations Executive at Storey's Gate, where the facilities had not been modernised since Churchill's day:

> Mountbatten was seen at the beginning of the crisis with an armful of maps and a handful of drawing pins, shouting for the 'Duty Captain' and looking for wall space to set up a proper situation map! A purpose-built Operations Centre was not provided until the present Ministry of Defence Main Building was occupied in 1964.[26]

The Kuwait operation was also a good test of the efficiency of the tri-service command headquarters recently set up at Aden and Cyprus. The necessary reinforcements, sea, land and air, including *Bulwark* and her Commando, were brought to the operational area within a few days. Mountbatten's assumption of overall operational control had got off to a good start, and the virtue of close coordination between overseas and defence policy in action was demonstrated.

However, if defence and foreign policy were shown to be two sides of the same coin (as President Kennedy memorably pointed out), rather than the former being the servant of the latter, both continued to be the slaves of economic policy. The capacity to intervene effectively in support of what was clearly a major economic interest of Britain could only be maintained if her economy could take the strain. In Europe a tri-service contribution to NATO was a fair price to pay for the UK's security against invasion or starvation by blockade; and the cost of a semi-independent strategic nuclear deterrent force could also be justified, even if not conceded by CND. But what about the cost of updating the arms, sea, land and air, which had protected Kuwait, and keeping them deployed east of Suez, let alone the expenditure of 'blood and treasure' to be faced if such 'regional deterrence' should fail? Was there any other economic interest around the Indian Ocean, or in South-East Asia, which could be quantified, like oil from the Gulf, and set against the cost of defending it?

The answer was 'no'. The assumption was that the preservation of peace and stability ensured the safety of British lives and property, and access on fair terms to raw materials and trade – important though not quantifiable. But, as the Oscar Wilde character remarked, 'a cynic is someone who knows the price of everything and the value of nothing' and the Treasury was nothing if not cynical, especially when faced with the rapidly rising costs of defence. For not only was new technology, with its associated R&D, multiplying by orders of magnitude the cost of new weapons and equipment, but modern armaments were being made available to the client states of the Sino-Soviet bloc. In the attempt to bring about a sharing of the defence burden east of Suez with allies, as in NATO, the British government had subscribed to CENTO (the Central Treaty Organisation), and SEATO (South-East Asia Treaty Organisation). But despite Harold Watkinson's (questionable) assertion that these treaties were on a level with NATO, that Britain was equally committed to all three, and that 'these three alliances are absolutely interdependent, and the failure of one is the failure of all',[27] it became increasingly difficult to determine the size and shape of the military forces which it would be in Britain's interests to maintain east of Suez.

If the 'size' was to be governed by what Britain could afford after meeting the demands of the welfare state and covering the NATO contribution, how was 'value for money' to be measured, in terms of 'shape', as between the various conventional force options? Given that the spectrum of situations to be coped with ranged from aid to the civil power to limited (non-nuclear, but also non-allied) war, how could the necessary flexibility and mobility be provided with the maximum economy of force? The success of the Kuwait operation seemed at first to provide a pattern for the future. But the core naval element had been the fleet aircraft carrier and her air group, with escorts and logistic support. The RAF, already scenting the possibility of losing what seemed to have become its *raison d'être*, namely to wield Britain's strategic nuclear deterrent (Skybolt was beginning to turn sour), sought to develop the case for substituting shore-based aircraft operating from islands in the Indian Ocean for aircraft carriers. With the end of National Service due in 1963, the Army faced restructuring as well as re-equipment problems.

Under Mountbatten's leadership, which included engaging the Treasury at an early stage in the preparation of defence budgets, the Chiefs of Staff worked for a time in fair harmony following the Kuwait operation, with one major exception. This was the refusal of the RAF, for no openly declared reason, to modify its operational requirements so they could be met by an adaptation of the NA39 (Buccaneer), already tested and flying at over Mach 0.9 at very low level, with a unit cost of some £800,000. The RAF's proposed TSR2 was reported to need £35 million for research and development, its all-up weight was to be about 85,000lb, unit cost would be about £1 million – and both weight and cost were escalating.

Mountbatten tried hard to persuade Watkinson to insist that the RAF should accept the NA39 and abandon TSR2, pushing his protests in private to the limits of propriety. But the minister remained adamant. It was the only matter, according to Mountbatten, on which they could not reach agreement. As things turned out, the TSR2 was cancelled in 1964 by Denis Healey, its weight having gone up to 100,000lb and unit cost to £4 million. Ironically, the first of a new generation of fleet aircraft carriers, known as CVA01, was cancelled shortly afterwards, and the Buccaneers transferred to the RAF when the Navy no longer had the carriers from which to operate them. It had been Mountbatten's contention that a better bet for the RAF would have been to make do with the NA39 until they could make use of the 'swing-wing' technology proposed by Barnes-Wallis and incorporated by the Americans in their F-111, which was eventually acquired to equip the RAF. It must be said, however, that much of the data obtained when developing the TSR2 was used in due course for the design of the European collaborative multi-role combat aircraft, the MRCA, later called the Tornado.

Although, when he was First Sea Lord, Mountbatten had promoted the case for the large 'fleet' carrier as embodying the mobility and flexibility of modern naval power, he had also been impressed with the potential of the VSTOL aircraft, the so-called 'jump-jet', and had envisaged a cruiser-size ship equipped with surface-to-air missiles and VSTOL aircraft as a valuable addition to the future fleet. He was also impressed by the anti-submarine potential of the helicopter. He was not, therefore, so dedicated to the retention of the large, fixed-wing aircraft carrier, per se, as were Caspar John and his Board. Interestingly, Vice-Admiral Sir Ian Hogg, who had served with Mountbatten as his Staff Officer (Plans) when he was Commander-in-Chief in the Mediterranean, recalled:

[Mountbatten] told me bluntly that he was responsible for my promotion to Captain, and after a year (1958) at the IDC [Imperial Defence College] he demanded me as the Naval representative on his newly formed staff of the embryo Chief of Defence Staff – a unified organisation which he had fought for, and which for so long had been resisted by the individual Service Chiefs of Staff. . . .

I enjoyed two years at Storey's Gate, except that Caspar John – then First Sea Lord – issued an order round the Old Admiralty that nobody was to discuss Naval affairs with me without the express permission of himself or VCNS. I told Caspar how foolish his attitude was, but it didn't have much effect. He once said to me: 'Mountbatten is 30 per cent brilliant; 30 per cent dark blue; and 40 per cent childish enthusiasm.' I didn't share his view.[28]

It was during this period that the author, having recently been director of a naval staff division, formed the opinion that it should not need four-and-a-half separate ministries to administer three armed services. Accordingly, he wrote a paper proposing the abolition of the Admiralty, the War Office and the Air Ministry, unifying the political control of the forces under the Secretary of State for Defence assisted by ministers of state for manpower, armaments, and supply and civil establishments. The identity of the three services was to be maintained and their professional heads would continue to be responsible, both individually and corporately in the Chiefs of Staff Committee, for military advice to the government.[29] On being sent a copy of this paper the permanent under-secretary at the Ministry of Defence replied courteously that he had read it with interest, 'but preferred simple solutions'. No doubt. As he (Sir Edward Playfair) had informed IDC students a few weeks earlier, his main qualification for his post was to have demonstrated in his youth 'a certain facility for writing elegant verse in a dead language'.

This self-deprecatory sally reinforced the comment of an independent student of British naval policy at that time:

> The standard complaint that the Civil Service is hampered by the strong Oxbridge emphasis on the classics and amateurism is not just academic criticism. An American observer can scarcely fail to sense the civil servant's stereotypical references to mythology, history, literature and Victorian England. It appears almost impossible for him to answer any question, no matter how simple, without painfully tracing its historical origins. He seems to respect precedent even more than does the tradition oriented culture as a whole. Moreover, the civil servant is often inclined to look down on the engineer or scientist.[30]

Radical reform of the central organisation for defence could not be expected from the civil service on its own initiative; hence, in Macmillan's savage restructuring of his Cabinet in July 1962, Watkinson was replaced by Peter Thorneycroft, the ninth Minister of Defence since Churchill in 1951 and, according to *The Sunday Times*, a man of 'vision and organising genius'. But, the writer added:

> In creating inter-Service unity and a central cohesive direction everything turns upon the overriding authority of the Chief of Defence Staff. The present holder of

the office is Admiral of the Fleet Earl Mountbatten, the last great war commander still at the summit of power with experience of directing the three Services as one. This year he completes 20 years as a member of the Chiefs of Staff Committee, and when he retires we shall have successive Chiefs of Staff who have never held high command in war, have had no responsible experience in combined operations and whose professional training gives them a prior commitment of loyalty to their own Service.[31]

Macmillan had toyed with the idea of making Mountbatten Minister of Defence, but the precedents for senior officers of the services in that essentially political role – Chatfield and Alexander – were not good, and Mountbatten had no wish to be involved in politics in any case. He did, however, agree to his term as CDS being extended for two years until July 1964, and with the strong backing of both Prime Minister and the new Minister of Defence he set about achieving the revolution in Whitehall which for so long he had believed to be necessary, and himself as the only person who could bring it about. Besides, Edwina's death had left him little else to live for.

Having obtained the approval of Macmillan and Thorneycroft to the first draft of a paper on his proposed reorganisation, Mountbatten retired to his Irish seat, Classiebawn Castle, and set about refining this seminal document. Apart from one or two personal staff officers the only people he consulted were Solly Zuckerman, as chief scientific adviser to the Minister of Defence, and Sir Robert Scott, lately Commissioner-General in South-East Asia, who had replaced Sir Edward Playfair as the Minister's permanent under-secretary. In view of the conclusions of Mountbatten's paper, which he signed on 9 October and sent to the Prime Minister via Peter Thorneycroft, it is not surprising that he felt bound to refrain from showing it to, let alone discussing it with, the service ministers and their Chiefs of Staff.

It was a fact that Caspar John, Dick Hull and Tom Pike, despite the Christian name terms, had all on various occasions used insulting language both to and about Mountbatten in the hearing of their staff officers and others. They disliked his propensity for pressing his views informally on ministers and others who might help get them accepted as policy, rather than a particular single-service proposal. Pike in particular, as Chief of the Air Staff, believed that Mountbatten always favoured the Navy although, according to Ziegler, Air Chief Marshal Sir Alfred Earle, who had been Deputy Chief of the Defence Staff and was therefore best placed to know, 'believed that Mountbatten was as nearly impartial on inter-Service issues as it was possible for him to be'.[32] Mountbatten was, without doubt, not only perceived by these men, the professional heads of their services, as a threat to their single-service sovereignty, but as 'not one of them'. In direct contrast to their inbred dislike of talking 'shop', especially in the mess, Mountbatten's eagerness to discuss every aspect of the profession of arms, whether a detail or a grand strategic concept, jarred upon his fellow Chiefs of Staff.

They found uncongenial, also, his un-British lack of restraint in describing his own achievements, as well as the evidence on all sides of his prodigious activity – so unlike the effortless superiority of Balliol men. But an Oxford (albeit not Balliol) man who as a civil servant saw Mountbatten at work, Sir Patrick Nairne, remembered:

> his executive drive and energy; his contacts with everyone who had a hand on a lever of power; his determination that the Navy should not lose out to the Army and RAF; his vision that the three Services could, nevertheless, work in a closer and more unified organisation. . . .[33]

Sir Patrick also referred to:

> a more engaging personal side – for example if I, as a very junior civilian from M Branch, sought to make a point at the [First Sea Lord's] briefing meeting, he would listen to me as courteously as to the VCNS; if he had pressed a point on Denis Healey as Defence Secretary, he would send for me afterwards to check personally how I was going to take action on the [Secretary of State's] behalf.[34]

Not until 9 December, when the service ministers and Chiefs of Staff were informed by Prime Minister's Personal Minute, did they learn officially of the drastic reform of the central organisation of defence Mountbatten had in mind:

> I have come to the firm conclusion that nothing short of the abolition of separate Service Departments and the creation of a single Ministry of Defence will get to the root of the problem.[35]

Well aware of the animus of the Chiefs of Staff and many senior civil servants, Mountbatten sought to distance himself from the decision-making process. Reaction to the proposals was predictably hostile, expressed in a sharply critical paper by the single-service Chiefs for which they claimed the support of, among other warriors, the retired Chiefs Harding, Slessor and Portal; also predictably, the Prime Minister ordered an independent enquiry to seek a resolution of the fierce conflict of views. The task was undertaken by Lord Ismay, Churchill's representative on the wartime Chiefs of Staff Committee, and Sir Ian Jacob, previously Ismay's assistant in the Military Wing of the Cabinet Office.

In the midst of these developments, news came through that the US Air Force had abandoned Skybolt. A Tri-Service Scientific Committee set up to study Skybolt replacement options could not resolve the inter-service conflict which was generated, and 'could only agree that whatever system was chosen must have mobility and instant readiness'.[36] Macmillan was due to meet President Kennedy at Nassau, in the Bahamas, on 18 December to discuss a wide range of topics:

> On learning of the cancellation of Skybolt I immediately (13 December) sent a message to our Ambassador in Washington on how the Nassau meeting should be handled. It seemed that it ought to start right away with the Skybolt question: 'My difficulty is that if we cannot reach agreement on a realistic means of maintaining the British independent deterrent, all the other questions may only justify perfunctory discussion, since an "agonising reappraisal" of all our foreign and defence policy will be required.'[37]

Neither Mountbatten nor his American opposite number as Chairman of the Joint Chiefs of Staff, General Maxwell Taylor, were present at Nassau. This was probably an advantage from Macmillan's point of view, since Britain could not afford to have more than one strategic deterrent system, whereas the USA felt bound to include all feasible systems in its nuclear deterrent armoury, lest the Soviet Union, by a scientific or technological breakthrough, should suddenly gain a decisive advantage; and the single system with the highest military credibility from the British point of view was certainly the submarine-launched ballistic missile system, Polaris. Not only did it offer mobility and instant readiness, but its capacity for total concealment ensured its invulnerability to a pre-emptive first strike, and hence its deterrent credibility.

Having thus ensured that any discordant Pentagon voices would be muted, Macmillan still had to argue against the State Department's persistent advice to Kennedy that it would not be in the best interests of the USA to let Britain have a stake in an American system while denying this to France, and indirectly jeopardising the cherished project of a mixed-manned European nuclear force. But Macmillan, briefed by Mountbatten, was determined to get Polaris, and clinched the matter by pledging that Britain would make her nuclear force available to NATO:

> Accordingly, the President and the Prime Minister agreed that the United States will make available on a continuing basis Polaris missiles (less warheads) for British submarines.[38]

On Christmas Eve 1962, the Admiralty Board reviewed the responsibility which would now devolve upon the Navy for mounting the strategic nuclear deterrent, and decided to implement immediately a project management scheme prepared and approved by the Board in June 1960. Since the execution of the British Polaris programme was not completed until five years after Mountbatten had ceased to be CDS, it is appropriate to record that on 6 April 1963 the Polaris

Agreement was signed, and a liaison officer newly appointed to the US Special Projects Office by the British Chief Polaris Executive (CPE), namely Rear Admiral H.S. Mackenzie (later Vice-Admiral Sir Hugh Mackenzie), arrived in Washington to start work. The British Naval Ballistic Missile Programme was under way, and would continue until it was thoroughly finished. The Polaris deputy controller, Rear Admiral C.W.H. Shepherd, commented:

> We planned in 1963 to fire our first missile at 11.15 EST [Eastern Standard Time] on 15 February 1968; we failed by 15 milliseconds. We were told in 1963 that there must be a continuous deterrent from July 1968; this was achieved.[39]

As to the cost, according to Professor Peter Nailor, who was for a time the Chief Administrative Officer of the British Polaris Project:

> . . . even given the increases in submarine costs and the decreases in missile purchases, there was overall a significant saving on the programme, in the sense that it eventually took less money to produce and deploy the force than had originally been envisaged.[40]

In the annals of major British defence projects, nothing like this degree of operational success, timeliness and cost-containment has ever been achieved before or since. It was a convincing testimony to the creative project management plan produced under Mountbatten's aegis, and facilitated in execution by the close professional relationship which he had initiated with the US Chief of Naval Operations.

During the spring of 1963 Mountbatten undertook a series of visits in South America, and was in Caracas on 1 March when he heard that the Cabinet had considered the recommendations in the Ismay/Jacob report. As old 'Jackie' Fisher would have complained, they did not amount to *totus porcus* – the whole hog. But the main thrust of Mountbatten's proposals was accepted, namely, the abolition of the Admiralty, the War Office and the Air Ministry (and hopefully the Ministry of Aviation). The Chiefs of Staff had felt it their duty to put forward every conceivable objection to the defence reorganisation proposals, but neither the Prime Minister nor the Minister of Defence would yield. And Thorneycroft was encouraged, as recounted by Macmillan in his memoirs, by a typically Churchillian intervention:

> Pray take no notice at all of any obstruction. You should approach this the way Lloyd George used to approach problems with dashing, slashing methods. Anyone who raises any objection can go, including Ministers.[41]

The government's intentions, given legislative form, were set out in a White Paper (Cmnd 2097) published in July 1963.

Ismay and Jacob had gone as far as they sensibly could to endorse Mountbatten's proposals. What they would not accept was the removal from the single-service Chiefs of Staff of their comprehensive personal responsibilities and status as the professional heads of their services by introducing the separate posts of commanders-in-chief, or inspectors-general, of the forces. This would have been disastrous. The differences between the three arms, sea, land and air, are profound and genuine. No one man can provide, at a critical juncture, the weight of responsible advice about some aspect of any service which is to be expected of a single-service professional head. However, when it comes to the conduct of operations at theatre level, in which all three services are involved, a single commander is best.

Proof of this was provided in 1963–65 when the confrontation in Borneo was well handled from the outset, carried through and successfully terminated thanks to prudent and professional direction by the Defence and Overseas Policy Committee of the Cabinet, advised by Mountbatten as Chief of the Defence Staff and the Chiefs of Staff, with the unified commander in Singapore acting as theatre commander in operational control of all three services. This was in effect the Macmillan–Thorneycroft–Mountbatten defence organisation in action.

It is of interest that Professor R.V. Jones, a connoisseur of bureaucratic tergiversation, observed:

> One of the most serious weaknesses with the Ministry was that I found myself almost cut off from the operational directorates of the Service ministries. . . .
>
> There was a substantial improvement by 1963, when I was asked to chair the Ministry's Working Party on the Future of Air Defence. One factor in this improvement was Lord Mountbatten's undertaking a second tour of duty as Chief of Defence Staff – he told me that it was during his second tour, now that he 'knew the ropes', that he was able to effect some key reorganisations. Despite the diminished status of Britain in the world, the Ministry now had far more sense of purpose than it had shown during my previous spell.[42]

Throughout 1963 the work of planning the new Ministry of Defence, to incorporate the three Service Departments as they now became, went ahead in parallel with crisis management, day-to-day administration and budgeting. It was a period of intense activity for all concerned. This in itself helped to generate a corporate spirit – the spirit of the hive, as Mountbatten called it. Within the year this monumental constitutional reform – the greatest of the century – had been given effect.

In March 1964 Mountbatten attended a Privy Council at which royal consent was given to the Bill, and on 1 April 1964 the service ministries closed down and the uprooted denizens of hallowed precincts moved into what is now the Ministry of Defence main building. There they were divided vertically into Navy, at the Charing Cross end, Army and Central Staffs in the middle, and Air Staff in their original place at the Westminster end. The real innovation was to improve on co-location, desirable in itself, by accommodating the entire defence staff horizontally by function: on the sixth floor were the ministers, chiefs, senior civil servants, the chief scientist, and their personal staffs; the seventh floor held the personnel and logistic policy people; on the fifth floor were the operational staffs and the Joint Operations Centre, and on the fourth the defence intelligence staff. This fell short of the optimum integration of the services; but when, on 7 April 1964, Mountbatten held his first Chiefs of Staff meeting in the specially appointed conference room, he had good reason to be content, for the time being, with what had been achieved.

As there remained much to be done, especially at the highest policy level, Macmillan asked Mountbatten to stay in office as CDS for another year, and he agreed. But in October 1964 the Labour Party was returned to power; although Denis Healey, the new Secretary of State for Defence, respected Mountbatten's abilities, now that the organisation of defence had been radically restructured he felt, and many in Whitehall and Westminster agreed with him, that Mountbatten was no longer indispensable. Mountbatten himself, while conscious that much had still to be done if his proposals for the central organisation of defence were to be fully carried out, had begun to look forward to retiring from active service as Chief of the Defence Staff. It was therefore agreed that his tenure of that office should not be further extended.

On the national defence front, by far the most critical issue facing the new Prime Minister, Harold Wilson, was whether or not to appease the left wing of his party, which strongly urged the abandonment of Polaris as Britain's earnest of a commitment to unilateral disarmament. Supposing he felt strong enough in the Cabinet and the party to keep the strategic nuclear deterrent, could Britain afford to do so? Writing to Wilson a few days after the general election to congratulate him, Mountbatten spoke of the *raison d'être* of Polaris:

> The part that the British deterrent has to play . . . is to dispel in Russian minds the thought that they will escape scot-free if by any chance the Americans decide to hold back release of a strategic nuclear response to an attack. Our own Polaris force will be capable of inflicting on the Russian homeland damage which the most hard-headed gambler could not regard as anything but utterly unacceptable.[43]

The outcome was that Wilson accepted the political credibility of this argument and, having done so, committed his administration to providing a force of four Polaris-missile-armed submarines – the minimum number with which a continuous deterrent patrol could be assured.

Given that over half of defence expenditure in peacetime is immutable in the short to medium term – pay, pensions and material overheads – the only measure open to a Secretary of State for Defence (the status dated from 1 April 1964) when called upon to make an immediate and drastic reduction in defence expenditure is to slash projects for new equipment.

Healey was therefore constrained by the economic stringency enforced upon him by the demands of the welfare state to impose a ceiling of £2 billion (at 1964 prices) in his first defence estimates. Major projects would have to go. At the celebrated 'crunch' meeting at Chequers on 20–22 November 1964 it was made clear that the 20 per cent reduction in defence estimates demanded by the Chancellor, James Callaghan, could not possibly be achieved unless both the RAF's most sacred of cows, the TSR2, and the Navy's equally sacrosanct project, the fleet aircraft carrier CVA01, were sacrificed.

The infighting during the Defence Review brought about by this ultimatum was in no way, it is sad to report, mitigated by the advent of the unified Ministry of Defence. By this time, however, the TSR2 project was beginning to lose some of its attraction for its RAF and other backers. A purchase of American F-111s offered an acceptable alternative. So Healey advised the Cabinet to cancel the TSR2, and that was that. The announcement was made by the Chancellor as part of his 'austerity Budget'. The case for the CVA01 seemed, for a time, somewhat stronger; the need for flexible and strategically mobile air cover for rapid-reaction forces east of Suez was convincing. But the cost of a carrier programme (one carrier does not make a viable force) could not possibly be accommodated without throwing the Navy completely out of balance. It was perhaps unfortunate that the Admiralty Board refused at that time to contemplate settling for the VSTOL carrier as the successor to the existing fleet carriers. These, however, were to have their operational lives extended into the 1970s. Because of the prolonged argument about CVA01 its demise was not finally decreed until after Mountbatten had ceased to be CDS. Although he was inclined to blame the First Sea Lord, Sir David Luce, for losing the carrier battle, the intransigence of some of the Navy's most senior aviators was to a large extent responsible. They allowed themselves to be inveigled into a competition in theoretical cost-effectiveness, instead of emphasising the essential absurdity of the island-bases concept and calling the RAF's bluff by settling for smaller and cheaper carriers with an anti-submarine potential.

During the remainder of Mountbatten's final year in office, the armed forces continued to be active in various operations. Early in 1964, for example, military mutinies in newly independent Tanzania, Kenya and Uganda were successfully quelled by Commandos landed from the carrier *Centaur* and troops from the strategic reserve in Kenya. The Borneo confrontation continued to employ major forces in deterring Soekarno's government, while British troops and aircraft were deployed to the Yemen where severe fighting was in progress as factions struggled for power following the announcement that Britain would withdraw from Aden in 1968. Writing in 1992 the historians of the Chiefs of Staff said:

In all these operations, the new Tri-Service Headquarters British Forces in Cyprus, Aden and Singapore responded quickly and effectively to the directions of the Operations Executive in the new Ministry of Defence and proved their worth. It was all a far cry from the cumbersome days of Suez less than a decade earlier, and from the improvisations of the Kuwait intervention. With Queen's enemies to be defeated or restrained, the Chiefs had no difficulty in co-operating wholeheartedly; and with Mountbatten in the Chair, ministers received clear and emphatic advice, and their decisions were swiftly implemented by the new command machinery.[44]

In March 1964 Mountbatten was asked by the Prime Minister to undertake a mission for the purpose of persuading a number of Commonwealth governments to help stamp out illegal immigration into Britain by establishing adequate controls and health checks. Denis Healey, with alacrity, urged his Chief of Defence Staff to take on the task. Having strong ideas of his own he doubtless felt that to be free for a time from Mountbatten's powerful and insistent advocacy of the services' viewpoint might be a relief. So Mountbatten undertook the uninviting job as a matter of duty. As usual, he tackled the problem resolutely and with tact. The civil servant who accompanied him produced a long-winded report. Mountbatten's own summary of the principles which should govern the action required to bring immigration under control were simple and sensible:

Commonwealth citizens would be treated wherever possible more and never less favourably than aliens;

Britain would always welcome *bona fide* students from the Commonwealth; and the right of a wife and dependent children to join an immigrant would always be observed.[45]

In the few weeks remaining to him as CDS, Mountbatten had to be content with only one more important step towards the creation of a fully integrated central defence staff: the merger of the three service intelligence directorates into a single defence intelligence staff, the director of which would be on the staff of the Chief of the Defence Staff. But he found it easier to get his way in minor matters. Captain R.W. Garson recalls that he was President of the wardroom mess at a 'Taranto' dinner in 1964, to celebrate also the 50th anniversary of the Fleet Air Arm, when Mountbatten was the principal guest. It took place in the shore establishment at Gosport formerly named HMS *Daedalus*, a naval air station and the alma mater of many of those present, but recently renamed by the Ministry of Defence (Navy) as HMS *Ariel*. On being told by the Flag Officer, Naval Air Command, Vice-Admiral Sir Richard Smeeton, of the resentment caused by this change, Mountbatten said 'Dick, we will change it back. You start the ball rolling and it will be one of my last acts before stepping down.'[46] He was, of course, as good as his word.

On 16 July 1965 Mountbatten was relieved as Chief of the Defence Staff by Field Marshal Sir Richard Hull. He was 65 years old, and had held the most important post in Britain's defence establishment for six years. Admiral of the Fleet Lord Lewin, Chief of the Defence Staff in 1980, giving the Mountbatten Memorial Lecture at the RUSI, summed up thus:

Perhaps no organisation should be set in concrete. Our Armed Forces are more closely integrated today than they have ever been. Our defence colleges and our training establishments preach the benefits and the essential nature of inter-Allied and inter-Service co-operation. All this is a tribute to the wisdom and energy of Earl Mountbatten. But defence is a dynamic business and there is no certainty that what appears basically sound today will meet tomorrow's needs. The debate will continue, and this would have met with the approval of Lord Louis. I did not intend to propose a radical new organisation. My intention, and my hope, has been to remind you of the debt that we owe to a great man.

I chose as the title of my address – the Common Cause. Our great privilege, I suggest, has been to be associated with a man who had the vision to see the common cause, and the courage to pursue it.[47]

EPILOGUE

> The whole earth is the sepulchre of famous men.
> *Thucydides*

The sailor who joined the Royal Navy as a cadet in 1913 as His Serene Highness Prince Louis of Battenberg retired from active duty 52 years later as Admiral of the Fleet the Earl Mountbatten of Burma, with a new family name. Having been deprived, when he was 17, of the title 'Prince', he had nevertheless brought to his professional career as a naval officer a princely style which combined the common touch with a commanding presence and leadership founded upon meticulous study of relevant technology, unbounded enthusiasm and relentless energy. General Sir John Hackett has this to say:

> In operations of war, to whose successful conduct all military activity is directed, management and leadership are both indispensable. They are not the same thing. Some part of the functional area covered by each is common to both . . . the higher the level of command and the greater the distance from . . . 'the sharp end', the higher the requirement for management; the lower the level and the closer the battle, the higher the need for leadership. Given that technical competence is a requirement everywhere . . . the good platoon commander must be a competent manager in a limited sphere but the demands upon his power of leadership can be very great. For an army commander the distribution of emphasis between management and leadership will be different.[1]

And different, yet again, for a Supreme Allied Commander. In order to be successful he must have 'in spades' the capacity to lead, the ability to manage, and the judgement to utilise both qualities in proportion. Liddell Hart said of Marlborough that he had 'the power to inspire affection while communicating energy'. That could equally be said of Mountbatten.

Uniquely, in the matter of technical competence a supreme commander must be quick to understand and evaluate the material factors affecting the operational strengths and weaknesses of the other arms besides his own. When Winston Churchill chose Mountbatten to be his Adviser on Combined Operations, he was well aware of the young captain's uninhibited interest in matters technical – 'you must make yourself into a triangular hermaphrodite, Dickie', he told him; and later, when Mountbatten had done so, Churchill proposed him as Supreme Commander South-East Asia on the grounds that he was 'young, enthusiastic and triphibious' (a locution which, incidentally, fell harshly upon the scholarly ears of General Hackett, as President both of the Classical Association and the English Association of the United Kingdom).

The author, being privileged on one occasion to precede Field Marshal Montgomery in the lecture theatre of the Army Staff College at Camberley, heard his celebrated talk on the art of the general. In the course of it he sought to establish the criteria by which *le grand chef* may be distinguished from *le bon général ordinaire*. No doubt he wished to make quite clear the category to which he belonged. To be accorded the status of *un grand chef* Montgomery declared, 'he must have conducted a successful campaign against a wep*u*table foe'. General Wolfe's victory at Quebec, for example, did not qualify him. Mountbatten, being still alive, was not eligible for inclusion with, *inter alia*, Alexander the Great, Hannibal, Marlborough, Napoleon and Wellington – nor, for that matter, was Nelson mentioned, even in passing. But, granted that 'Monty' himself must now be included with the greats, there can be no question that Mountbatten also qualifies. He was the theatre commander who conducted the campaign against the Japanese, which drove them out of Burma – and the Japanese were surely a 'wep*u*table' foe.

Mountbatten's reputation as a naval leader has evidently suffered from his being judged not as a captain of war, but by the pattern of the Navy's senior officers prevalent before 1914 and which persisted between the wars, characterised by Churchill as:

> competent administrators, brilliant experts of every description, unequalled navigators, good disciplinarians, fine sea-officers, brave and devoted hearts . . . more captains of ships than captains of war.[2]

This misjudgement of Mountbatten by his seniors was compounded by his propensity to swim strongly against the still-flowing tide of technophobia, recognised by Captain Roskill as

> the long-standing British belief that a good seaman was by definition a more valuable asset than a good engineer, and the pronounced tendency of the Executive Branch to regard their technical colleagues as inferiors, professionally as well as socially. . . . The navy of 1918 was proud of and confident in the great traditions it had inherited from the past; but tradition can too easily be made the excuse for not facing up to the need for change when change is obviously needed. . . . I now feel that in the education and training of officers of my generation it was exaggerated to the detriment of professional study and profound thinking about the problems of

the day and the future. I am sure the senior officers of those times were anti-intellectual. They mistrusted the officer who showed originality of thought or a tendency to question the accepted view, and above all one who committed his thoughts and ideas to paper.[3]

The reaction of Sir Andrew Cunningham, for example, to Mountbatten's constant probing of the frontiers of conventional naval wisdom, was to question his 'judgement'.

If the erstwhile prince did not match up to the accepted model of an admiral, by how much less could he be accorded the acclaim owing to a general or an air chief marshal; hence it is only in the persona of *un grand chef* that Mountbatten's military reputation was made, founded though it was upon a thorough grasp and active experience of sea warfare, followed by that of combined operations. As far as the pantheon of British military leaders is concerned, Mountbatten was uniquely qualified; and not only in having commanded land, sea and air forces at theatre level, but in having done this when so young. Not since Prince Rupert of the Rhine, who commanded an army at the age of 23, or Prince Eugene of Savoy, a field marshal at 29, had there been so youthful a great commander. But, whereas in the 17th and 18th centuries to be a prince was to have a chief command by right, in the 20th it was a handicap to be royal. Promotion in the officer corps of the all-regular, volunteer armed forces was by merit, harnessed to a career structure which owed more to bureaucratic orderliness than determination to advance a potential 'captain of war' with the rapidity which he might deserve. Hence the discomfort, even resentment, felt in the higher ranks of the British armed forces, especially in the Royal Navy, at the over-leaping advancement of Mountbatten to flag rank, and its equivalent in the other two services.

This resentment was exacerbated by Mountbatten's no doubt tiresome insistence upon the tightness of his views and decisions, coupled with the evident delight which he took in Machiavellian manoeuvres to achieve his ends in the face of hidebound hostility. But the records prove his invariable respect for the constitutional limits of his authority, and the care he took to preserve intact the monarchy of which, as an institution, he was so proud to be a part.

Criticism of Mountbatten, which in fairness must not remain unanswered, has persisted in regard to four episodes in particular: his handling on certain occasions of HMS *Kelly*, and the 5th Destroyer Flotilla; his part in mounting the Dieppe raid; the dismissal of General Leese from the post of Commander-in-Chief, Allied Land Forces, South-East Asia (ALFSEA); and the accusation that, when Viceroy of India, he was responsible for the communal mass killings, and connived at changing the award of the boundary commission to favour India. What has been written in this book should go a good way towards disposing of these criticisms.

To sum up, the all-round performance of the destroyers he commanded in peacetime, HMS *Daring* and *Wishart*, was pre-eminent; in war, as Captain (D) 5th Destroyer Flotilla, in its leader HMS *Kelly* and, when she was out of action, in one or other of the flotilla, Mountbatten set an inspiring example of offensive action against the highly skilled and in some ways technically superior German navy and air force.

In the case of Dieppe, the aim of which was to carry out a reconnaissance in force, the necessity for such an operation as a preliminary to re-entry into western Europe was accepted by the Chiefs of Staff; the decision to employ Canadian troops was politico-military and not made by the Chief of Combined Operations; the decision to remount Operation RUTTER as JUBILEE, in conditions of quite exceptional security, was taken by Winston Churchill and the Chiefs of Staff, and surprise was achieved; features of the plan which led to heavy casualties, namely inadequate naval bombardment and air support, and the decision to make a frontal attack, were contrary to Mountbatten's advice and were not his responsibility. The lessons learned from JUBILEE were acknowledged by the war leaders to have been indispensable to the success of OVERLORD. Montgomery, in his *Memoirs*, concluded:

> My own feeling about the Dieppe raid is that there were far too many authorities with a hand in it; there was no one single operational commander who was solely responsible for the operation from start to finish, a Task Force Commander in fact. Without doubt the lessons learnt there were an important contribution to the eventual landing in Normandy on the 6th June 1944. But the price was heavy in killed and prisoners. I believe that we could have got the information and experience we needed without losing so many Canadian soldiers.[4]

As to the Leese affair, the matter was surely laid to rest in a letter from Leese to Ronald Lewin, biographer of Slim, dated 25 April 1973:

> On no account do I want you to think that I am blaming Mountbatten for what happened. He certainly gave me no authority to sack Slim.[5]

Finally, India. The central fact is that once an impending date for handing India over to her peoples had been pronounced by the British government, the government of British India could not guarantee beyond that date the pay, pensions and conditions of service of the Indians employed (and they were the overwhelming majority) in civil administration; nor, in the likely event of civil disorder, could the Indian army, composed of mixed ethnic and religious elements, and faced like the civil services with an uncertain future, be relied upon to support the civil power if and when called upon to do so. By the time Mountbatten arrived in Delhi as Viceroy there was no longer any power to hand over. Speed in achieving a settlement was of the essence if civil war throughout the subcontinent was to be avoided.

As to the charge against Mountbatten that he was pro-Indian in carrying out the duty laid upon him by the British parliament, and through it by the British people, this has proved hard to substantiate. Evidence has been derived mainly from his alleged interference with the award made by Sir Cyril Radcliffe, chairman of the boundary commission. In his biography of that eminent lawyer and great public servant, Edmund Heward sums up:

> Radcliffe might well have been persuaded by the arguments put forward by Mountbatten and Ismay. What is certain is that he could not have been persuaded against his better judgement. He found Mountbatten arrogant: did not care for him personally and had already shown his independence by refusing Mountbatten's request to delay the Award until after 15 August.[6]

Emanating from a former Chief Master of the Supreme Court, this opinion may safely be held to exonerate Mountbatten of bias. It testifies to the fairness of the independence settlement negotiated on behalf of Great Britain by Mountbatten that the last British Chief of Naval Staff in India did not depart until 1958, nearly 11 years after independence; and destroyers of the Pakistan Navy were deployed to operate under Mountbatten's command in the Mediterranean when he was Commander-in-Chief there, in the 1950s.

Lawrence James, writing in 1995, said:

> At least Britain had parted company from India with dignity and a sense of achievement, whereas abandonment of old spheres of influence in Iran and Egypt had been retreats in the face of insults and brickbats.[7]

In the case of India, Mountbatten's advice to his Prime Minister was in accordance with government policy, of which he became a skilled and determined executant; in the Middle East, by contrast, his advice to his political masters was rejected. In the case of Egypt, the damage to Britain's standing in the world was only limited by the exemplary fashion in which Mountbatten conducted the Suez operations, in obedience to orders with which he profoundly disagreed. James concludes that:

> Few empires have equipped their subjects with the intellectual wherewithal to overthrow their rulers. None has been survived by so much affection and moral respect.[8]

It would be false to the muse of history to deny for any reason, or unfairly diminish, the immense and unique contribution of Louis Mountbatten to this achievement.

For a few months after retirement from active duty Mountbatten, now Earl Mountbatten of Burma, was fully occupied in organising the archives of his papers, and in maintaining a vast correspondence with all and sundry who sought his interest in personal matters or charities. Then began the epic enterprise of filming his life and times for television, most ably produced by Peter Morley with the rigorous scripting of John Terraine, a military historian of high repute. This presentation of Mountbatten's world-spanning activities, much of it filmed on the original locations, was a substitute for the customary autobiography provided by political and military leaders. And with that 'in the can', Mountbatten turned to the many tasks he was asked to undertake.

Before long he was presiding over some 200 or so associations or institutions covering an extensive range of interests; accepted the invitations of successive governments to carry out missions of goodwill to foreign rulers; paid visits to the countries of the Commonwealth; founded Atlantic College, at which young people of many nations were to complete their schooling together in the name of international understanding; reported on the reform of the prison service and the design of high security prisons; resisted the temptation to be involved in plans to form a government of national unity in the event of a breakdown in public order, which certain press barons professed to fear; refrained from speaking in the House of Lords as an election approached, lest the monarch should thereby be associated with party politics; and made public time and again his view of the dangers inherent in the deployment of tactical nuclear weapons – as witness his profoundly important speech at Strasbourg on 11 May 1979:

> . . . the nuclear arms race has no military purpose. Wars cannot be fought with nuclear weapons . . . by a reduction of nuclear armaments, I believe it should be possible to achieve security at a lower level of military confrontation.[9]

He also did his best to encourage the growth of a world-class electronics industry in Britain, as well as urging industrial leaders to improve dramatically their approach to man-management.

Captain Raymond Dreyer recalled, in this context, that:

> Mountbatten was the prime mover in getting a Royal Charter for the British Institute of Radio Engineers (BritIRE). This meant that members were entitled to the title of Chartered Engineer (CEng). . . . A few years ago the Institute of Electrical Engineers (IEE) absorbed the BritIRE, so I am now a Fellow of the IEE, which is a broadly based and excellent institution. . . . That was one way in which Mountbatten helped us along, when we retired and went into industry. And this was true of the whole Commonwealth, where BritIRE got a lot of members.[10]

Mountbatten's credentials as a leader of Europe's mariners were recognised in his election, in 1975, as an Associate Member of the French Académie de Marine, which, at the reception marking the occasion, was described by its president in these words:

> *Héritière de l'Académie royale de Marine fondée sous le règne de Louis XV, notre compagnie ainsi que vous le savez, a reçu mission, suivant ses statuts, de favoriser le développement des hautes études concernant les questions maritimes de toute nature: qu'il s'agisse de marine militaire ou marchande, de sciences et techniques maritimes, de navigation et d'océanologie, d'histoire, lettres et arts ou de droit et d'économie maritime.*
>
> [As heir to the Royal Naval Academy founded in the reign of Louis XV, our company has thus, as you know, been given the statutory mission to promote the development of advanced studies concerning maritime matters of all kinds: whether it be the armed or merchant navy, maritime science and technology, navigation and oceanography, history, literature and the arts, or maritime law and economics.]

In his speech of thanks for the honour, Mountbatten delighted his hosts:

> *. . .Helas! au contraire de l'anglaise et de l'allemand que l'on m'a enseigné dès le berceau, je n'ai appris le français qu'á l'école. Et tout le monde sait ce que donne dans ces conditions le français d'un Anglais!*
>
> [Alas, unlike English and German, which I was taught from the cradle, I only learned French at school! And everyone knows the kind of French that this produces from an Englishman!]

And he went on to tell of his sojourn in France as a young commander when qualifying as an interpreter:

> *. . . Notre professeur, Madame Callède, était formidable. Elle avait même reussi à enseigner aux commissaires du bord les termes nécessaires au maniement d'une tourelle de quinze pouces!*
>
> [Our teacher, Madame Callède, was splendid. She even managed to teach the pursers the requisite terms for the handling of a 15-inch gun turret!]

His peroration was both elegant and pleasing to those present:

> *L'amiral Amman a parlé de ma spécialité d'ingénieur des transmissions et de mon intérêt pour l'électronique. C'est très aimable á lui et je tiens á lui dire que la Société d'Encouragement pour la Recherche et l'Invention de France m'a décerné sa médaille d'or. Après la cérémonie et pendant le vin d'honneur, j'ai demandé au Président de la société si la France souffrait de ce que nos appelons 'la fuite de cerveaux'. C'est-a-dire l'emigration des chercheurs et des savants vers des pays mieux équipés et plus fortunés. Sa réponse indignée ne s'est pas faite attendre: 'Mais non,*

Monsieur, et cela pour trois raisons – notre langue, notre cuisine et nos femmes!' Et ce sont justement trois des raisons pour lesquelles j'aime tellement la France!'[11]
[Admiral Amman has talked about my specialisation as a communications engineer and of my interest in electronics. It is very kind of him, and I am pleased to tell him that the French Society for the Encouragement of Research and Invention has awarded me its Gold Medal. After the ceremony and during the toast, I asked the President of the society whether France was suffering from what we call the 'brain drain' – that is to say the emigration of researchers and scientists to richer and better equipped countries. His indignant reply came back without hesitation: 'Certainly not, Sir, and for three reasons – our language, our cooking and our women!' And those are precisely three of the reasons why I love France so much!]

But the well-being of the servicemen of Britain and the Commonwealth and their families, was never far from Mountbatten's mind. The testimony of Lieutenant General Sir Napier Crookenden affords a good instance:

In 1973 I was sent for by Mountbatten and paraded at his flat in Wilton Crescent mews one September day. He said he wished me to take over from General Jack Denning as Chairman of the SSAFA [Soldiers, Sailors and Airmen's Families Association] Council . . . he persuaded me to accept.

Six years later he was foully murdered by the IRA. Next day I read through my fat file of correspondence with him as our President and at the back I found a letter to Jack Denning which read as follows: 'I saw Napier Crookenden yesterday. I think he will make a good Chairman. He agreed with everything I said.'

Going on to recall several occasions in which Mountbatten had provided immediate and effective support to SSAFA, General Crookenden ends with a comment arising from research that he was doing for the Air Force Historical Society:

. . . as I go through the histories of the preliminary planning through 1942, 1943 and early 1944 I am struck by the enormous debt owed by all the planners, including COSSAC, to Mountbatten and his Combined Ops Staff.

Apart from the development of materiel and techniques, the most important legacy of his work to my mind was the idea and practice of fully integrated staffs, in which inter-Service rivalries disappeared.[12]

And so the never-ending round of public service continued; but family life, revolving round his daughters, sons-in-law and grandchildren, was never neglected. Then, just before noon on 27 August 1979, Mountbatten took a family party out in a small motor launch, *Shadow V*, which he kept in the little harbour of Mullaghmore, hard by the old mansion, Classiebawn Castle in County Sligo, left to him by Edwina and used for family holidays 'away from it all'. The plan was to recover some lobster pots set the day before. In the launch with him were Lord and Lady Brabourne (daughter and son-in-law), Lord Brabourne's mother Doreen, and the Brabourne's twin sons, Nicholas and Timothy, plus a local lad, Paul Maxwell, who helped to look after the boat. Just as *Shadow V* slowed down on reaching the lobster pots, a bomb which had been placed below the engine was detonated, probably by remote control from the shore. Mountbatten himself, Nicholas and Paul were killed instantly, and 83-year-old Lady Brabourne was so severely injured that she died a little later. Timothy was blown clear but badly hurt; his parents' legs were broken, with many lacerations from splinters of wood and metal.

The Provisional Irish Republican Army claimed responsibility for the murders, but in Dublin's Special Criminal Court, on 23 November 1979, one Thomas McMahon was convicted of the murder of Mountbatten and sentenced to life imprisonment.

The state funeral which took place followed to the letter the comprehensive and meticulous instructions given by Mountbatten in response to a request from the Lord Chamberlain made some years previously. For the author, who witnessed the cortège passing down Whitehall, the most moving sight was that of Earl Mountbatten's charger, immaculately turned out, carrying his Lifeguards' jackboots reversed in the stirrups. But sailors drew the gun-carriage whereon lay the Union Flag-draped coffin, and naval uniforms predominated in the ceremonial, as befitted the obsequies of a princely sailor, Admiral of the Fleet the Earl Mountbatten of Burma, KG, PC, GCB, OM, GCSI, GCIE, GCVO, DSO, ADC, FRS, DCL, LL.D, DSc, Personal ADC to the Queen.

Appendix I

CENTRAL ORGANISATION FOR DEFENCE (BASED ON CMND 476 OF JULY 1958)

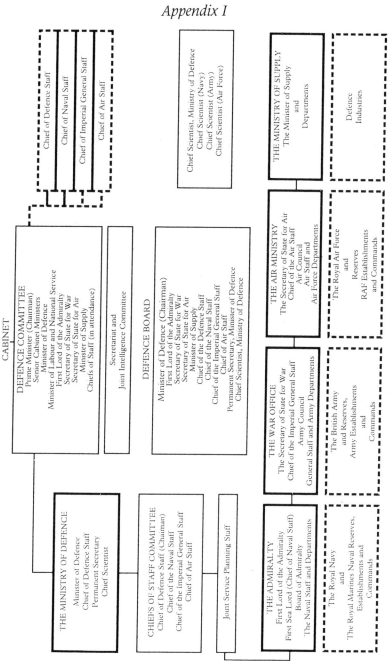

Fig 1. Central Organisation for Defence, 1958

Appendix II

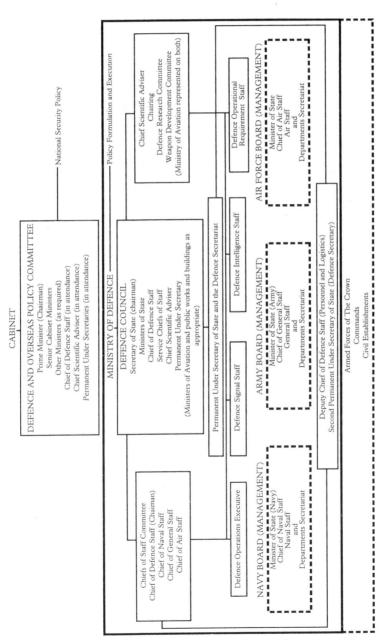

CENTRAL ORGANISATION FOR DEFENCE (BASED ON CMND 097 OF JULY 1963, IMPLEMENTED 1 APRIL 1964)

CABINET

DEFENCE AND OVERSEAS POLICY COMMITTEE
Prime Minister (Chairman)
Senior Cabinet Ministers
Other Ministers (as required)
Chief of Defence Staff (in attendance)
Chief Scientific Adviser (in attendance)
Permanent Under Secretaries (in attendance)

— National Security Policy

— Policy Formulation and Execution

MINISTRY OF DEFENCE

DEFENCE COUNCIL
Secretary of State (chairman)
Ministers of State
Chief of Defence Staff
Service Chiefs of Staff
Chief Scientific Adviser
Permanent Under Secretary
(Ministers of Aviation and public works and buildings as
appropriate)

Chiefs of Staff Committee
Chief of Defence Staff (Chairman)
Chief of Naval Staff
Chief of General Staff
Chief of Air Staff

Chief Scientific Adviser
Chairing
Defence Research Committee
Weapon Development Committee
(Ministry of Aviation represented on both)

Permanent Under Secretary of State and the Defence Secretariat

Defence Operations Executive

Defence Signal Staff

Defence Intelligence Staff

Defence Operational
Requirement Staff

NAVY BOARD (MANAGEMENT)
Minister of State (Navy)
Chief of Naval Staff
Naval Staff
and
Departments Secretariat

ARMY BOARD (MANAGEMENT)
Minister of State (Army)
Chief of General Staff
General Staff
and
Departments Secretariat

AIR FORCE BOARD (MANAGEMENT)
Minister of State
Chief of Air Staff
Air Staff
and
Departments Secretariat

Deputy Chief of Defence Staff (Personnel and Logistics)
Second Permanent Under Secretary of State (Defence Secretary)

Armed Forces of The Crown
Commands
Civil Establishments

Fig. 2. Central Organisation for Defence, 1964

NOTES

Chapter 1

1. W.G. Perrin (ed.), *Boteler's Dialogues* (1685) (London, Navy Records Society, 1929), p. 3.
2. Lieutenant Commander the Reverend Hugh St Aubyn Wake RN, in conversation with the author, 1992.
3. The Navy Records Society, *The Beatty Papers*, vol. 1, p. 23.
4. The Battenberg Course Indicator, invented by Prince Louis in 1892, was a mechanical device for determining the course and speed of other vessels in relation to the user's own ship. It proved particularly useful for convoys in the Second World War.
5. Randolph Churchill, *Winston Churchill: Young Statesman 1901–1914* (London, Heinemann, 1967), p. 552.
6. Ibid. p. 540.
7. Michael Howard, *The Lessons of History* (Oxford, Clarendon Press, 1991), p. 113.
8. Randolph Churchill, op. cit., p. 552.
9. Richard Hough, *Louis and Victoria: the First Mountbattens* (London, Hutchinson, 1974), p. 281.
10. Randolph Churchill, op. cit., pp. 717–18.
11. Richard Hough, *Mountbatten, Hero of our Time* (London, Weidenfeld, 1980), p. 25.
12. The Navy Records Society, op. cit., p. 149.
13. Stephen Roskill, *Man of Secrets*, vol. 1 (London, Collins, 1980), p. 134.
14. MB1/A364.
15. William James, *Admiral Sir William Fisher* (London, Macmillan, 1943), p. 13.
16. Philip Ziegler, *Mountbatten: The Official Biography* (London, Collins, 1985), chapter 8, *passim*.
17. John Terraine, *The Life and Times of Lord Louis Mountbatten* (London, Hutchinson, 1968).

Chapter 2

1. Captain Jack Broome, DSC, RN, *Make a Signal* (London, Putnam, 1955), p. 171.
2. Nicolas, Sir N.H. (ed.), *The Dispatches and Letters of Lord Admiral Viscount Nelson*, vol. 4 (London, Chatham, 1997–8), p. 236.
3. Lieutenant Commander Langton Gowlland, RN, letter to the author, 8 November 1992.

4. Stephen Roskill, *Naval Policy between the Wars*, vol. 1 (London, Collins, 1968), p. 236.
5. The Navy Records Society, *British Naval Documents 1204–1960*, p. 946.
6. MB1/C93.
7. Ibid.
8. Stephen Roskill, *The Naval Review* (April 1980), pp. 151–4.
9. Rear Admiral George Ross, *The Naval Review* (January 1981), pp. 21–2.
10. Stephen Roskill, *The War at Sea 1939–45*, vol. 1 (London, HMSO, 1954), p. 267.
11. Corelli Barnett, *Engage the Enemy More Closely* (London, Hodder & Stoughton, 1991), p. 48.
12. Winston S. Churchill, *The Second World War*, vol. 1, App. II (London, Cassell, 1948), pp. 589–90.
13. Martin, Gilbert, *Finest Hour: Winston Churchill 1939–1945* (London, Heinemann, 1983), p. 33.
14. Charles Poynder, *Of Frigates and Fillies* (London, Nautical Publications, 1993), p. 24.
15. Ziegler, op. cit., p. 127.
16. Vice-Admiral Sir Louis Le Bailly, KBE, CBE, letter to the author, 25 July 1995.
17. Gus Britton, letter to the author, 21 December 1993.
18. MB1/A110.
19. Lieutenant General Sir Adrian Carton de Wiart, VC, *Happy Odyssey* (London, Cape, 1950), p. 174.
20. Terraine, op. cit., p. 72.
21. MB1/B11D/f1.
22. Ziegler, op. cit., pp. 138–9.
23. MB1/B11D/f1.
24. Ibid.
25. Adrian Seligman, letter to the author dated 11 March 1996.
26. Quoted in Ziegler, op. cit., pp. 138–9.
27. Roskill, op. cit., p. 443.
28. Winston Churchill, *The World Crisis*, quoted in Randolph Churchill, op. cit. (London, Thornton Butterworth, 1923–9), p. 544. See also single volume edition, Churchill, *The World Crisis 1911–1918* (New York, Simon & Schuster, 2005).

Chapter 3

1. Dwight D. Eisenhower, *Crusade in Europe* (London, Heinemann, 1948), p. 75.
2. John Terraine, op.cit., p. 85.
3. MB/1/B14.
4. Ibid.
5. Ibid.
6. Quoted Ziegler, *Mountbatten: The Official Biography* (London, Collins, 1985), p. 152.
7. Bernard Fergusson, *The Watery Maze* (London, Collins, 1961), p. 60.
8. MB1/B15.
9. Winston Churchill, *The Second World War*, vol. 3 (London, Cassell, 1950), pp. 480–1.
10. Brian Loring Villa, *Unauthorised Action: Mountbatten and the Dieppe Raid* (Toronto, OUP, 1989), p. 163.

11. Fergusson, op. cit., pp. 88–90.
12. Directive by Chiefs of Staff to CCO, dated 16 October 1941.
13. Fergusson, op. cit., p. 90.
14. MB1/B13.
15. Fergusson, op. cit., p. 108.
16. R.V. Jones, *Most Secret War* (London, Hamish Hamilton, 1978), p. 245.
17. Ziegler, op. cit., p. 168.
18. Martin Gilbert, *Road to Victory: Winston S. Churchill 1941–1945* (London, Heinemann, 1986) p. 113n.
19. Operation SLEDGEHAMMER was the code name for a limited Allied invasion of France in 1942. The main objective was to capture either Cherbourg or Brest as a foothold, before a larger landing. After the costly Dieppe raid in August 1942, SLEDGEHAMMER was abandoned.
20. Operation GYMNAST was the early code name used in 1941 for the plan for an Allied landing in North Africa, later named TORCH.
21. MB1/B13.
22. Villa, op. cit., p. 18.
23. Ibid., p. 248.
24. Ibid., p. 3.
25. Roskill, *The War at Sea 1939–1945*, vol. 2, p. 310.
26. Villa, op. cit., p. 200.
27. Ronald Lewin, *Ultra Goes to War* (London, Hutchinson, 1978), p. 64.
28. Gilbert, op. cit, vol. 4, p. 150.
29. F.R. Hinsley, et al., *Intelligence in the Second World War: Its Influence on Strategy and Operations*, vol. 2 (London, HMSO, 1981), p. 695.
30. Gilbert, op. cit., p. 150.
31. Ibid., pp. 210–11.
32. Ibid., p. 211.
33. Ibid.
34. Chief of the Imperial General Staff, Sir Alan Brooke (later Field Marshal Lord Alanbrooke).
35. MB1/B17.
36. Hinsley, op. cit., p. 185.
37. MB1/B26.
38. Gilbert, op. cit., p. 185.
39. Lord Lovat, *March Past* (London, Weidenfeld, 1978), p. 252.
40. MB1/B18.
41. Ibid.
42. W.S. Chalmers, *Full Cycle: The Biography of Admiral Sir Bertram Ramsay* (London, Hodder & Stoughton, 1959), pp. 131–2.
43. Ibid.
44. Operation ROUNDUP was the code name given to a plan for an Allied invasion of France across the Channel in the spring of 1943. On 8 April 1942 General Marshall and President Roosevelt's personal representative, Harry Hopkins, visited London to put the plan to Churchill, who agreed in principle. The plan was later abandoned in favour of OVERLORD.

45. Chalmers, op.cit., pp. 131–2.
46. Kenneth Edwards, *Operation Neptune* (London, Collins, 1946), p. 29.
47. Rear Admiral R.E. Horan, *The Naval Review* (January 1961), p. 23.
48. Gilbert, op. cit., p. 225.
49. Chalmers, op. cit., p. 138.
50. Ibid., p. 146.
51. Ibid., p. 149.
52. MB1/B26.
53. MB1/B14.
54. MB1/B17.
55. Horan, *The Naval Review*, op. cit., p. 40.
56. Ibid.
57. Fergusson, op. cit., pp. 275–6.
58. Ibid., p. 282.
59. Ibid., p. 238.
60. Solly (later Lord) Zuckerman OM KCB FRS (1904–93) was a South African-born zoologist and anatomist, who undertook a number of research projects for the British government during the war and was Chief Scientific Adviser to the Ministry of Defence, 1964–71. During the Cold War he was opposed to the nuclear arms race.
61. Roskill, op. cit., vol. 3, I, p. 119.
62. Air Marshal Sir Arthur Tedder, Commander-in-Chief RAF Middle East Command. Under him, the RAF played a key role in the victory at El Alamein, after which he was promoted to Air Chief Marshal. He subsequently became Marshal of the Royal Air Force and received a peerage in 1946.
63. Fergusson, op. cit., pp. 241–2.
64. Ibid., p. 246.
65. Gilbert, op. cit., p. 464.
66. Ibid., p. 465.
67. Ibid.
68. Ibid., p. 467.
69. Ibid.
70. The Whitworth Papers, cited Ziegler, op. cit., p. 222.
71. Ziegler, op. cit., p. 222.
72. Janet Morgan, *Edwina* (London, HarperCollins, 1991), p. 222.
73. Ziegler, op. cit., p. 224.

Chapter 4

1. Field Marshal Viscount Slim, *Defeat into Victory* (London, Macmillan, 1956), p. 534.
2. Ronald Lewin, *Slim: The Standardbearer* (London, Leo Cooper, 1976), p. 128.
3. Lewin, op. cit., p. 129.
4. MB1/C SC3/47/c.
5. David Rooney, *Wingate and the Chindits* (London, Arms & Armour Press, 1994), p. 99.

6. 'Directive by the Prime Minister and Minister of Defence', 'Most Secret', sent as COSSEA No. 1 OZ 3331, 29 October 1943; Cabinet Papers 120/707, cited Martin, *Road to Victory*, p. 519.
7. Slim, op. cit., pp. 200–2.
8. Brigadier M.R. Roberts, 'The Campaign in Burma, 1943–45', in *RUSI Journal* (May 1956), p. 241.
9. Lewin, op. cit., p. 136.
10. Gilbert, op. cit., p. 695.
11. Rooney, op. cit., pp. 118–19.
12. Ibid.
13. MB1/C189.
14. Cited Lewin, op. cit., p. 173.
15. David Rooney, *Burma Victory* (London, Arms & Armour Press, 1992), p. 60.
16. Ibid.
17. Ibid., pp. 44–5.
18. Mountbatten, *RUSI Journal* (November 1946), p. 477.
19. MB1/C189.
20. Ibid.
21. Rooney, *Burma Victory*, p. 75.
22. John Costello, *The Pacific War 1941–45* (London, Collins, 1981), p. 466.
23. Lewin, op. cit., p. 188.
24. Rooney, *Burma Victory*, p. 139.
25. Winston S. Churchill, *The Second World War*, vol. VI, *The Tide of Victory* (London, Cassell, 1954), p. 12.
26. Mountbatten, op. cit., *RUSI Journal*, p. 479.
27. Gilbert, op. cit., pp. 883–4.
28. Ibid., p. 885.
29. Mountbatten, op. cit., *RUSI Journal*, p. 479.
30. Captain J. Hans Hamilton, letter to the author, 26 March 1996.
31. MB1/C229.
32. Rooney, *Burma Victory*, p. 183.
33. Mountbatten, op. cit., *RUSI Journal*, p. 481.
34. Lewin, op. cit., pp. 214–15.
35. Ronald Lewin, *The Ultra Story* (London, Hutchinson, 1978), p. 305.
36. Lewin, *Slim: The Standardbearer*, p. 222.
37. Mountbatten, op. cit., *RUSI Journal*, p. 482.
38. Lewin, *Slim: The Standardbearer*, p. 231.
39. MB1/C43/21.
40. Lewin, *Slim: The Standardbearer*, p. 241.
41. Ibid., p. 245.
42. Gilbert, op. cit., p. 1348.
43. Lewin, *Slim: The Standardbearer*, p. 246.
44. Ibid., p. 250.
45. MB1/C43/26.
46. The historical name of 'Siam' was first changed to 'Thailand' in 1939, but reverted to 'Siam' between 1945 and 1949 when 'Thailand' was definitively adopted.

Chapter 5

1. Duff Cooper (Viscount Norwich), *Old Men Forget* (London, Hart-Davis, 1953), p. 57.
2. Kenneth Harris, *Attlee* (London, Weidenfeld, 1982), p. 381.
3. Ronald Lewin, *The Chief* (London, Hutchinson, 1980), p. 238.
4. Edmund Clerihew Bentley, in *The Oxford Book of Quotations* (London, OUP, 1943), p. 27.
5. Thomas Babington Macaulay, *Complete Works*, vols XI–L, *Speeches, Poems and Miscellaneous Writing*, p. 588.
6. *Encyclopaedia Britannica*, 15th edn, vol. 9, p. 416.
7. Ibid., vol. 3, p. 305.
8. Quoted in Lewin, op. cit., p. 227.
9. Lewin, op. cit., p. 237.
10. Harris, op. cit., p. 273.
11. Ziegler, op. cit., p. 346.
12. Harris, op. cit., p. 375.
13. Ibid., p. 376.
14. Ibid., p. 379.
15. Ibid., p. 380.
16. Gilbert, op. cit. (1945–65), pp. 301–2.
17. Harris, op. cit., pp. 381–2.
18. Lord Ismay, *Memoirs* (London, Heinemann, 1960), p. 411.
19. Ibid., p. 415.
20. MB1/D254.
21. Ibid.
22. Ziegler, op. cit., p. 356.
23. Harris, op. cit., p. 375.
24. Ismay, op. cit., p. 417.
25. Ibid., p. 418.
26. Richard Hough, *Edwina: Countess Mountbatten of Burma* (London, Weidenfeld & Nicolson, 1983), p. 190.
27. Ziegler, op. cit., p. 385.
28. Ismay, op. cit., pp. 424–5.
29. Ibid., p. 425.
30. Ziegler, op. cit., p. 387.
31. MB1/D267.
32. H.V. Hodson, *The Great Divide: Britain-India-Pakistan* (London, Hutchinson, 1969), p. 347.
33. Ismay, op. cit., p. 428.
34. Ibid., p. 429.
35. Mountbatten to Attlee, quoted Ziegler, op. cit., p. 408.
36. MB1/D297.
37. Alastair Lamb, *Kashmir – A Disputed Legacy* (Hertingfordbury, Roxford Books, 1991, and Karachi, OUP, 1992); see also Lamb, *Crisis in Kashmir 1947–1966* (London, Routledge & Kegan Paul, 1966)
38. MB1/D267.

39. Ibid.
40. Ibid.
41. Ibid.
42. Ibid.
43. Hodson, op. cit., p. 351.
44. Ziegler, op. cit., p. 423.
45. Ibid., p. 426.
46. Ibid., p. 427.
47. MB1/D320.
48. Ziegler, op. cit., p. 428.
49. Ibid., p. 428.
50. Ismay, op. cit., p. 432.
51. Ibid., p. 433.
52. Ibid., p. 434.
53. Ibid., p. 435.
54. Ibid., p. 436.
55. Ziegler, op. cit., p. 451.
56. Ibid., Mountbatten cited, p. 450.
57. Ibid., p. 460.
58. Lewin, *The Chief*, p. 238.
59. Andrew Roberts, *Eminent Churchillians* (London, Weidenfeld, 1994), p. 56.
60. Ibid., p. 55.
61. Slim, *Defeat into Victory*, p. 384.
62. Nirad C. Chaudhuri, *Thy Hand, Great Anarch* (London, Chatto & Windus, 1987), pp. 50, 68.
63. Roberts, op. cit., p. 132.
64. Hodson, op. cit.

Chapter 6

1. Lord Carrington, *Report on Things Past* (London, Collins, 1988), p. 111.
2. Admiral of the Fleet Lord Tovey, letter to Rear Admiral Paffard, 20 December 1958.
3. Commander W.J. Crowe Jr, USN, *The Policy Roots of the Modern Royal Navy*, PhD dissertation (Princeton, Princeton University, June 1965).
4. *RUSI Journal* (May 1948), p. 34.
5. Commander Geoffrey Greenish, RN, letter to the author, 21 November 1992.
6. The Reverend Lovell Peacock, *With Those in Peril* (Worcester, SPA, 1979), p. 224.
7. Journal of Midshipman J. Watson, RCN; extract sent to the author by Commander J. Watson, RCN.
8. Martin Gilbert, *Winston Churchill*, vol. VIII, *Never Despair, 1945–65* (London, Heinemann, 1988), p. 467.
9. Ibid., p. 673.
10. Vice-Admiral Sir Hector MacLean in conversation with the author, 26 November 1992.
11. Lady Mountbatten papers, 19 September 1952, quoted Ziegler, op. cit., p. 512.

12. Recollection of the author.
13. Sir John Colville (1915–87), Private Secretary to Winston Churchill 1940–41, 1943–45, 1951–55.
14. Sir John Colville, *The Fringes of Power*, cited Gilbert, op. cit., vol. 8, p. 679.
15. Ziegler, op. cit., p. 522.
16. Captain W.R. Lapper, RN, letter to the author, 9 November 1992.
17. Ibid.
18. Quoted Ziegler, op. cit., p. 522.
19. Ibid.
20. Lapper, op. cit.
21. MB private correspondence, 6 November 1954.
22. Vice-Admiral MacLean, op. cit.
23. Rear Admiral P.G. La Neice, *Not a Nine to Five Job* (Yalden, Kent, Chattertons, 1992) p. 127.
24. Phillip Darby, *British Defence Policy East of Suez, 1947–68* (London, OUP, 1973), p. 55.
25. Field Marshal Lord Bramall and General Sir William Jackson, *The Chiefs* (London, Brassey's, 1992), p. 294.
26. Keith Bartley and Edward Lynch, 'The Political Economy of UK Defence Expenditure', in *RUSI Journal* (March 1981).
27. Vice-Admiral MacLean, op. cit.
28. Rear Admiral La Neice, op. cit., pp. 127–8.
29. Cmnd 9691, paraphrased.
30. Captain J.O. Coote, letter to the author, 8 November 1980.
31. Mountbatten, note to the author, 1973.
32. Andrew J. Pierre, *Nuclear Politics; the British Experience with an Independent Strategic Force* (London, OUP, 1970), p. 139.
33. Recollection of the author.
34. Mountbatten, in conversation with the author, 1973.
35. General Sir John Glubb (1897–1986), known as 'Glubb Pasha', led and trained the Arab Legion in Transjordan (later Jordan) from 1939 until 1956.
36. Sir Anthony Nutting, Minister of State for Foreign Affairs, 1954–56. He resigned over Suez.
37. Evelyn Shuckburgh, *Descent to Suez: Diaries 1951–56* (London, Weidenfeld, 1986), *passim*.
38. Nuri Es-Said was Prime Minister of Iraq before the 1958 revolution that overthrew the monarchy. Pro-British, but unpopular in Iraq, he was murdered by forces loyal to General Kassem, the leader of the coup d'état.
39. Anthony Nutting, *No End of a Lesson* (London, Constable, 1967), pp. 47–8.
40. MB1/N106.
41. Quoted by Bernard Levin, *The Times*, 5 November 1980.
42. Draft in MB1/N106.
43. Quoted in Ziegler, op. cit., pp. 539–40.
44. Dwight D. Eisenhower, *Waging Peace* (New York, Doubleday, 1965), p. 92.
45. William Clark, quoted in *The Times*, 22 November 1979.
46. MB1/N106.
47. Eisenhower, op. cit., p. 88.
48. Nutting, op. cit., p. 145.

49. Sir Antony Acland, lecture on 'The Relationship, between Foreign and Defence Policy', in *RUSI Journal* (May 1983).
50. Eisenhower, op. cit., p. 92.
51. Shuckburgh, op. cit., p. 357.
52. Quoted in Levin, op. cit., p. 363.
53. Shuckburgh, op. cit., p. 363.
54. Ibid., p. 366.
55. 363 HC Deb, quoted Phillip Darby, op. cit., p. 107.
56. Eric Grove, *Mountbatten as Chief of Naval Staff* ('Aspects of British Defence and Naval Policy in the Mountbatten Era', Conference at the University of Southampton, 25–26 September 1990).
57. Ibid.
58. Captain J.O. Coote, RN, *Lord Louis*, US Naval Institute, *Proceedings* (March 1981), p. 16 et seq.
59. Grove, op. cit., p. 8.
60. David Brown, 'Mountbatten as First Sea Lord', in *RUSI Journal* (June 1986), pp. 67–8.
61. Transcript of speech provided by Captain D.S. Wyatt, RN, to the author, 2 June 1975.
62. Captain D.G. Robertson, letter to the author, 30 January 1996.

Chapter 7

1. Sir William Hayter, *The Diplomacy of the Great Powers* (1960), p. 46, quoted Phillip Darby, *British Defence Policy East of Suez* (London, OUP, 1973), p. 142n.
2. 238 HL Deb, 21 March 1962, col. 579, quoted Phillip Darby, op. cit., p. 214.
3. Dean Acheson, speech at West Point Military Academy, USA, 5 December 1962.
4. Minute by Prince Louis of Battenberg, Director of Naval Intelligence, in Adm. 1/7859, quoted Nicholas d'Ombrian, *War Machinery and High Policy* (London, OUP, 1973), p. 76n.
5. W.S. Chalmers, *The Life and Letters of David Beatty* (London, Hodder & Stoughton, 1951), p. 411.
6. Field Marshal Lord Bramall and General Sir William Jackson, *The Chiefs* (London, Brassey's, 1992), p. 105.
7. Ibid., p. 127.
8. Ibid., pp. 128–9.
9. *The Times*, 16 April 1942.
10. Bramall and Jackson, op. cit., pp. 271–2.
11. Cmnd 476, Introduction.
12. Ibid., para 13.
13. Ibid., para 10.
14. Ibid., para 19.
15. Bramall and Jackson, op. cit., p. 323.
16. L.W. Martin, 'The Market for Strategic Ideas in Britain; the "Sandys Era"', in *American Political Science Review – 1962*, p. 39.
17. Peter Foot, *Mountbatten as CDS: Budgets, Organisation and Policy* ('Aspects of British Defence and Naval Policy in the Mountbatten Era', Conference at the University of Southampton, 25–26 September 1990).

18. Lord Zuckerman, *Six Men Out of the Ordinary* (London, Peter Owen, 1992), p. 145.
19. Bramall and Jackson, op. cit., p. 330.
20. Martin, op. cit., p. 39.
21. Darby, op. cit., pp. 171–2.
22. Letter from the Chief of Naval Operations, Admiral Arleigh Burke, to the First Sea Lord, Earl Mountbatten of Burma, 'Top Secret and Personal', dated 28 February 1959.
23. Bramall and Jackson, op. cit., pp. 331–2.
24. Captain R.D. Franks, letter to the author, 20 January 1994.
25. Bramall and Jackson, op. cit., p. 333.
26. Ibid.
27. Darby, op. cit., p. 224.
28. Vice-Admiral Sir Ian Hogg, letter to the author, 20 January 1994.
29. Captain I.L.M. McGeoch, 'The Political Control of the Armed Forces', in *RUSI Journal* (May 1961), pp. 218–20.
30. William J. Crowe, Jr, op. cit., p. 363.
31. *The Sunday Times*, 12 August 1962.
32. Ziegler, op. cit., p. 586.
33. Sir Patrick Nairne, letter to the author, 24 October 1994.
34. Ibid.
35. Prime Minister's Personal Minute No. M330/62. MB 1/496, quoted Ziegler, op. cit., p. 612.
36. Bramall and Jackson, op. cit., p. 343.
37. Harold Macmillan, *At the End of the Day* (London, Macmillan, 1973), p. 349.
38. Bahamas Meetings, December 1962, *Cmnd* 1915, Statement on Nuclear Defence Systems, 21 December 1962, para 8.
39. Rear Admiral C.W.H. Shepherd, quoted in Vice-Admiral Sir Ian McGeoch, 'The British Polaris Project', MPhil dissertation, University of Edinburgh, 1975.
40. Peter Nailor, *The Nassau Connection* (London, HMSO, 1988), p. 68.
41. Macmillan, op. cit., p. 349.
42. Professor R.V. Jones, lecture at RUSI on 'Science, Intelligence and Policy', 8 November 1978.
43. Mountbatten to Harold Wilson, Prime Minister, 19 October 1964, MB/J61; quoted Ziegler, op. cit., p. 627.
44. Bramall and Jackson, op. cit., p. 347.
45. MB1/K144.
46. Captain R.W. Garson, letter to the author, 18 March 1994.
47. Admiral of the Fleet Lord Lewin, The Mountbatten Memorial Lecture, RUSI, 7 July 1980.

Epilogue

1. General Sir John Hackett, *The Profession of Arms* (London, Sidgwick & Jackson, 1983), p. 184.
2. Randolph S. Churchill, *Winston S. Churchill: vol. II: Young Statesman 1901–14* (London, Heinemann, 1967), p. 544, citing WSC in *The World Crisis*.

3. Captain S.W. Roskill, *Naval Policy between the Wars* (London, HMSO, 1978); The National Maritime Museum, *Maritime Monograph*, No. 29, p. 2.
4. Field Marshal the Viscount Montgomery of Alamein, KG, *Memoirs* (London, Collins, 1958), p. 77.
5. Lewin, *Slim: the Standardbearer*, p. 238.
6. Edmund Heward, *The Great and the Good* (London, Barry Rose, 1994), p. 51.
7. Lawrence James, *The Rise and Fall of the British Empire* (London, Abacus, 1994), p. 577.
8. Ibid., p. 629.
9. Mountbatten, speech on the occasion of the award of the Louis Weiss Foundation Prize to the Stockholm International Peace Research Institute at Strasbourg on 11 May 1979.
10. Captain Raymond Dreyer, letter to the author, 6 December 1992.
11. Script sent to the author by the naval attaché, British Embassy, Paris, 25 October 1993.
12. Lieutenant General Sir Napier Crookenden, letter to the author, 15 November 1993.

INDEX